Emergency Deep: One man's life in the Submarine Service
Published by Richard A Smith

Copyright 2012, Richard A Smith

All rights reserved.

My sincere thanks to Jamie Swimm for assistance with the front and rear covers.

Introduction
08

Chapter 1: The long road to the sea...12

Chapter 2: You're in the Navy now...19

Chapter 3: A Little Nukie never hurt anybody...34

Chapter 4: What am I doing here?...69

Chapter 5: So *that's* a submarine...88

Chapter 6: Techno-jargon makes me horny...115

Chapter 7: Only as good as her crew...122

Chapter 8: You non-qual puke...167

Chapter 9: Puss rockets and sail rabbit...182

Chapter 10: Mother may I...205

Chapter 11: Seaman Snerd, fetch me a bucket of steam...217

Chapter 12: May the ORSE be with you...240

Chapter 13: So close to war...249

Chapter 14: The Bonnie Land...266

Chapter 15: No, really...what am I doing here?...300

Chapter 16: Yer outta here!...327

Chapter 17: The long road back...359

Chapter 18: The Silent Bastards and the Rolex Watch...390

For my Dad,

Oh, if you only knew.

For my Mom,

For all the times I made you worry.

For Yvette,

For being my rock and anchor during the worst, but most interesting times of my life.

Disclaimer

Memoirs are, by definition, an exercise in memory. No one's memory is flawless, except for that woman in the police show on TV. Mine is no different, being at least equally flawed. Having said that, I would like to make the following pledge to the reader:

Every event, emotion, statement, or location detailed in this book is transcribed to the very best of my knowledge. I have made every possible effort to double check any elements that could be verified. In some instances, the identities of United States Navy vessels have been changed for security reasons. Some circumstances and time frames have been slightly altered for security reasons, and to keep my pretty face out of prison. These alterations have no effect on the flow or validity of the events being described, and only those present at the time will notice these slight differences. I am telling this story to the absolute best of my ability, with no deliberate "augmentations" to increase the "pucker factor", or get me a free drink at McCarthy's.

I have decided to change the names of the crew members and other significant people described in this book. This is for three very important reasons:

1) To protect the innocent.

2) To protect the guilty.

3) To make things easier for me, since I really suck at remembering peoples' names.

I would also like to make the following pledge to the Federal Government:

I have taken every possible precaution to ensure that no classified information of any kind has been revealed in this book, regardless of any likelihood of it being obsolete. As far as I'm concerned, if it was classified twenty-six years ago, it's classified today. So, there.

I would like the reader to sit back, relax, and enjoy this memoir with the complete confidence that I am telling it with the highest possible degree of accuracy. Liars *always* get caught, and when they do, it *never* goes well.

So, why take the chance?

Introduction

I grew up in a military family. A *very* military family. It wasn't just my Dad. My brother was military. My cousins were military. My uncles were military. One fought in Italy in World War II. And, it wasn't just military. Many of them worked in elite or covert fields. My Dad was in Air Force Intelligence. He was one of the best analysts they ever had. He was once brought in to brief the Vice President of the United States because the commissioned officers involved couldn't "handle it".

I know. I've heard the jokes. Military intelligence is a contradiction in terms. Very funny, very camp, but very inaccurate. The intelligence community has saved more of *our* folks' lives, and taken more of *their* folks' lives, than any bomb, bullet, or brigade. And, here's something you don't hear every day: Many gave their own lives. When my Dad was in Viet Nam, the Intel personnel were *prime targets*. They were the ones who told the pilots where to drop the bombs. The VC really, really wanted those guys dead.

My Dad related three stories to me when I was a child.

1) My Dad got off a plane in a foreign country. Like so many others, he hailed a cab. It was obvious he was military, but there were military people all over the place. He could have been in any line of work. He got in a cab, and the driver took off. During the drive, the cabbie asked my Dad what he did for a living. My Dad told him he was a cook. The driver turned around and said,

"I thought you were in intelligence."

My Dad leaned forward, and said,

"Pull this cab over this instant, or I'll blow your fucking brains out, right here."

The cabbie felt his survival instinct kick in, pulled over, and let my Dad get out. Mission *not* accomplished.

2) At Ton Son Nhut airbase, near Saigon, they farmed out the Intel people to a variety of barracks, as opposed to keeping them all together. The reason was simple: if all the Intel guys were in one barracks, all the enemy would have to do is blow up *one* building to kill *all* of them. So, they put one here, one there, etc...

One of my Dad's guys went out drinking one night. In true military fashion he really tied one on. He came home, got into bed, and fell asleep. At some point he rolled off his cot, and in his alcohol induced slumber, rolled *under* his cot. That's where he spent the rest of his night. In the morning when he woke up, he discovered that the throat of *every* man in that room had been slit in their sleep. Who lived there? Cooks. Typists. Mechanics. "Wing wipers" every one of them. People of no strategic value. People not worth killing quietly in their sleep.

It was obvious what had happened. They knew he lived there. But, they didn't know *where* he slept. The answer was to kill every man in the room, to make sure they got *him*. But he rolled under his cot, and they missed him. Every other man in the room died *because* of him...but they missed *him*. Needless to say, that man's little red choo-choo went chugging around the bend. He was sent back to the U.S. soon thereafter.

3) A group of people went into Saigon for lunch. My Dad was with them. They could have been anybody. Intel people didn't wear any special uniform or insignia. They

pulled to the side of the road. While they all still sat in their jeep, a vehicle raced by. A telltale clatter they all recognized told them what had happened. A grenade had been rolled under their jeep. They all bailed out just in time. Well...*almost* all of them. One guy didn't make it. He got a piece of shrapnel right up his ass! Don't worry. It wasn't my Dad. He's still a "perfect asshole".

That is a little known hazard intelligence types have had to deal with since the intelligence community came into existence. Yes, they've had their blunders. But, the good far outweighs the bad. Next time you meet an Intel guy, buy him or her a drink. Let's move on. Back to my military family...

My brother went into the submarine service. My cousin was a Naval Aviator. Yes, it's true, fly-boys and bubbleheads are practically natural enemies. A mutual respect still exists. One can't be a Naval Aviator by scratching the dot off a ticket. Another cousin was a crew chief on A-10s. In case the reader doesn't know what a crew chief is, without them, pilots would spend their time twiddling their thumbs. Pilots are smart enough to *fly* high-tech aircraft, but not necessarily smart enough to *maintain* them. Another cousin worked with nuclear tipped ICBMs. My uncles were either trigger pullers, Intel types, or communications types. By communications what I really mean is, one person talking into a little box, to another person on the other side of the world, listening to a little box. Sure, that happens all the time now. It didn't, in the *1960's.* Another uncle was responsible for a classified listening post on the tiny island of Ascension, in the middle of the South Atlantic. There's a pattern forming here. Submarines...covert. Intelligence...covert. Classified communications...covert. Cold war flight operations...classified. ICBMs...not covert...but highly classified.

My family wasn't just military, it was *dark*. It was spooky. My father was prepared for a nuclear conflict. He had stockpiled food, water, radiation surveying gear, weapons, ammunition, medical supplies (including those for "invasive" procedures), decontamination supplies, fuel...you name it. My Dad deliberately selected a house that would survive a direct nuclear attack on the Air Force base twenty miles away. This is the environment in which I was steeped. My life revolved around all things military. I would say this happened to a fault. In reality, it extends far *beyond* that.

This is the environment in which my life began, and my adventure was germinated. These are the sources of the little voices that followed me through my life, from the time I was old enough to listen, to the present day. Those shouting whispers,

"You can't tell your friends, without telling your enemies."

"It's easier to *keep* them out, than *get* them out."

"Everything you do, affects everything you do."

"You can tell someone what to do, and you can tell someone what to say. But, you can't tell someone what to think."

"Always consider the past, the present, and the future."

"ALWAYS."

So...you have the map. You speak the language. Let the journey begin...

Chapter 1-
The long road to the sea.

The sea is woman, the sea is wonder. Her other name is fate.

– old sailors' proverb

People often ask me when I first realized that submarine duty had changed me for the rest of my life. One particular moment comes to mind. It was shortly after I received my official notice that I had been discharged. Yvette and I were living in our apartment in West Springfield, Massachusetts. That would put it at about...mid 1988 or so. We were lying in bed. Yvette turned to me and said,

"Rich?"

"Uh - huh?"

"What does it mean to 'prime the diesel'?"

I rolled over and looked at her. That was a phrase I hadn't heard or said in quite a while. Where did that come from? Did she read it somewhere? Had she heard it somewhere? Was she thinking about a story I had once told? Was "priming the diesel" now a vague sexual term? This was truly odd. I explained the requirement and procedure for priming the fuel system for the diesel engine that drove our emergency generator. I explained why and when it would be used.

I asked her if that answered her question. She told me that indeed it had. I laid there for a few moments, trying to figure out where her question might have originated. I was baffled. Why ask *that* question? Why ask it *then*? What made her think of that at such a peculiar time? I turned to her and asked,

"What made you ask that? I mean, that's a pretty obscure question. Especially for pillow talk."

She looked at me and said, quite matter-of-factly,

"Oh...you were yelling it in your sleep last night."

The little voice in the back of my head was whispering: Oooooh, that's *different*.

Let's flash back six years. I'm not saying I was required to join the military. That certainly was not the case. Neither was it in any way preordained. I could have followed any career path I wanted, as long as it began at the age of eighteen and didn't involve me being financially dependent on my parents.

College was a possibility, but a remote one. Not that it was discouraged in any way. Education was extremely important in our family. But, the subject of higher education was so remote I never even felt the smallest drive to even take the SATs. So, I didn't.

Independence was very strongly stressed in our family. It was assumed that, upon reaching adulthood (i.e. the age of eighteen), we would leave the house and follow our chosen paths. Where that path might take us was unimportant. It was equally assumed we would be popping in on a regular basis, frequency being determined by the distance from home. So, the dominant undercurrent in my family was that military service was just... *natural*. What else would I do? Why on earth would I contemplate anything else? My life was so anchored in military culture nothing else seemed a proper fit. I always waffled back and forth regarding what my path would be. But the options were always different aspects of the military.

Even if I didn't make the military a career, my life would certainly include at least a portion of time in the military. For that reason, my father always stressed the importance of choosing a field with a civilian counterpart. What I did in the military would determine what I did as a civilian. Conversations like this were a constant occurrence:

"Hey, Dad...I think I want to be a missile technician."

"Oh? Sure about that? Did they open up a Missiles R Us down the street?"

"No."

"Fred's Rent-A-Missile?"

"No."

"Oh, I know...Missile Repair Man! Thank God you're here!"

"Okay, Dad. I get it."

Or maybe this one:

"Hey, Dad! I'm thinking about becoming an Intel guy like you. You did say I'd be good at it."

"That's true. I did say that. And, you *would* be good at it. Where do you want to live when you get out?"

"Probably right around here. I like it here."

"You won't be able to live around here. You'll be living in either the D.C. area, or St. Louis. That's where the Intel jobs are."

"I don't want to live there. I've heard it sucks there."

"Well, so much for the Intel field."

Planning ahead was crucial when making decisions like this. I quickly learned that a seemingly casual move like this would have far reaching ramifications years in the future. Those kids who wanted to be policemen or firemen their entire lives had it made. The ones who wanted to be doctors or teachers were sitting pretty good. The ones who wanted to be astronauts were sitting on a fragile bubble. Ballerinas were just plain screwed.

So, it would appear that my Fairy Godmother had pledged me to Uncle Sam. There were so many things I wanted to do. So many of them had a good civilian counterpart. Some I would have to eliminate right away. Flying was out. I wore glasses. Special Forces was out, for the same reason as Missile Repairman. Another obstacle was a complete and total lack of any guarantee I would receive the training I wanted. For so many people, "needs of the Pentagon" determined that many promising mechanics were instead cooks, and many budding chefs were heavy equipment operators.

So, it became a dual purpose mission. I would need to find a career path with a good civilian counterpart, with training guaranteed in writing, that I also liked. The assortment was better than we planned. Convincing recruits to enter hard to fill areas by putting training in a contract was becoming more popular. Of course, dubious fields like Satellite Tracking Technician still occasionally reared their ugly heads. Logic prevailed.

My older brother, Steve, proved to be the key element. He was tip-toeing through the same minefield I was. But, he was a few years ahead of me. I paid close attention to his options and choices. That was when the clouds opened. God's voice roared down,

"SUBMARINES".

Then the majestic voice continued,

"And, stop playing with yourself so much."

Okay. That was...awkward. Good thing no one else heard that.

Hold it. I know what you're about to say. I know how your beady little mind works, dear reader. And, I'm counting on the slim chance you're actually paying attention to all this mind numbing drivel going on and on. You're about to say,

"Submarine Repair Man! Thank God you're here!"

No! It's not like that! Really! Let me explain. Here's why submarines became such a good idea:

1) Guaranteed training in a critical field: nuclear propulsion. And what sits right next to nuclear propulsion? Nuclear generation of electricity. At the time, nuclear power plants were extremely popular. They were springing up like Uranium enriched dandelions! They needed people to run

them. Those people were paid an awful lot of money. They had to be extremely reliable people. They had to be smart, stable, and able to stand stress as if it was a misty rain on a morning picnic. Where were they getting most of their operators? The Navy! Yup. Navy nukes were the first choice for anyone trying to staff a nuclear power plant. I'll explain more about that later. (Chapter 8 - May the ORSE be with you.) I couldn't ask for a better civilian counterpart.

2) The submarine service is an elite service. Very few applicants are selected for that duty. Now granted, one must be a complete lunatic to volunteer (yes, it's always been a totally volunteer organization) for duty on a ship designed to sink. A vessel going below the surface of the water violates every primal instinct humans possess. I've heard that all before. But, only the highest quality loonies are accepted into this field of service. It has been estimated that ninety-eight percent of the country's population couldn't qualify for submarine duty, for a number of reasons. In a submarine, you're dealing with an entirely different caliber of person. Well...for the most part. Hey, Dad! I won't have to slit some commie's throat in the middle of the jungle to be someone as important as you! Bargain! Yes, I have to admit it. My Dad has always been the Gold Standard to which I have always compared myself.

3) The submarine service has always been extremely secretive, extremely exclusive, and extremely dangerous. Even in the best of times, several submarines have been lost with all hands. The United States, the Soviet Union/Russia, Great Britain, and France have all lost submarines and entire crews. Data regarding the Chinese is relatively unknown. And best of all...women love daring men!

Is it any mystery why this appealed to me so much? My Dad was involved in dangerous and classified work for twenty years. Now I would be able to follow in his footsteps while still fulfilling all the requirements for ensuring a successful future. Could this get any better?

Oh...if I only knew what I had gotten myself into.

Chapter 2-
You're in the Navy now...

Ask not what your country can do for you, but what you can do for your country.

-JFK

"Everybody off the bus! Everybody off the goddam bus! Get off the fucking bus, now!"

It was late evening, January 18, 1983. The bus from O'Hare International Airport had just come to a halt at Great Lakes Recruit Training Center. That was my introduction to military service in general, and the Navy in particular.

Up to that point, the process was hardly a soothing one. It started with a test. Physical exams and an extensive background check followed. Once they realize they have a potential NF (Nuclear Field) candidate in their clutches, everything changes. More tests and another background check. Wait! Did he say submarines? Better do a background check. Documents and more documents. Sign here. Now here. Now here. This one says if you do *this* you're going to prison. This part says if we find out you did *this*, you're most *definitely* going to prison. Holy smoke! I wasn't even in the Navy yet!

Briefings were conducted regarding how we will travel, what we can and cannot do or say, what to do if things go wrong. A heads-up on how absolutely nasty everything will be when we get there. It didn't help. All the forewarning in the world doesn't help when you pull up to the Recruit Training Center in that bus. Oh, I had lots of forewarning. My Dad talked to me. My brother talked to me. The recruiter talked to me. Total strangers on the street talked to me. There were all kinds of advice.

1) It's all a head game.

2) Don't take it personally.

3) Just do what you're told.

4) Pay attention. It's all about attention to detail.

None of that really helped. When that Petty Officer stepped onto the bus and let loose, we became a big bunch of deer, each with his very own set of headlights. Things went downhill from there.

We were all brought into a large room, and told to sit down in high school style desks. They rattled off a long list of things we weren't allowed to bring in with us. Anyone with such articles was to walk to the front of the room and place the items on the table. Some guys had to be told numerous times that they really couldn't bring that nip bottle of Jack Daniels, no matter how bad they might need it.

There were weapons, booze, cigarettes, pot (yes, I said pot.), dirty magazines (they went into a separate pile for special examination later), and other items. We gave up all personal items except the clothes on our backs. Those items were very carefully checked before being put into storage. More than once we heard,

"How many fucking times do we have to tell you...no fucking booze!"

We were marched from building to building, going through a head spinning variety of activities. The slightest mistake or misbehavior was greeted with a tooth rattling tirade of obscenities. Time continued to pass with no end in sight. Few things are as bad as being disoriented, exhausted, and terrified all at the same time. We finally arrived at our barracks right about 0300. We were allowed to get into bed.

We actually slept. Until 0600. Then it all started again. The lights came on, and a garbage can was thrown down the center isle of the barracks. Then came the greeting we were to hear many times over the next eight weeks,

"Alright, you fucking idiots! Get your lazy asses out of bed! Drop your cocks and grab your socks! Hey!! I...said...get...out...of...fucking...bed!"

The process of induction continued. We were allowed to eat breakfast. Then it was inoculations, uniform fittings, lectures, equipment issue, and so on. We were given toiletries. That was a good sign. Our sorry group was given the official label of Recruit Company 021. Anarchy changed ever so slowly into a recognizable routine.

Along with all the physical exams were the psychiatric exams. The military used the same Personality Inventories as the civilian community, with a few extra curves thrown in for their own special purposes. It was very important to the Department of Defense that they had no one in their midst who wanted to kill their mama, have sex with a sumac bush, or say...launch a nuclear missile at their old elementary school. (Damn you, Mrs. Perkins! I told you I'd make you pay!")

To that end, we were all sat down in a room with a Navy shrink and a couple of corpsmen. The mechanics of the test were explained. Then we were told to turn our test booklet over after we finished everything else, and draw a normal looking person on the back. This was repeatedly stressed. A *normal* person. This struck me as very odd. (I later discovered that a great deal can be discovered about someone just by how they draw a person.) We were very specifically instructed that it could not be a stick figure. It must be a full figured drawing. Well, that just *sucked*. I couldn't draw people to save my life! I was good at technical drawing. I was barely passable at sci-fi art. But people? They were setting me up to fail. I expressed my concern to one of the corpsmen,

"Excuse me, sir. I don't know the first thing about drawing people. Isn't there something else I could draw? This is really going to be a horrible drawing."

He looked at me. He obviously had heard this countless times before. Just do your best, was his advice.

So, I opened my booklet and started my test. It was pretty typical stuff. Did I love my Mom? Did I like sex? More specifically, did I like sex with girls? What would I do if I found a crying child? I found the test to be pretty routine. Then came that last question. I turned over the booklet, and stared at the blank white sheet. Come *on*. There had to be an alternative. They would take one look at my lame attempt and throw me out. Then it hit me. I picked up my pencil, and began to draw...

"Seaman Recruit Smith!"

My head jerked up.

"Yes, sir."

"Come...here."

His voice and face were icy. My alternative obviously was not acceptable. I walked up to the front of the room, and stood at rigid attention before his desk. He was looking at the drawing on the back of the booklet. He looked up at me. Back down to the paper. Back up at me. The expression on his face said I was definitely *not* in a position to screw with him.

"You drew this?"

"Yes, sir."

But I wasn't screwing with him! I just wanted to give them a decent drawing. I can't draw people, plain and simple. I had to put it in a context that would make me more...comfortable. He looked at me one more time. One more glance at the paper. My days old naval career was flashing before my eyes.

"I guess you can...sit...down."

I did an about face, and returned to my desk. Let me just point out, for the record, that naval medical personnel have no appreciation for sincere, exhaustive effort. I have absolutely no idea what could have been wrong with that drawing. Let me state my case:

1) The spacesuit was *perfectly* drawn.

2) The helmet had just the right combination of size and rakishness to look impressive, but not dorky.

3) I made it a point to place the hoses in a location where they would not catch on anything. After all, this needs to be believable.

4) The backpack had lights, knobs, and antennae, but not *too* many.

5) I thought the addition of a "blaster" type sidearm was quite plausible.

I really put a lot of work and thought into this. Mrs. Sherman would have given me a solid B+ on that work! And some tight-ass Navy shrink was panning it, for what? All I've ever heard was all these earthy-crunchy-squishy people saying,

"Now, now. There's really no such thing as normal, is there? None of us are (finger quotes) *normal.*"

Attention. Attention, population of the fantasy world of goodness and light. There apparently *is* such a thing as normal, and if any of you mouth-breathing dweebs went in the military, *you'd know that*!

Gratefully, my military career survived. I'd be willing to bet that if that shrink hadn't gotten laid the previous night, this story would have a very quick ending!

As the days, and eventually weeks passed, we all began to adapt. Life became a steady stream of exercise, inspections, lectures, tests, and disciplinary actions. One thing quickly changed: if someone did something wrong, the punishment wasn't a verbal dressing down. The punishment was physical. *Very* physical. The Navy actually had a special term for it. MASH. It stood for Make A Sailor Hurt. Used in a sentence:

"That bastard mashed me for a whole hour, just for being out of step."

The activity of choice for most Company Commanders was the push-up. The military has elevated the humble push-up to the status of high art, for the purpose of disciplinary action. We knew it was going to be bad when the CC told us to move our racks back against the walls. He wanted us to have extra room. But, one mashing session will always stick in my mind.

We were practicing our marching. Things went very, very badly. The junior of the two CCs was with us, and things deteriorated to the point that he simply gave up. He was absolutely despondent. If a bus drove by at that instant, he would have thrown himself under it. I know it. I just *know it*. Finally, he just stood there looking at us. He told us to form up and return to the barracks. We knew we were in for it, bad. This was going to be one for the books. We filed into the barracks, and before anyone could do anything, he walked into the office and shut the door. We were left out there, sitting in an eerie silence.

We began talking quietly amongst ourselves. We speculated over what he could be doing or thinking. Then the hushed conversation took a bizarre turn:

"Man, we were really bad out there."

"I know. We really, really sucked."

"We couldn't do *anything* right!"

"I never seen him look like that before."

"Me neither. I wonder if he's okay."

"Yeah. And he isn't mashing us. It's weird."

"We really do deserve a good mashing. I mean, we stunk!"

"Man, it's quiet in there."

"Well...we could mash ourselves."

"Uh..."

"No. Really. It's the right thing to do."

And so it was decided. We all assumed the position, and began doing push-ups. The RPOC (the recruit designated by the CCs to be in charge) began counting them off.

"Down...up."

"ONE, SIR!"

"Down...up."

"TWO, SIR!"

We continued for a few more, then someone realized we were making a horrible mistake.

"Wait! We can't call him sir! The CCs are called sir!"

"Well then, what do we call him?"

"We should call him...mate."

So we started over. The RPOC returned to his duty of counting off push-ups. Things seemed a little more normal now.

"Down...up."

"ONE, MATE!"

"Down...up."

"TWO, MATE!"

Suddenly the door to the CC's office flew open! Petty Officer Slater bolted into the room, a look of complete disbelief on his face,

"What the fuck are you people doing?? What is *wrong* with you people?? Have you lost your fucking minds??"

We all froze. We thought this would make him feel better. The RPOC stuttered out an explanation. Slater stared at the room full of people all motionless, in varying degrees of "push-up".

"Knock that shit off. Just sit there!"

A number of meek "yessirs" floated through the room. He walked back into the office slowly shaking his head.

As the weeks passed, we made our way through different stages of instruction. Some of it made absolutely no sense. Did they really have to teach a step by step method for brushing one's teeth? Or bathing? Really?

I also learned some amazing things about "nukes", as we became to be called. First of all, "nuke" was only *half* of the term. The entire term was "fuckin' nuke". We heard that term over and over. For some reason, it was easy to determine which recruits were NF candidates. Any time one of these people did anything incorrectly or weirdly, the response was immediate,

"Fuckin' nuke!"or, "He's gotta be a nuke."

As it turns out, the reason for that was nukes had a reputation for having particular characteristics:

1) Very, very smart.

2) Absolutely no common sense.

3) Socially, completely inept.

Put them all together. You have someone who could calculate your chances of being struck by a bus by using a copy of the London Times, a weather chart, and a calculator. They were constantly tripping. What would you expect from someone who couldn't tie their own shoes? Never go out in public with them. They'll be the one scratching their ass with one hand and picking their nose with the other. It's anyone's guess which finger will go in their mouth first.

Now add in the knowledge that they'll be paid more, and promoted faster, just because they're a *fucking nuke!* Sadly, my bunkmate did absolutely nothing to dispel this myth. He was, in fact, extremely smart. I usually ended up making his bunk during inspections because he was completely incapable of doing it himself. He was the one who sat at the lunch table and blew a pound of flem into his hands, turned to his nauseated neighbor and said,

"If you aren't going to finish your dessert, can I have it?"

In spite of my ability to blend in and disappear virtually anywhere, I still had my nuke moment. I'll always remember it. We were attending a lecture on birth control and sexually transmitted diseases. Why on earth would a sailor need to know anything about *that*? These guys were over thinking everything! Wasn't tooth brushing bad enough? The instructor was telling us about the lack of reliability of "withdrawal" as a form of birth control. He asked if anyone knew why this was. I raised my hand, and was recognized. Before I could stop myself, I professed,

"You always excrete a small amount of semen before you ejaculate."

He looked at me for a few seconds, and said,

"Exactly. You always dribble before you shoot. You're a fucking nuke! Aren't you!"

BUSTED!

Everybody got a huge laugh out of that one. Well...almost everybody.

We went through a week of service, ironically called "Service Week". The recruits were given a dose of "normal" military routine, working jobs around the base they really couldn't screw up. I realized the recruits who did things like helping us size our uniforms during our first days were working their Service Week. My place in Service Week turned out to be at the chow hall, working in the "After Hold". That was where the syrup canisters for soda and bug juice (the military version of Kool-Aid) were stored. My title was "After Hold Captain". However, I was never called that. Anyone who came to the hatch for a package called me the "Monkey Man". The ceiling in the After Hold was very low. The result was that I constantly walked around hunched over like, well...a monkey. I spent the entire week working with one recruit who was obviously tasked with making sure the soda machines worked properly. Cooped up under the chow hall, I would hear his distant summons,

"Monkey Man, Monkey Man...come out of your hole!"

Finally, we were in the end game. We were doing fewer and fewer push-ups. Marching was practically second nature. Everyone knew how to swim, recognize rank, and tie a neckerchief. If it moved, we saluted it. If it didn't, we polished or painted it. Of course, we all had our occasional glitches, right up to the very end. As I recall, mine was quite spectacular.

In the military, especially in basic training, things must be done in a very specific way. Small details are critical. Here's a good example:

When told to report to the CCs, one goes to the door, stands at attention, and knocks three times. When the CC tells them to enter, they walk in a certain number of steps, come to attention and say,

"Good morning, sir. Seaman Recruit <u>fill in the blank</u> reporting as ordered, sir."

Obviously, afternoon or evening can be substituted for morning, depending on the time of day.

And so it happened. One of the guys came over and told me Chief Holt wanted to see me. I went to the door. I knocked three times. I was told to enter. I walked in the proper number of steps, came to attention, and said,

"Seaman Recruit Smith report -"

That's as far as I got. Chief Holt stood up, leaned over his desk, and *screamed*,

"GOOD MORNING TO YOU, TOO!ASSHOLE!!!"

But, graduation day finally came. We made it through the ceremony without making complete asses of ourselves. I had a very nice overnight visit with my Mom and Dad. And it was time to move on to the next step of the journey.

Chief Petty Officer Holt and Petty Officer First Class Slater were a priceless guiding influence during those first shaky days in the Navy. I will always remember them with sincere fondness.

Now I was in the regular Navy. I moved from "recruit side" of the base, to "main side". I moved into a huge barracks comprised of four blocks arranged in a square with a courtyard in the center. Appropriately enough, it was known to everyone as Snipes' Castle. Almost all propulsion engineering students on the base lived in this monstrous building. Engineering personnel are known in the Navy as "snipes". Do the math.

I started with PEB, which stood for Propulsion Engineering Basics. A few weeks there got the ball rolling. From there, I went to my Class A school. Since I had selected the mechanical aspect of the Nuclear Field, I went to Machinist Mate "A" school. A few weeks later it was time for training on a "live steam" plant. It was essentially a land locked ship propulsion plant. This was a bittersweet time. It felt good to actually get my hands dirty. Sadly, it was the beginning of my slow downward spiral into the quicksand of depression. I made my first mistake. During a shutdown of the system I was responsible for, I forgot to shut a critical valve. I was absolutely devastated. The instructor told me this was the place to make mistakes. That was the purpose of the school. It didn't matter. The seed had been sown.

By May of 1983 I had finished my first round of schools, and met my first contractual obligations. In return I was promoted to Petty Officer Third Class. I was now authorized to sew Third Class "Crows" onto all my uniforms. I was now officially a Non Commissioned Officer.

The Navy finally gave me a much deserved rest. I was able to go home on leave before continuing on to NTC Orlando. I was looking forward to it. Orlando had the reputation for being a party town. If someone couldn't have fun in Orlando, they had nothing to live for. I was luckier than I thought. Those waiting for their slot in the nuclear program were assigned temporary duty. That duty could be anywhere. My brother, for example, was sent to the U.S.S. Lexington. She was based in Pensacola, Florida. The Lexington, or Lady Lex was the Navy's training aircraft carrier. After serving there for several months, Steve was able to transfer to Orlando for school.

Another friend of mine got stuck in Mayport, up the coast from Orlando. Apparently, duty at Mayport was like watching paint dry. Then there were the ones who still had painful karma to burn off. They stayed in Great Lakes until their slot opened up.

But not me. The duty gods smiled on me. Apparently all that clean living and flossing between meals paid off. I was assigned to Public Works NTC Orlando. My partying could get off to an early start. Good thing, too. Once school started things would change drastically, and not for the better.

So, for about three months my routine resembled the life of Riley. I worked an easy job on day shift, five days a week, with every weekend off. My roommate and I hit it off pretty well. The escapades quickly began. My life became a blur of bars, nightclubs, parties, and strip clubs. I quickly learned there was a distinct advantage to living in a tropical climate if one was determined to drink to excess on a regular basis. For one thing, if one drank themselves into a stupor and passed out behind some bushes, they probably would not die of exposure during the night. Can't say that about New England! But the day of reckoning would finally arrive. It was time for me to face the purpose of going through all this crap in the first place:

United States Naval Nuclear Propulsion Program, or as it was more widely known...Nuke School.

Chapter 3-

A little Nukie never hurt anybody.

The difference between "E=mc2" and "Let there be light" is you'd never get Charlton Heston to star in a movie based on the former.

- Unattributed

My increasing exposure to other candidates allowed me to start forming a profile of the kind of person who would willingly enter such a program. It was someone who couldn't resist a challenge. Once they accepted it, they could not and would not stop until they succeeded. Failure was simply not an option. Many felt a strong family obligation to finish the program. Over the months, I would hear countless students say if they failed, they could never go home. They would be unable to face their families. They would be a total failure. Absolutely worthless. Passing this program was *everything*. They would rather die than fail. I found myself wondering if a family could actually put that kind of pressure on someone, or if it was generated from within. It just didn't seem to make any sense.

For now.

Finally, the day came to start United States Naval Nuclear Propulsion School, or NPS. I was officially part of NPS class 8401, along with two to three hundred other lost souls.

We were all brought together in the auditorium in one of two school buildings housing our program. A Chief Petty Officer walked to the podium. A grim assessment of the upcoming six months was laid out for us. We were entering one of the most demanding military academic programs in the world. If we survived, we would be one step closer to joining a very small, very exclusive group. The Chief said,

"I want every one of you to turn and look at the man sitting on your left. Now turn and look at the man on your right. At the end of this phase of the program, neither of those men will be here."

Attrition was expected to be at least fifty percent. Stress would be astronomical. The tempo would be brisk. The minimum passing grade would be 2.5...a C+ in civilian schools. There would be no squeaking by with a D, like the old high school days. The typical course of study for subjects would be eight to twelve weeks, depending on complexity. Subject matter would begin with basics, and finish up with material well into college level. All notes would be taken verbatim. Notebooks would be inspected regularly. Every page of our notes were required to be stamped CONFIDENTIAL NOFORN at the top and bottom. That meant not only was it classified, but it couldn't be viewed by any foreign nationals. All notebooks were required to have red covers, so standard military protocol for classified material could be followed. We had an awful lot of sensitive material floating around, and we needed to keep track of it. All classes, study, and homework would be done in the secure confines of the school buildings. No notes would be allowed out of the buildings, and personal effects were searched regularly. Infractions would probably mean immediate discharge and possible imprisonment.

We would need to be very careful regarding stress, and how we dealt with it. Obviously, drugs were strictly forbidden. Drinking was not advised, but it was understood that that was a lost cause. Advice was simple and to the point.

1) Learn the signs of stress in yourselves and those around you.

2) Rely on each other for support. Talk to each other. A friend is better than a bottle.

3) Exercise. It will help keep your stress level down, and your resistance high.

4) You're going to have to work hard. Don't be afraid to play hard. Just don't be stupid about it.

5) Don't start any new serious relationships. For Pete's sake, don't pick this time to get married. You'll quickly be divorced. This program will bring out things in you that you didn't even know existed. Your own mother won't even recognize you after this.

No punches were pulled regarding what would probably happen to some of us. The program was designed from the outset to be extremely difficult to pass. They needed to weed out the weak and unstable candidates. If someone was going to snap, they wanted it to happen here. Two miles off a hostile coast would be a very inconvenient location.

There would be nervous breakdowns. There would be arrests. There would be medical emergencies. Yes, there was a very high probability of suicides. All these things had happened before, and would undoubtedly happen again. Whether or not it happened to any specific individual was determined by how they chose to deal with the unrelenting stress and pressure that would follow.

We then went through a week long program called NASAP with a group of therapists. That stood for Naval Anti Substance Abuse Program. It was a touchy-feely attempt to get us accustomed to the idea of opening up to each other during times of extreme stress, instead of drinking ourselves to death. Apparently opening up was something I had a problem with.

I remember this event like it was yesterday, and will always remember it. We were sitting in a circle of chairs about twenty feet in diameter. Our "facilitator" was a former alcoholic and drug addict who had turned her life around, went to school, and became a successful therapist. She had a huge nasty scar on one of her legs, a memento of less happy times. She was liberal in her telling of stories about how things could be turned around, no matter how bad they looked. She was essentially the "don't give up" poster child. She was a good match for the program, and I genuinely liked her.

She was sitting about six people away from me. I was sitting there, listening to the conversation, basically just taking it all in. Everything seemed normal. Suddenly the talking stopped. I didn't realize it right away, and it took me a moment to notice how quiet it was. I looked around and saw she was staring at me. She spoke to me, not harshly, but intensely,

"I can't read you. I just can't read you. I can't get any emotion from you. It's like there's a wall up. I feel like I'm trying to get feelings from a stone."

No one in the room said anything, or even seemed to find her remarks unusual. I must have missed something somewhere. I never did figure out what that incident meant.

Finally it was time for classes to start. We were brought into the school building that housed the first three months of the program. We were shown around, and told the basic rules of security. We met some of our instructors. They told us what was expected of us. Most of them were pretty laid back, but a few were run of the mill pricks. We learned what our daily routine would be; what time we had to be in class, when we could break for lunch, and when assisted study hours would be held.

Official instruction began. We all fell into the routine fairly easily. I watched the people around me. They all seemed to be in the same boat as myself. Sure, it was going to be bad, but not impossible. We didn't have anyone picked out yet as a straggler. Then, one morning we had an empty seat. Danny was nowhere to be seen. That was odd. Was he sick? Was there a family issue? We all knew he ignored that critical advice, and got married shortly after arriving in Orlando. Speculation continued until our section advisor, Chief Carson walked in. The room quickly fell silent. The Chief looked around the room for a few seconds, and then said,

"You guys have probably noticed that Danny is missing this morning. Right now he's in the psych ward at the hospital. He tried to kill himself last night. Obviously, he won't be back. He'll be okay. But, maybe you could consider him an example of what could happen if you let things get out of hand."

Not a word was said. Then a hesitant voice spoke up in the silent room,

"What did he do...I mean, how did he try to do it?"

"I heard he took a bottle of pills. Pills of some sort."

We had suffered our first casualty. Danny was the first to "nuke out", as we called it. Initially, I found the going pretty easy. I had a good physics background. I knew my way around mathematics, though I wasn't great at it. Chemistry wasn't a problem. My head was above water, and it looked as if it would stay there. When HTFF started, I started to bog down a little. HTFF stood for Heat Transfer and Fluid Flow. It was a combination course of thermal dynamics and fluid dynamics. It was a killer for many of the students. So much so that it had its own nickname: Fleet Transfer and Student Flow. At least I wasn't alone.

Then two things happened at the same time. First, I failed my HTFF final exam. That came as a serious blow. That was the beginning of the end for many students. Second, I had my lower wisdom teeth removed. This procedure is very different in the military to what it is in the civilian community. The procedure can be very complicated at times. One of mine came out like a regular tooth, quick, neat and easy. The other one was the problem. It was still inside the jaw, and sideways.

The dentist had to cut away the gum, cut away the jaw, chisel the tooth in half, and take it out in pieces. The gum was then stitched back up. This happens a lot. That isn't what makes it so different. Here's what makes it so different. In the civilian community, the oral surgeon puts you to sleep for the procedure. That way you don't have to gag on the blood and bone chips. You don't have to watch the guy leaning over you, pounding on your jaw with a screwdriver. You don't have to feel your jaw on the verge of snapping. General anesthesia is the norm. It's just a decent thing to do.

In the military, they give you a couple of shots of *Novocain*.

It was one of the most terrible experiences in my life. The patient is then given pain killers, one day off (which some recommended you not take, because you'd get behind in school), and the advice that you might want to skip the pain killers. They might cause problems with concentration in school.

I did take the day off. Just as they predicted, I *did* get behind in school. How would I catch up? That was *my* problem. Having wisdom teeth removed is a requirement for everyone going into submarines. Did they have to do it *then*? Of course not. It could have been done at any point. That's the military for you.

Things quickly went downhill. My grades went down. My mandatory study hours went up. That meant less sleep. The possibility of failure loomed. I just couldn't catch up. I fell further and further behind. The depression returned. I quickly fell into a downward spiral. I would never make it. I would fail. My brother made it through, but I wasn't good enough. I was inferior. He had what it takes to do something special, like my Dad. I didn't. I would end up like so many others. I would fail out and become what we called other failed students. Nuclear Waste. Conventionals. Haze grey and underway. Nuked out.

Even if I stayed in submarines, I would go as a conventional. The stigma would mark me for the rest of my career. My family would never see me the same again. Oh, they wouldn't say it. But they would be thinking it. I knew it. I was absolutely miserable physically, mentally, any way a person could be. I just wanted it to end. But I couldn't fail. That was unacceptable. Everywhere I looked, I saw doors closing. The spiral became a free fall. Only one option seemed to make more and more sense.

Suicide.

It all made perfect sense now. These guys *weren't* crazy! They had figured it out! What the others felt now made perfect sense to me. The suffering would be over. I wouldn't have to face failure, or even worse, my family. Could it actually be that easy? It certainly seemed that way. No more sitting in a classroom for twelve hours a day, watching myself slowly slip under. No more worrying about how I could possibly face anyone . What would they say? What would I say? No more concerns about going through life constantly faced by reminders of how I failed to measure up. It would all be over with for one very convenient reason:

I'd be dead.

One small spark of sanity remained, like a solitary star on a cloudless winter night. I feared the unknown nature of death. That little spark kept me mesmerized just long enough for salvation to arrive. And, it arrived in a most curious form, a most unexpected form, quite out of context...

Pain.

Carpal Tunnel Syndrome was still a fairly obscure issue in the early 1980s. The world wasn't filled with computer keyboards like it is today. It was still caused by repetitive actions, just not in the same daily context it is now. It was this ailment that gave me the critical break I needed, and it was caused by one of the key factors of Nuclear Power School: verbatim taking of notes.

We students did a lot of writing in school. There were no recorders, no iPads, or any other buffer between us and our instructors. Some classes weren't so bad. Those involving math were a welcome break. But, others made up for it. It was a regular event to have an instructor walk into the classroom and say,

"Okay guys. Get out your liquid cooled pens. Today's going to be a rough one."

As it turns out, handwriting was the repetitive motion that drove my right hand nuts. I had a little helper, though. In my teens, I had a previous operation in that wrist. The doctors thought it might have changed things just enough to push the situation over the edge. Not that they wanted to admit anything was wrong.

It's a cliché caricature of military medicine to look at someone sick or injured, and say,

"It's all in your *mind*."

The story was that a military doctor (you want a contradiction in terms...*you got one*!) would avoid pulling a person out of service for treatment by convincing the patient it was all in their imagination. Got a sore ankle? It's all in your mind. One of your eyes getting dim? That's okay. It's all in your mind. This sarcastic remedy is very prevalent in older service members and veterans.

So, let's set the scene. I was talking to my Mom and Dad on the phone one day. I mentioned this irritating pain growing in my right hand. My Dad's immediate response was,

"So? Switch to your left hand, dummy. It'll feel like someone else is doing it."

This drew the prerequisite groan from my Mom, and my Dad got down to business. He explained the nature of Carpal Tunnel Syndrome, and the simple operation that cured it. I would be fine in no time. We finished up our call, and decided that I would go to sick call soon.

My visit to sick call was to be an eye opening experience. I expected the doctor to look at me, and quickly come to the same conclusion my father did. He gave me a quick exam, and proclaimed,

"There's nothing wrong with you. It's all in your mind."

I almost fell out of my chair! Oh Jesus, Mary, and all the orphans!! They actually *say* that! I thought that was all a joke. Well...I was wrong. He went on to explain that I was obviously feeling doubts regarding the line of work I had chosen. I was creating the pain myself so I wouldn't have to finish the program. I stared at this man. He was a Captain. That's one step down from an Admiral of one sort or another. I accepted his diagnosis and left.

I called my Mom and Dad again, and told them what my "problem" was. My Dad's response?

"Of course he's going to say that! What else did you expect? Go back again, and they'll realize they actually have to treat you."

I went back. I was given a much more thorough exam. Nothing was found, but the doctor said it would be a good idea to do a nerve conductivity test. It required a specialist, and the Navy had a contract with one in town. The test was arranged.

Now, let's talk about nerve conductivity tests. The name pretty much says it all. It involves nerves. It involves conductivity. Conductivity involves electricity. What they don't tell you is the part about the needles. Yes, I said needles. What the test essentially involves is sticking needles in various parts of the patient and running an electric current through them. I'm going to start a grassroots movement to rename the test the "wire-you-up-like-a-stereo-speaker-and-shock-your-sorry-ass" test. It might take up more space on the billing form, but at least folks would know what they were really in for.

The test was inconclusive. All that for nothing, a total waste of time.And even worse, the specialist was kind of creepy. The naval hospital wanted to look at me one last time. I went in for my appointment. Another Captain...oh, wonderful. But this time it was different. He was a kindly older man, coming up on his retirement. We sat and talked. He asked me a few questions about how it hurt, when it hurt, was I doing a lot of anything manual. I answered his questions. He sat for a moment. Then he did something quite odd. He opened his desk drawer, and took out a soup spoon.

He told me to join my index finger and thumb. He held up his own hand in the "A-okay" sign to show me what he meant. I did as he asked. He stuck the spoon in the circle my finger and thumb made.

"Don't let me pull this through."

He pulled it through. He tried it again. I was trying to keep my fingers together, but he pulled it through with ease each time. He looked at me,

"Just as I thought. You have Carpal Tunnel Syndrome. Probably from all the hand writing."

He explained the problem, just as my Dad had. He explained the operation to fix it, just like my Dad had. Then he said something that made my heart sink,

"You won't be going back to class. We'll schedule the operation, and I'll let you know when to come back for the pre-op."

Just what I needed! Another period away from class to make doubly sure I failed! I told him about my concerns, and asked if the issue could be held off with drugs until I was through with the program. His response took a few minutes to comprehend,

"Oh, you're out of the program. You'll be on medical hold. We'll do the surgery. You'll go on convalescent leave, and when you're finished healing you'll rejoin with a later class."

This was too good to be true. But, apparently that was how it worked. The Universe had just done me a huge honking favor. I was getting a rest. I was getting a second chance. I just might consider not touching myself so much after all.

And so the operation was scheduled and performed. Strangely enough, I was dating the OR nurse at the time. It would have been a little awkward if I had died on the operating table. Happily, everything went exactly as it was supposed to. I went back to have the stitches removed. I was assigned light duty and physical therapy. I reported to the records department at Nuke School. I would be spending my light duty sorting and alphabetizing records. I just had no idea what kind of records I'd be dealing with. It turned out I would be reorganizing records of civil complaints, arrests, and cases of students claiming homosexuality to leave the Navy.

Wow! Was that ever an eye opener. I had no idea so many seedy events took place behind the scenes at Nuke School. It was like a police blotter and soap opera fell in love and had a baby. Just when the day was getting dull, I would come across a batch of records for the people claiming homosexuality to get discharged. People nowadays have no idea how easy they have it. When these poor guys went in to drop the bomb, the Navy was ready and waiting. They wanted it all. They wanted names, dates, times, locations, and specific activities. All in proper chronological order. Obviously, the Navy wanted to make it as stressful and embarrassing as possible. They wanted to cull out the fakers just trying to get out easy. I decided if I ever truly felt I was gay, I'd just keep it to myself, thank you very much.

After a few weeks of that routine, I was transferred down to the Maintenance Shop. I joined another group of students lost in Limbo waiting to hear their fate. It was mostly light repairs, some cleaning, and strangely enough, construction of award plaques. That was a pretty interesting process. After a couple of weeks in the shop, I discovered the Universe decided I hadn't gotten enough rest just yet.

One night, I was showering before going to bed. I discovered a small bump, about the size of a pea, at the base of my spine. I wasn't crazy about the idea, but I figured I'd keep an eye on it to see what happened. For all I knew, it could be a bug bite. Central Florida was full of all kinds of strange little critters that liked the taste of people. I went to bed. I awoke in the small hours of the morning to a pain unlike any other I had ever felt. The lump on my bum grew from the size of a pea to that of a grape! Any contact, however slight, brought a wave of searing pain. I couldn't lay on my back or my side. Not that it mattered. I'd need a shot or two of morphine to get anywhere close to sleep. I toughed it out for the rest of the night. I'd go to the hospital in the morning.

By the time I got to the hospital I could barely walk. The doctor brought me in right away, and looked at my back.

"Oh, yeah. You've got a Pilonidal Cyst. That's a big one. It grew that much overnight?"

I confirmed all the elements of the story. He said it would have to come out, but he could lance it right then and there to buy a little time. My absolute glee at being sliced with a scalpel, in a very painful area, without any anesthesia was quite apparent. He said he'd make it quick. I only yelped a little. Then I was on my way back down to the lab to start another round of pre-op tests. I was getting to know the routine pretty well.

As it turned out, the nurse drawing my blood was a cute red head I'd met during my previous pre-op workup. I quickly got her number, and then just as quickly lost it. Women never will understand the intense sense of loss a guy feels when that happens. It was a happy reunion. She gave me her number again, and this time I did *not* lose it. It came in quite handy later.

I was a little more nervous this time going into the operating room. The doctor told me he would be attempting a new type of operation that would improve the healing of the incision. I wasn't happy about being the subject for a military medical experiment. I suppose I should just be grateful he didn't tell me it was "all in my head".

I checked in to the hospital the night before the operation. There was a very unique aspect of the prep for this procedure. A nurse came in that night and shaved my ass! Yes, you read that correctly. *Shaved my ass*. All of it. Every possible square millimeter. I ended up in some very unusual positions during the process, but she managed to complete the project. After that I was told to take a shower. I had some very unique impressions and insights soaping up and washing my freshly shaved bum. I'm not exactly sure I should discuss them. No. I think not.

The cyst came out without too much protest. It was time for some more convalescent leave. If there was any payoff for being hacked up by a Navy doctor, it was the free leave. But, the sense of urgency regarding my re-entry into the program was never far from me. All this time was put to very good use. I knew I would need to completely reassess how I was doing things. I would need to come up with a new routine. I would need to find a better way to combat the stress, and give myself some kind of break. I would soon have an opportunity to put these theories to the test.

Class 8407. That was to be my new home. I discovered they were actually ready for me a little earlier, but my return had been delayed for a very specific reason...by a very specific person, Chief Carson. As it turns out, he was keeping distant tabs on my medical issues and recovery. When he realized I was close to returning to the program, he pulled some strings. He explained that it would be beneficial for me to reenter into a familiar environment. 8407 had a vacancy in *his* section. The devil you know is better than the devil you don't. It was a good move.

Class8407, section 1 was where I belonged, as it turned out. Nuke School was divided up into specific sections, based on two criteria:

1) Rating. (the specific job one holds in the Navy)

2) Test scores. The theory was that the teaching environment would be more efficient if the students had similar learning abilities.

I started out in section 7 out of 13 sections in 8401. I returned to 8407 in section 1 out of 13. Section 13 was the highest scoring section. It doesn't take a rocket scientist to figure out what section 1 was. It was called the "Rock Section" for obvious reasons. When I spoke with Chief Carson later, I theorized that they had figured out exactly how stupid I really was. It was then that he informed me of his little "adjustment" to my schedule. There was an added benefit. The better instructors were assigned to the lower sections. It would give me a little better chance of success.

Section 1 was quite a group of guys. When I joined them, we numbered forty six. They had already lost several of their group in the weeks before my arrival. They all wished me luck. These guys deserve special recognition, if for no other reason than they had to deal with a whack job like me. These were my companions on this new road of trials and tribulations.

Petty Officer Straus: he looked like the stereotypical "Joe Cool". Rakish good looks, blow dried black hair, and dark aviator sunglasses that he wore as often as possible, unless he was ordered to remove them. He was known for the "joules" incident. He sat in the back of the room, and was prone to sleeping. During one of those periods, he was zonked out at the back of the room, aviators on, an unlit cigarette dangling from his lips in preparation for an upcoming "smoke-and-coke" break. The instructor had enough, and asked Straus a question in a very loud voice. Straus, rudely roused from a sound sleep, said the first word that popped into his head,

"Joules!"

And the crowd goes wild!! Fireworks spread across the sky! Sailors kiss random nurses in Times Square! The instructor stood at the front of the room in mute astonishment.

It was the correct answer.

For the remainder of the program, if a questions was posed to Petty Officer Straus, and he was hurting for an answer, someone would urge in a stage whisper,

"Joules."

Petty Officer Sturges: A little blonde guy, he was bright and sarcastic. His quick wit was his best defense. Once however, he made one wise ass remark too many. To me. I was left without an equally crafty comeback. I did the only thing I could think of at the time. I quickly reached down and grabbed the glasses off his face. I took a slobbering lick off both lenses. I carefully placed them back on his face. The room was silent. Finally, cries of "gross", "blech", and "yuck" filled the room. They were absolutely correct on all counts. His glasses tasted absolutely horrible. To this day, I have never done that again.

Petty Officer Funk: he never had a moment of peace. With a name like that, how could you? He was a soft spoken, good natured man. One of the few to survive.

Harry Reems: man, was he a cool guy. He was like a big teddy bear. Very even tempered, it was rare to see him ruffled. The only time I saw him angry was when we were sitting in a bar, and he was complaining about how quickly his wife spent his paychecks. He was an avid shooter, and part of one of the most memorable shooting outings of my life.

Petty Officer Puch: we called him anything but his real name! He was known as Petty Officer Pork, Puke, Poke, Peep, you name it. Another married student, he was usually ready with a story about his latest domestic escapade.

There were others, whose names I sadly have forgotten. But, their faces will live in my mind forever. One guy moved down to Orlando with his wife. I said *wife*. They were already married when they arrived. She was fifteen. Face it. Some of those stereotypes are based on fact.

There was the guy who earned a thrashing from his wife for substituting a pickle (fresh from the fridge) for a vibrator during a recent sexual interlude.

One of our guys used to do an impression of a "twidget", the slang term for an Electronics Technician. ETs and MMs were always fighting, unless drinking was occurring. We MMs had no shortage of abuse to pile on our black magic inclined shipmates. This guy would put on his black Navy issue raincoat. He would don his sailor's hat (called a white hat in the Navy), stretched to insane proportions. Then he would commence the critical part of his act. He would begin to drool. To this day, I swear at least one of his parents was a St. Bernard. This guy would stand there and drool until a single strand of saliva stretched from his mouth to the floor! Unbroken, it would waver like a silver thread in the subtle breeze. Then he would laugh,

"Ahore, ahore, ahore, (snort) ahore!"

We would be breathless in convulsive laughter. For men constantly on the verge of the mental breaking point, activities like this were crucial. If that didn't happen...*this* happened:

It was a typical school day. We had just come back from a quick break. As the instructor started into the next part of the lesson, we heard the distant wail of a siren. It got louder. The instructor listened for a few seconds, then made a dismissive gesture and continued talking and writing. It was getting quite loud now. The instructor started talking louder to remind the students that there was a *class* in progress. The siren stopped. We returned our attention to Lt. Mathias. He breathed a sigh of relief, and started talking again. Not so fast, Mr. Mathias! As he was writing on the board, his back to us, a crew of EMTs raced past the door with one of those neat wheeled stretchers and boxes of medical equipment. We all got up and raced to the door! Mr. M turned around with a look that said *Oh, come on guys! Really?* Finally, even he couldn't resist the urge and joined us at the door. Using rank as a cow catcher, he pushed his way to the front. The EMTs screeched around a corner, and were gone. Mr. Mathias herded us all inside. Then, in a moment of clarity, he closed the door before continuing the lesson. A few heads turned as muted radio traffic raced past the door as the EMTs and their package departed.

Later, we found out what had happened. One of our classmates decided it would be a good idea to see if he could leap over the desk near the door, usually occupied by the Study Hours Watch after hours. He expertly sized up the situation. Eying the distance, his "leaping off" point, and the convenient elevated starting point, he decided it would be no problem. His audience insured him he had figured everything correctly. Sadly, the elevated starting point would be a part of the problem. You see, that same elevated starting point that allowed him to achieve the needed altitude to clear the desk, also set up a perfect trajectory between his forehead and the top of the door frame.

Actually, I heard it was quite spectacular! His head made an almost cartoonish sound as it smacked into the door frame. Blood went everywhere. His unconscious form landed on the linoleum floor with a gratuitous bounce. No applause, though. I guess they figured that would be a little tacky. Officers and Chiefs ran, obscenities were shouted, and phone calls were made.

Yes, he survived the program.

Classes continued. Courses were taught. Tests were taken. Sadly, the number of students in our section continued to drop. They dropped like flies, actually. One student after another either failed out, nuked out, or had to be removed due to some kind of medical or mental stress. I still recall one particular student. As the courses progressed, he became more and more consumed by eczema. He would come into class with his face covered with ointment. As his stress level increased, so did his ailment. Finally, he couldn't take it anymore. He was dropped from the program. I ran into him later. I asked him how he was doing. He told me it was as if a huge weight was lifted from his shoulders. I looked closer at him. All the eczema was gone. He looked happy. Sadly, seeing him like this had no effect on the pressure I felt to pass the program. Even making the connection between leaving, and the improvement of health and sanity, made no impact. Stupidity can be so powerful.

Another group of characters was our instructors. What a colorful and diverse bunch they were. They were a mixture of commissioned and enlisted submarine veterans, career officers who had never seen sea duty, and junior officers fresh from the program themselves. They had secured a position as instructors as their next duty assignment. The men would eventually go to sea. The women would be instructors or administrative staff in one form or another.

Lt. Sopp: he could have a sense of humor from time to time. Sadly, he bought in completely to the Academy philosophy regarding enlisted personnel. He had to be addressed as "sir" at all times. We were not allowed to question his previous comments, unless they were specifically phrased. But, he had his moments. In spite of his attempts to be a machine, we all knew he was human. The occasional smile or laugh gave him away.

Petty Officer McClister: he was one of our favorite instructors. His field of expertise was MTMO. That stood for Mechanical Theory for Mechanical Operators. He was an intuitive instructor, and everyone grasped his lessons with ease. The only problem was that he found himself at a very difficult crossroads. He had just made Chief. He also just got accepted by the NECP. That was the Nuclear Enlisted Commissioning Program. So, he had just achieved the rank that would make him the "big frog in the little pond" when he started a program that would make him an ensign. In other words, the "little frog in the big pond". I have to wonder how he dealt with that. He became a little "twitchy". His demeanor changed. He also developed a very unusual habit. While lecturing and writing, he would stop and whistle at key points in his statements. It was just a little two note whistle. But, it became disturbing for most of us. When we realized it wasn't going to stop, we would often look at each other with concern as he lectured. The saddest part happened when I went to him with a question after class. He was in the faculty office area, and I sought him out for clarification on something he said earlier. He looked at my notes, took my paper and began to speak and write. Standing there alone, just the two of us, he whistled as he spoke just as he had in class. I suddenly felt very sad. I didn't even listen to the rest of what he had to say. All I wanted to do was reduce the discomfort by leaving as soon as he was finished.

Mr. Mathias: he was a hoot! He was our math instructor. He had a natural knack for teaching. Our math curriculum started with fractions, and ended with college level Calculus. When I studied Algebra Two and Calculus in high school I floundered. I had no grasp of anything going on. I actually worried about entry into the Nuclear Field because I squeaked through Calculus with a D.

Not so for Mr. Mathias. I had no issues at all grasping the principles he explained. I surpassed the level of mathematics I struggled with, and continued further under his instruction. We enjoyed his classes. As a compliment, one of the students drew a caricature of him on the chalk board, as he would appear on TV. He drew the TV around him as well, with great skill. Next to it he wrote,

"It's time for the Mr. Mathias show!"

We sat there, admiring his expert work. Mr. Mathias walked in, took one look, and walked out. Next, Chief Carson walked in. He took one look at the chalk board, froze, and walked out. At class time, Mr. Mathias returned and started class. He wrote on the chalk board as usual. But this time he avoided writing on the board with the artwork. Finally, as the lesson continued, he had no choice. He stopped and admired the picture. He commented on its quality of likeness. Then he erased it and continued with the lesson. When the lesson was finished, we chatted for a minute or two before he left.

Between classes, Chief Carson returned. He lectured us sternly, telling us how lucky we were that Mr. Mathias had a sense of humor. We might not be so lucky next time. We were to be much more careful from now on.

Mr. Mathias told us this story one day before class. He was still in college. Being a math major, he was coming in for the first day of one of the more advanced classes. To his complete surprise, the room was packed! Was this some kind of mistake? Maybe a joke? This class had six or seven students during a busy semester. Why all the people? The professor for the class was popular. Was that it? The class waited for their professor to arrive.

Things did not turn out as expected. Instead of the well-known math professor, a little old Indian man walked in. He looked like he was 120 years old. Gandhi himself could have been one of his students. He situated himself in the room, paused, and then spoke in a very thick Hindi accent,

"My name...Oman Opadid. I teach you...mathematique. Your professor have...as you say...dysentery. He no come back."

He then proceeded to begin writing mathematical equations. He wrote non-stop until all the chalk boards were full. He was totally silent the entire time. When the boards were filled, he stopped, erased them all, and started over. Again, he filled the boards. He didn't even turn around to face the room. He simply wrote. Again, he filled the boards and erased them. And again. The room was totally silent. At the end of the class, Mr. Oman Opadid turned around. Six students remained. He gathered his personal effects and walked out. The next day, the regular professor returned. He walked in to see a normal compliment of six students, greet the class, and start a perfectly normal semester of class. It was unknown whether or not he was ever told about Oman Opadid.

Chief Henderson: He was our instructor for ETMO, or Electrical Theory for Mechanical Operators. He spent a few years on one of our ballistic missile submarines, the U.S.S. Will Rodgers, also known as the "Willie R". He was quite a colorful individual. With years of sea experience, he was never short of a few sea stories if things were slow. During one of these periods he told some stories about one of his shipmates (who will be known as Joe) that I will *never* forget. This tale is forever etched in my mind:

Chief Henderson was walking along a pier, with his friend. They were headed back to their boat after a few hours ashore. As they walked along, they passed a local man fishing off the pier. In a large plastic bucket was a fish he recently caught. Joe stopped abruptly, and looked in the bucket. The man turned around to see a CPO staring at the fish in his bucket. Joe said,

"That's a neat fish! Can I have it?"

The man looked Joe up and down. Not knowing Joe's degree of sanity, he reluctantly agreed to relinquish the fish. As they continued down the pier toward their submarine, Joe crammed the fish into his trouser pocket as far as it would go. They got to the boat, and climbed down the torpedo room hatch. Joe held up a finger, as if to say *now watch this*. They walked toward the Wardroom. As they went, Joe transferred the luckless fish from his pocket to inside his pants and shirt. Finally, they arrived at the Wardroom door. Joe politely knocked. They were told to enter. The officers were having lunch, all seated around the table. Joe greeted the roomful of officers. Then he walked over to his division officer, a Lieutenant. He stood close to the table. He announced,

"Hey, Lieutenant! I got something for ya!"

With that, he opened the fly of his pants. The head of the fish flumped out onto the table, its mouth still gulping for air. The room erupted in pandemonium, half crying out in horror, and half laughing hysterically! The Ensign sitting next to the Lieutenant, in true Ensign fashion, *vomited*. I guess submariners have an odd sense of humor.

Our physics instructor was a young Lieutenant Junior Grade. I can't recall his name. He was an avid football fan. We delighted in getting him caught up in involved debates about football as soon as he walked into the room. Ten minutes later, he would suddenly stop and shout,

"You bastards did it *again*!"

He made full Lieutenant during our period there, for which we heartily congratulated him.

Our chemistry instructor was another Electrician's Mate Chief, whose name I have sadly forgotten. He was good natured. A typical middle aged, balding, fast talking man, his most notable feature was the degree to which he would profusely sweat as he wrote on the black board. It would be difficult to keep up with his staccato bursts of information. It wasn't just the speed at which he spoke. We would be enthralled by the sight of him leaning into the black board, almost looking at his writing sideways. Chalk would fly, and the sweat would *run* off him. He always kept a hand kerchief in his non writing hand, which he used to regularly mop the sweat off his balding head and face.

He was also very, *very* military. Our courses were divided up into subjects called Topical Guide Objectives. Some of our instructors referred to them casually. Some ignored them completely. Not our Chief! Oh, no! Not only did he refer to each and every one, not only did he call each one by its full designation, he also used the phonetic alphabet religiously. I can still recall him pointing rigidly at the black board, belting out in true military precision,

"Next, Topical Guide Objective Bravo..."

Before chemistry class, one of us would invariably point rapidly at various objects around the room shouting,

"Alpha! Bravo! Charlie! Delta!"

This menagerie of characters was responsible for our welfare and instruction during the first leg of our trip through hell. It was they who would be mostly responsible for our success. Sadly, their record was not perfect, especially with us. Our number continued to drop. One student never had a chance. He studied so long each day, he couldn't sleep at night. He constantly fell asleep at his desk. Our remedy for times like that was to stand in the back of the room. After dozing off several times, he would finally get up and walk to the back of the room, his face saying "I know, I know. I'm going." Toward the end of his time with us, he would walk to the back of the room. A few minutes later we would hear his pen or notebook hit the floor. He was falling asleep on his feet. Finally one day his seat was empty. It was only a matter of time.

We also lost two more students from other sections. One went to the top floor of his barracks, and dove headfirst off the balcony. Amazingly, he survived. Another got on his motorcycle, wound it up as fast as he could, and ran directly into a dumpster. He did *not* survive.

My second chance enabled me to perform much better the next time around. But, not *that* much better. I still ended up with mandatory study hours. It eventually got up to thirty five hours a week. These study hours were taken very seriously. Violating them usually meant disciplinary action of some kind. Some students falsified the study logs. A couple of my friends took that route. These people were always found out. When they were, they were immediately kicked out of the program, and demoted. One thing could always get a student kicked out, no matter how smart they were. That one thing was Demonstrated Unreliability. A DUI was an immediate ticket to the fleet. Too many speeding tickets had the same effect. An arrest was a sure thing.

My mandatory study hours were thirty five hours a week. That was the maximum amount that could be assigned. I had no choice but to comply. But that caused a problem. One of the changes I made to my routine was my mandatory time off the base, or at least out of the school building. Taking a regular break of some kind would be critical to my success. That time was going to be the weekends. There were still times when I would need to spend hours in the school building on a Saturday or Sunday. But, I was able to spend enough time in class during the week to have some kind of regular time off. This is how I did it...

Normal school hours were eight hours a day, five days a week. That's your typical forty hour week. My mandatory study hours were thirty five hours a week, all of which had to be spent in the classroom as well. So, break out your calculators. That came up to seventy five hours a week in the school building. But, I still needed to have my weekend free. How was I going to pull *that* off? Don't put those calculators away! It didn't take long to figure out that all the school time needed to be satisfied in five days. So, I would need to spend at least fifteen hours per day in the school building. Eight hours of class, and seven hours for study would be my daily routine. I steeled myself for a very nasty time for the remainder of my time in Orlando.

But it worked.

I kept my head above water. The days were long, and the nights were very short. Actual time spent in class was roughly seventeen hours a day. The flip side was that I had free time on the weekends to do anything I wanted. I was actually able to get a room at the nearest fancy hotel. I spent time at the beach, either with relatives or friends. Sometimes I just laid in my room and read or listened to music. It was then that I discovered WLOQ, and the new love in my life. Jazz!

The end of the program was growing near. These six months of torture culminated in what was known as...

THE COMP.

The Comp was the final exam for Nuke School. It was a four hour test that included everything and anything covered in the last six months of having information crammed down our throats. Anything involving physics, math, chemistry, nuclear fission, corrosion control, radiation control, electricity, thermal dynamics, fluid dynamics, schematics or technical diagrams. It was all fair game. It was also the make-or-break period for a budding Nuke. That one test determined whether or not one had a career. It was an extremely stressful prospect.

Preparations for the Comp began about two weeks before the actual test. Comp test study packs were handed out. These were essentially practice tests for the real event. Each one had to be completed and handed in, when they would be analyzed by the instructors. It finally got to the point that classes were finished, and all we did was study packs. In the last week before the Comp, I received some very interesting news:

My brother was getting married. I was the best man. He was in Maine. I was in Florida, preparing for the most important test of my entire life. Would I be able to make the wedding?

Sure. I would just tell the Chief.

"ARE YOU OUT OF YOUR FUCKING MIND??"

Chief Carson's eyes were the size of baseballs. Out of the question. Absolutely out of the fucking question. I had a

Comp to prepare for, in case that detail slipped my mind. But...but...I had it all figured out! I could fly up Friday night. The wedding was on Saturday. I could fly back Sunday. It was fully contained within the constraints of the weekend. I didn't have duty that weekend. It would work. I pulled out all the stops. Pulled every heartstring I could imagine. It was now that I would find out if Chief Carson actually *had* a heart.

He did. *Kind of.*

This was his final decision,

"Okay, I'm telling you... you can't go. But I can't physically restrain you, or watch you every hour of the day. If you go, I know nothing about it. But, you listen to me. If you're not here Monday morning, and I have to tell my boss you're 1300 miles away, I'll be hanging. And, you'll be hanging right next to me. But, there will be one major difference between you and me. *You won't have an ass!"*

I delivered the good news to my brother. The flights were arranged. It was one of the most distracting weekends of my life. Every glitch was an indication I wouldn't make it back. Logan International Airport should have a sign outside proudly proclaiming:

LOGAN INTERNATIONAL AIRPORT! HOME OF THE GLITCH!

Monday morning I walked into Chief Carson's office. I shrugged and gave him a reassuring smile that said "See? It all worked out." All he did was growl. So much for appreciation for all my hard work.

The day of the Comp finally arrived. Every surviving member of Class8407 Section 1 was present. All sixteen of us. The empty feeling in the room was lost on no one. There were forty six of us when I joined them. They had lost guys before I arrived. I was struck dumb by the attrition rate. I can only imagine what these guys felt. We all wished each other luck. Then the room got very quiet.

The Chief came in and gave us a pep talk. All unnecessary materials were removed from the room. All calculators had to be powered down and turned on again in the presence of the proctor. This insured that no student had preprogrammed formulas in their calculators. All formulae had to be remembered by heart. The test booklets were passed out. We were specifically ordered to keep them closed. Every heart in that room was pounding. I know mine was. The proctor cleared his throat.

"Begin."

The test was actually a little anticlimactic. That's probably what the staff intended. By this point, you would either fail or succeed. Every once in a while the heavy silence would be broken by a despondent sigh. Apparently I wasn't the only one having "Oh, shit" moments. I finished the test. I went through it again, checking every possible thing I could think of. I sat there for a moment, and then did it again. This was it. I could think of nothing else I could doubly triple check. I had either passed or failed. I looked up at the clock. Ninety minutes had passed. *Ninety minutes?* This was supposed to be a four hour test! There was no way in Hell, Heaven, or Earth I could have properly completed that test. But...I could think of nothing else. I stood up, walked to the proctor's desk and passed in my test. He looked at the clock, and back at me. I shrugged and walked out.

Chief Carson was standing outside the classroom. He heard the door open and spun around. He saw me, and his face held a mixture of shock and rage. He looked at his watch, then back at me. All I could do is shrug,

"Sorry, Chief. I checked it over and over. There was nothing else I could do."

"You finished the test?"

"Yeah."

"You had better have *aced* that mother fucking test!"

He was still grumbling as I walked away. It was lunchtime. I walked down the concrete strip that separated the chow hall from the school buildings. I only got halfway there. How the hell could I eat at a time like this?

The only thing more dramatic than the day of the Comp...is the *night* of the Comp. The tradition was firmly entrenched. Early in the evening, the scores for all students would be posted in the huge window at the end of one of the first floor corridors. A huge section of glass was completely concealed by sheets upon sheets of computer printed results.

What would normally happen was that a student would go up to the window, find his section, find his score, and find out if he had any future worth as a human being. Someone not having experienced going through the program simply cannot understand the life changing significance of that pivotal moment. A crowd of people was permanently located around that window, jockeying for position to see their particular page. The occasional whoop of joy or cry of pathetic despair would be heard. I will always recall one sight I witnessed while walking back to my barracks that night. A young man was there by the window. He was on his knees in the grass, his head bowed to the ground. He was sobbing uncontrollably. It didn't take a rocket scientist to figure out which way his test went.

The next part of the tradition was optional, and didn't matter whether a student passed or failed. It was the Navy Nuke equivalent of a stoned rock star smashing his guitar. The student would then take several steps back from the wall...and throw their calculator into the bricks as hard as he possibly could. The next day, the lawn would look as if it was covered in confetti. Upon closer inspection, one would see it was calculator keys. It was the impromptu memorial to those sacrificed products of Sharp, Texas Instruments, National Semiconductor, and Hewlett-Packard.

I chose to avoid the wall that night. Either I passed or failed. Going to the wall wouldn't change anything. I'd find out one way or the other tomorrow. As it turns out, I didn't need to. I was walking out to the main gate to get picked up by the OR nurse. On the way, Harry drove by in his old dingy white Pontiac. He leaned out the window and shouted,

"We all passed! We all passed the Comp! We all made it!!"

A huge weight had been lifted off my shoulders. I then ran into Sturges, walking back from the taxi stand. He ran up, threw his arms around me, and planted a huge kiss on my bearded cheek! The scent of beer was strong. He obviously started celebrating early.

"We all passed! You! *You* son of a bitch! You got a *3.4!*"

I couldn't even feel my feet on the ground! It was all over. I survived. *We* survived. Out of the forty-six I started with, we graduated sixteen. That part sucked. But, it really was over.

For now.

The few remaining days were filled with busywork, duty watches, cleaning, and waiting. You know what they say. The waiting is the hardest part. We were provided the distraction of a graduation ceremony. All candidates worthy of special attention were called up to shake Captain Gorman's hand, and receive their diploma personally. My name was called. It was then that I learned I had attained a 3.2... top standing for my section.

The Navy was now determining the next part of our respective journeys. The next step was called "Prototype". We would go to one of the Knowles Atomic Power Laboratory sites for hands on experience running an actual nuclear propulsion plant. We would go to Idaho, New York, or Connecticut. I was hoping for the S1C site in East Windsor, Connecticut. Two reasons drove that. First, it meant I could live at home instead of running around looking for an apartment, and worse, roommates. Second, it was the site my brother, Steve, qualified on.

We all carefully filled out our "dream sheets". The Navy pretended we had some say in where we were going. It was actually just a cruel hoax, as we'll see later. The day finally arrived. The Chief came in waving a paper, saying it would be posted on his door. He almost got pressed flat to the door as he tried to get tape out of the dispenser. We crowded into him, trying to get a peek at the printout. I weaseled my way to the paper. I found my name, and traced my finger across the page. That couldn't be right. Someone bumped my finger. Try it again. Find my name...trace across...slooooowly...S1C.

Chapter 4-
What am I doing here?

Adversity introduces a man to himself.

- Anonymous

"Rotary! Rotary!! What the fuck is a *rotary*? I drove around that friggin' thing six times before I figured out how to escape!"

Hysterical laughter erupted through the locker room that first morning at S1C, officially known as Knowles Atomic Power Laboratory, East Windsor Site.

"Welcome to New England!"

Many of the students from the northeast told him he passed his rite of passage. New England girls might actually talk to him now. Our first day was frantic and chaotic. We were shown where to show up each day for quarters, which is the naval equivalent to roll call. We were separated into sections, and section leaders were assigned. We met our advisors, also known as our "Sea Dads". We picked up all study materials needed. We learned our schedules. The next six months were going to be very, very tough. Each day would be at least thirteen hours. That was if everything went perfectly. Each work week would be seven days long. Days off were staggered. The entire cycle would be seven days on and two days off. Then seven days on and one day off. Then seven days on and three days off. Then it would start all over. We would rotate through day shift, swing shift, and midnight shift.

Standards would only get tighter. The minimum passing grade would now be 2.8, or about a B-. Mandatory study hours were back in effect. The same penalties used in Orlando would apply if we tried to skip them. If someone had to stay for study and couldn't make the drive home, there was a place for them to sleep and shower. It was a Quonset Hut dubiously named The Hilton. I never used The Hilton. A lot of guys did. Some guys used it a lot. Some used it too much, like one student from our group who decided to use it as the setting for his death. He was found the morning after he overdosed on sedatives, about halfway through the program.

Our exposure to the prevailing attitudes began early, and came from a source as old as the military itself: graffiti on the bathroom walls. Military historians are quick to point out the graffiti on the walls of bathrooms in Roman barracks. The only element that changed over time was the equipment referred to. Three expressions of contempt and desperate frustration will remain in my memory forever. Let's discuss.

The first was a work of art that obviously took a long time to construct. If it wasn't finished over a period of days, then the student had fallen into a zen-like frame of mind during his respite in the stall. Neatly printed on the wall, from seated shoulder height to seated knee height was:

WAKE UP WORK
GO HOME SLEEP
WAKE UP WORK
GO HOME SLEEP
WAKE UP WORK
GO HOME SLEEP
WAKE UP WORK
GO HOME SLEEP
WAKE UP WORK
GO HOME SLEEP
WAKE UP WORK
GO HOME SLEEP
WAKE UP WORK
GO HOME SLEEP
WAKE UP WORK
GO HOME SLEEP
WAKE UP WORK
GO HOME SLEEP
WAKE UP WORK
GO HOME SLEEP
WAKE UP WORK
GO HOME SLEEP
WAKE UP WORK
GO HOME SLEEP
WAKE UP WORK
GO HOME SLEEP
WAKE UP WORK
GO HOME SLEEP
WAKE UP WORK

Another was a play on Navy-speak. The military is infamous for its rampant use of abbreviations and acronyms. The Navy was no different. Everywhere we looked, we saw NAVSHIPS, NAVPERS, NAVSEA, etc. One creative student found the perfect way to express his unhappiness.

NAVSUX

Last but not least was a particularly artful arrangement of letters and numbers that I found quite imaginative. The wit and artful design almost brought me to tears.

S1C

SUX

D1C

If our Roman predecessors could have figured out what we were talking about, their hearts would have burst with pride.

The prototype phase of our training started with classroom work. We learned the history and basics about our plant. Combustion Engineering was asked to develop a nuclear propulsion plant for a small submarine. The idea was that a small propulsion plant utilizing direct drive would power a small, extremely quiet hunter/killer submarine. Direct drive means there is no reduction gear assembly.

Perhaps it would be easier if we laid a little ground work...

A typical nuclear propulsion plant includes a reactor, a steam generating system, two sets of steam turbines (one pair generates electricity), and a reduction gear system. The reduction gears act as a link between the two rapidly spinning propulsion turbines and the much slower turning propeller shaft. Think "transmission" between the engine and drive shaft on an automobile. Reduction gears allow more power to be transferred to the screw, making the vessel faster. But, the reduction gears make noise. In the submarine community, noise is very, very bad.

Now let's look at the system developed by Combustion Engineering. The two propulsion turbines that would normally be fitted to the reduction gears are instead each linked to a generator. Those two generators drive a Main Propulsion Motor attached to the shaft. The system isn't as powerful, making the vessel slower. But, it's *much* quieter.

The Navy used several different types of reactor plants back in the 1980s. The Nuclear Propulsion Program only taught one, the S5W plant. The overwhelming majority of our submarines used this plant. Sadly, there was no land based prototype plant to train on. That was for a couple of different reasons. First, by the time the S5W was designed and built, we had pretty much figured out what we were doing. A prototype wasn't really necessary. Secondly, land based prototypes were usually used for oddball designs that needed more exhaustive testing before being deployed in service. The downside to all of this was that a student learned the S5W plant in NPS. Then they had to learn a totally different system to qualify at a prototype site. Then they had to *re-learn* S5W, or another different system if they were going to a surface ship. My brother had it easy. He qualified on S1C in East Windsor, and then went to the U.S.S. Tullibee. She was the only submarine in the entire Navy using...you guessed it! The S1C plant. I did *not* have that luck, as the reader will later discover.

Our first morning at quarters was very interesting. All departments reported in with student and staff in formation. The Chief read the watch bill for the day. Then we noticed a small group of men standing at the front of the room, facing the Chief. He read through a list of each of them, announcing which position they had qualified for during the overnight. Each man had qualified for either Mechanical Operator, Electrical Operator, or Reactor Operator. He shook their hands one by one. Then, everyone took a step back. Here's when it got interesting! All the people in the ranks each pulled out a handful of pennies, and flung them at the backs of the newly qualified operators! There was a round of applause, and quarters was dismissed. I quickly realized what my next goal would be. I would set my sights on being pelted in the back with a shotgun blast of currency.

We started the classroom phase by leaning about the basic principles and systems of our propulsion plant. We quickly learned one unusual characteristic of our plant. It contained four main coolant pumps. But, one of them was valved out. It was inoperable, and KAPL was still deciding its fate. We needed to know the actual condition of the plant for safe operations to be insured. But that also gave the instructors an interesting kink to throw at a student.

"Describe the immediate actions for a loss of flow casualty in the starboard loop. Oh...assume pump three is operational."

Yes, we had to know those actions as well. System parameters, procedures, schematic layouts, and component purposes all had to be learned before we could work "in-hull". Along with classroom work came the tests. Initially, I did well. Then the most important part of our training began. This was the part that would prepare us for qualification on a submarine. This is how things would be done in the fleet. It was time to go in-hull.

In words alone, it's difficult to convey the image of what a prototype plant is. Most of the people I've described it to have difficulty forming a mental picture of what I'm trying to describe. It's best to think of it in purely technical terms. Try it this way:

When designers want to produce a new aircraft, they go through a specific order of steps.

1) Produce an illustration of how the finished product will look.

2) Use principles and equations to determine how the product will operate.

3) Build a test model for use in a wind tunnel. This will test those assumptions formulated on the drawing board.

4) Build a full sized prototype to test fly, and modify if necessary.

The propulsion plant for a ship or submarine is designed and built in much the same way. First, the operational requirements for the plant are decided upon. The designers determine the size of the plant. They decide the size and shape of the hull that will enclose it. The components need to be arranged in a certain way to fit the plant into the given space. Will it fit? Will the shapes and paths of the piping work as advertised? Does anything need to be moved? If so, is there room to move it? There's only one way to find out. They build an exact copy of the plant. They enclose it in a hull the exact size and shape of the real submarine hull. Any systems fed by sea water are fed by a system of fresh water piped into the hull. Instead of a propeller working against water, the Main Propulsion Motor shaft turns a generator supplying the same resistance. That generator's power output is fed through an enormous bank of resistors.

From the outside, it looks as if the rear half of a submarine has been pulled off and plopped on the ground. The rudders and stern planes have been removed. There is a building at each end. For everyone inside, it's an exact replica of what they'd see in the real submarine. If they didn't know better, they would be *on a submarine*.

Just as accurately reproduced is the method by which someone will qualify as an operator. The student must qualify on all the watch stations they will operate. In order to qualify on those stations, they must qualify on all the systems making up that watch station. For example, as a Mechanical Operator I would need to become intimately familiar with all cooling systems, the condensate system, all steam systems, the turbines, all lube oil systems, air conditioning systems, and anything involving a pump, pipe, fluid or valve. These systems would be broken up into separate watch stations such as Engine Room Upper Level, Engine Room Lower Level, and Machinery Space Lower Level.

I would need to know the location, power supply, purpose, and operating parameters of every component. I would need to know how to put the system into a safe state in the event of any conceivable emergency. I would need to know the effect each component would have on any other component in the event of a failure. I had to know all these things instinctively, without stopping to think. It's a lot to know! How does one learn it all? As any submariner can tell you, it's very simple:

The Checkout.

What is a checkout? It goes like this:

Let's say you need to get a checkout on the Main Condensate System. Here's how it goes.

1) Get a copy of the SOPs. This stands for Ship's Operating Procedures. This is broken up into several extremely large, heavy volumes. They can tell you virtually anything you need to know about virtually any system. Look up the chapter on the Main Condensate System, and read it. Several times. Know it forwards and backwards. Every speed, temperature, pressure, power supply, procedure, and component location. Then learn to produce a detailed schematic drawing of the system from memory.

2) Go in-hull. Find the system. Trace it out. Find *everything*. Every pump, motor, valve, breaker, and pipe. Trace it out one foot at a time.

3) Find an operator designated to give checkouts on that system. More specifically, find an operator designated to give checkouts on that system who isn't already giving a checkout to someone else. That could be a problem. If you find someone, you'll sit down with them. They'll usually start by asking for that detailed schematic drawing we were talking about. Draw it. Make it pretty, neatness counts. If you've done it correctly, he'll ask you about the locations of the components. This might involve going in-hull to show him directly. He'll ask you about all the operating parameters. He'll ask you about procedures and power supplies. The checkout will usually last about an hour. If you get everything right, you'll get a "sig". That's a signature on your qual card showing you're "checked out" on that system. If it doesn't go so well, you'll miss

questions. The answers to those questions will become "look ups". Go find the answers to those questions. Then you'll get your precious sig.

4) Move on to the next system.

Here is some extremely important advice. If you fail or get lookups from one instructor, *DO NOT* go to another instructor! If you *start* a checkout with an instructor, *end* with that instructor. Failure to do so is found to be in particularly poor taste.

After you've finished your checkouts for a watch station, it's time to go in-hull and actually stand the watch. All watch stations are staffed by instructors. The student takes the watch, and is removed only if the instructor wants to take over. That doesn't necessarily mean the student made a mistake. There are many different circumstances when an instructor will utter the words,

"I've got the watch."

So, the student stands the watch with an instructor over a period of days or weeks, depending on the complexity of the watch station. The system is operated in a wide variety of circumstances, including every conceivable emergency. That is when the hapless student is introduced to that ever present facet of Navy life: The Drill.

Oh, yes. We have drills for virtually everything in the Navy. One can tell the drills are about to begin when the Drill Monitors arrive. They are plainly labeled by red ball caps. They are the ones who run and later critique the drills. Seeing those red hats is never a good sign. In some instances, when the first red hat is sighted, someone will discreetly pick up a sound powered phone and softly say,

"Red hats aft."

Some will tell you learning what to do in drills is more difficult than learning to run the process in the first place. Sadly, as much of a pain-in-the-ass as they may be, they are critical to surviving those instances when things go to hell. When the student has displayed an adequate level of knowledge, they are declared:

Qualified in (fill in the blank).

This process goes on for each watch station the student will stand in the execution of their duties. The occasional test still rears its ugly head. But for the most part, the vast majority of work is done in-hull at this point. If everything goes right, if you don't get disciplined, if you don't fail out, if you don't commit suicide, you'll get to that pivotal, climactic moment:

Your Oral Board.

There are certain traditions surrounding the boards. They are always held in the wee hours of the morning. They know that is when a student is at their very worst. But, the strange part is the donuts. Well, maybe that part isn't so strange. After all, the Navy runs on donuts. Anyway, the candidate is required to bring a dozen donuts to his Oral Board. Perhaps *required* is a little too strong of a term. He's only required to bring them if he wants to *pass*. Dunkin Donuts were the best. I might be losing focus here. The donuts are presented, and the Board begins.

A Nuclear Propulsion Engineer (the civilian supervisor in charge of all operations), a Chief, and at least two staff Petty Officers proceed to grill the living hell out of this poor student. They want it all. Procedures, parameters, locations, schematics, and donuts. The process lasts about two hours. If the student passes, he gets to carry for the first time in his naval career, the following title...

Qualified as an Operator.

The candidate's status immediately changes. No more tests. No more watches. No more drills. No more study hours. They have officially made it through a year of sheer hell, and survived. In that year, they have received the rough equivalent of an engineering degree, served up in a manner that very few can survive.

So, how did my personal experience at Knowles compare? Think of it this way... rough periods of a person's life are often referred to as "a roller coaster ride". That metaphor would apply to my time at S1C. But, there would be some minor changes:

1) The roller coaster cars wouldn't have any restraining bars to lock down over your lap.

2) The ride wouldn't break smoothly to a halt. You wouldn't be told to exit to the left. Instead, it would run into a sturdy brick wall.

3) Covered in road kill.

4) On fire.

My time at S1C would be disturbingly familiar to my adventure in Orlando. Sadly, this time there would be no breaks for dreamy trips to the hospital. As mentioned previously, the training started with classroom work. This started out smoothly, but soon bogged down. The length of the workday, the extreme stress, and the daily commute soon took a toll on my performance. I wasn't failing tests, but my head was barely above water. All the same fears returned. My ability to sleep took a major hit.

I made it through the classroom phase. It was time to go in-hull. I quickly regained my footing. Seeing the principles in action has always been the key to my success in learning anything complex. My Sea Dad was impressed with my performance. During those periods when he stood watch with me, he began talking about recommending me for one of the advanced schools available to graduates with high standings or superior aptitude. The alternatives for Mechanical Operators were either Nuclear Grade Welding, or Engineering Lab Technician. Both would make for an interesting fleet assignment, and a supremely impressive resume'. Things were really looking up.

Not so fast, Squidly! Those demons from your past were only napping. I was on watch in-hull. I was manning the Feed Station, when I made a critical error. My Sea Dad was standing watch with me when it happened. Like most of my mistakes, it was spectacular. Why screw up just a little if you can go big, and get *everyone's* attention? My Sea Dad went ballistic. I got the speech. Not just the "I'm so disappointed" speech, either. It was time for,

"What the fuck is wrong with you? Are you fucking stupid? Did you think *at all* before you did that? Not only did you make yourself look like an idiot, you made *me* look like an idiot! I can't trust you at all! Don't you *ever* do something that stupid again!"

That was all it took. I was on the edge of being nuts to begin with. That just pushed me over the edge. It was the beginning of a trend that would follow me through the rest of my life. It was based on some simple ideas:

1) You don't think before you act.

2) Even if you *do* think, you don't think *enough*.

3) Don't do anything until you've analyzed it from as many angles as possible. Always consider everything. No, that's *not* impossible. Everyone else does it *all the time*.

4) You're going to screw it up, anyway. Prepare to be wrong. No matter what you do, the result is virtually guaranteed.

5) Cheer up. No one likes a sourpuss.

Actually, number five never occurred to me. But, it looks nice so I'll leave it in. That inner voice became an anchor around my neck. It took me longer to do things, even simple things. It took me longer to learn. It took me longer to process information and act on it. I was always the slow one. No one else knew I was getting the same answer as everybody else; I was just rethinking it over and over and over...

The rest of my period in-hull was satisfactory. But, I never truly recovered. I learned to think faster, that way I would just look slow, not stupid. My confidence and performance dropped to the point that I was pulled to the side and told there was no way I would be recommended for *anything*. It was hopeful that I would pass, that was it. I was totally crushed. Thoughts raced through my mind. My family telling me how proud they were for me being recommended for a special part of an already special field. My brother telling me how great it would look on my service record and resume'. I had already told my fiancée about my potential. I kept it together long enough to get home. The house was empty. My parents were in Florida, house hunting. I called them at my aunt's house, and proceeded to have a complete and total emotional breakdown.

It became evident that my current performance was as good as it would ever get. I still plodded away toward the ultimate goal of standing my Oral Board. I looked back on my watch standing experience, and gleaned as many positive elements from it as I could. I began studying my notes and drawings. I went back in-hull and retraced and reviewed piping systems. I brushed up on my procedures. I would be as ready as I possibly could. I would get the highest grade possible. I would do everything in my power to reposition myself to go to the fleet on the right foot. The only thing standing in my way was a hellish two hour meeting, with four people, at three o' clock in the morning.

And a dozen donuts.

The night finally arrived. Because a student couldn't be examined by their own crew, boards were almost always held during a student's time off. That would facilitate the participation of another crew. I walked into the room, donuts in hand. I walked up to the folding table at which they were seated. I presented the donuts as if I was giving Frankincense and Myrrh to the Baby Jesus. No going back now.

The first question came from the NPE,

"Okay...you're taking your logs in Engine Room Lower Level. You check a sight glass in the piping for Shaft Lube Oil. You see that it's full. What are your actions?"

If there was one single statement drilled into the minds of Mechanical Operators, it would be that a full sight glass is certain indication that flow of oil has ceased. That means some very expensive, very critical component was about to seize up tighter than a nervous nun. Any hesitation to recognize that, and act on it, was grounds for failure. I immediately said,

"A full sight glass is the sign of a loss of lube oil casualty. I'm going to call it away as loss of Shaft Lube Oil."

"Okay, then what?"

I then proceeded to describe my immediate actions, and the immediate actions of the other watch standers to avoid permanent damage to the system. They then went on to the next question. And the next. And the next. The next two hours became a blur of drawings, temperatures, pressures, power supplies, and procedures. Finally, it came to a close. I felt that I had done very well. Everything felt right. Everyone seemed happy. So...how had I done?

"Petty Officer Smith...we were going to fail you right away after the first question. But, we decided to continue to see how you'd do on the rest of them. You did good enough that we decided you were good enough to pass. But, I want to make it clear we're giving you the *minimum* passing grade. By rights, we could have failed you after the first question."

I stood there in complete shock. I was speechless. I couldn't believe what I was hearing! What had I done wrong? I finally found my voice,

"What happened? What was wrong with the first question?"

"We specifically told you the sight glass was full. You failed to recognize that was a sign of loss of lube oil flow.

That's grounds for immediate failure under these circumstances."

"What are you talking about? Those were the first words out of my mouth! I called it away as a loss of Shaft Lube Oil!"

"Well...we didn't hear you. We're giving you a 2.8 and I suggest you be content with that. You've passed the Board. You should be happy we allowed you to do *that*."

The discussion was over. My mind was racing! I couldn't believe it! After all the effort, all the stress, all the long days and sleepless nights! All that was for nothing. It was meaningless. Even worse, my naval career almost came to a screeching halt. Everything on that crowded, chaotic slate that represented my life was almost wiped clean. By one man. For one reason:

THE...DIPSHIT...DIDN"T...FUCKING...*LISTEN*!!

Later on, one incident came to mind. It seemed the perfect symbol for my period at S1C. It happened during one of the bad periods a few weeks earlier. I had gotten off midnight shift. I went through the usual routine. I changed out of my uniform, into my civilian clothes. I turned in my badge and dosimeter, placing them in their proper slots in the rack at the gate. I went through the radiation frisker, and walked out to my car in the parking lot. I started my car and began to drive the familiar route...

And *woke up* in my *driveway*.

I had no memory of the drive home. All the ramifications of what happened hit me. Shakily, I got out of my car. I had better try to get some sleep. Ten hours later I'd be doing this all over again.

"...qualified Electrical Operator, Petty Officer Smith qualified Mechanical Operator, Petty Officer Collier qualified..."

I braced myself for the barrage of coinage. It didn't hurt as much as I'd thought. Then there was the shaking of hands, pats on the back, and congratulations. I looked back on everything that had happened. I thought about all the sweat, pressure, tension, shame, sorrow and frustration. I was still spinning my wheels, even on a good day. And for what?

"What the unholy fuck am I doing here?"

Another wind down. One last party to celebrate. One more visit from the Enfield Police Department. It was time to fill out another "dream sheet". I already knew I was going subs. That narrowed the possibilities, and made the process easier. I really had only two real desires, either a fast attack boat out of Groton, or a ballistic missile boat out of Groton. If I had my "druthers", I'd take the missile boat. That was what I wrote down.

Sailors are as full of superstitions as a pomegranate has pips. Number one on the list...the Jinx. Oooh, yes. It's real. I've seen it! That's one reason why great care must be exercised when filling out a document of this importance. Make sure the writing looks happy. You don't want to piss off the Detailer. He picks your next assignment. And for God's sake, don't tell them what you *don't* want! They'll give you that just out of spite. Think I'm kidding? Think I'm deranged? The following actually happened:

One of the guys we graduated with at Knowles was very adamant concerning what he *didn't* want. He made those feeling clear on his dream sheet. He wrote,

"Nothing on the west coast. And, anything but a carrier!"

When our orders came in, we all crowded around the posting on the bulletin board. He found his name...

"What? Oh, great. Just fucking great! *Enterprise*...out of...*San Diego*!! What the fuck! What the *fuck*!!"

That's the Navy for you. That's the jinx for you. He baited them both, and shouldn't have expected anything less. Then it was my turn. I found my name. Slowly I traced the line across...

U.S.S. Skipjack SSN585   Homeport: New London Submarine Base, Groton, Connecticut.

I got my second choice. Not bad.

Chapter 5-

So *that's* a submarine.

Not all ships are designed to sink...some require our assistance.

-Unattributed

In 1979, one of my childhood dreams came true. No. Suzy Morton's swim suit top did *not* miraculously fall off at the public pool. Like so many other young kids, I loved building scale models. Unlike so many other kids, I concentrated *only* on military hardware. No dune buggies for me. No Camaros, Stingrays, or '56 Fords. The only reason I would have built a Jaguar is because one of the latest British attack jets was named the Jaguar. For me it was aircraft, tanks, ships, and because of my renewed interest...submarines. The closest I ever got to building an automobile was a Jeep...towing an anti-tank gun, of course.

But here's the problem. With my Dad being an intel type, I wanted to build modern equipment. World War Two subs were good, but a new nuke boat would be better. A Soviet boat would be the best. Sadly, the plastic model kit selection back then was pretty mundane. The only Soviet hardware available in kit form was aircraft and armor. What did a young honest American kid have to do to get a nuclear submarine?

Our luck broke when Steve found an old Renwal kit of the U.S.S. George Washington, the nation's first SSBN (nuclear powered ballistic missile submarine). It was one of those "cutaway" models showing the "highly secret" interior. It was all rubbish, of course. But, if one closed up both sides of the hull, it looked just like the real thing. That was great, but what about a nuclear fast attack boat?

Ask, and you shall receive! In 1979, the Monogram model company bought all the molds from the Aurora model company when the latter went out of business. They began retooling and releasing some of the old Aurora kits, some of which hadn't been seen in decades. One of them was...*TAA DAAAA*...a fast attack boat named:

U.S.S. Skipjack.

I instantly snapped up a few of them, just in case I pranged one. I lavished attention on this submarine as if it was a girlfriend. It was the pride of my collection. I still have one in my collection today, albeit for a different reason.

I stood in that hallway at Knowles, staring at the paper on the bulletin board. Two things struck me. My first thought was,

"Man, that boat is *old*."

My second thought was,

"It'll be ridiculous if I can't recognize her!"

Early in July of 1985, I drove down to Groton. I checked in, got assigned a room in the BEQ (Bachelor Enlisted Quarters), went down to the COMSUBRON2 building. I found out two things. First, that funny word stood for Commander Submarine Squadron 2. Second, the boat wouldn't be back in port for two more days. I asked if I could go back home until they got back. Sure. Why not.

I turned back around and drove right back to Feeding Hills. Yvette and her family were surprised to see me back so soon. I explained I would be driving back down on Friday morning to report aboard. I spent two more days of domestic bliss at home, then drove back down to try again.

I had better luck on Friday. The boat was tied up in port. I found her immediately. As I walked down the pier, I smelled for the first time that smell that would bring back so many memories. The smell of a working wharf. It's a mixture of sea water, oil, tar, diesel fuel, and sea weed. I can never smell that odor again without a flood of memories washing over me. I explained to the pier sentry and topside watch that I was reporting aboard. A Petty Officer was sent up to get me, and I followed him onto my first real submarine.

Across the brow (gang plank), over the rounded hull, to the forward escape trunk. The hatch was about three feet in diameter. Down a very short ladder to another nearly identical hatch. Then another ladder. This one wasn't easy. I had a folder full of records in one hand, and the ladder was covered in a very thin film of some kind of grease or oil. I landed at the bottom with an unceremonious thump.

I was in an entirely new world. Nothing I had ever experienced could prepare me for this. I had toured a Second World War submarine when I was much younger, but even that was nothing like this beast. The first thing to hit me was the smell. Nothing else on earth smells like a submarine. Imagine being in a place where you smell oil, diesel fuel, food cooking, sweat, steam (yes, steam has a smell.), and sanitary tanks. Topping it all off is Amine, a chemical used in the CO_2 scrubbers, lending its own unique tinge to all of it. Once one has smelled the inside of a submarine, they'll never forget it. I instantly understood why submariners had a special appreciation for fresh air.

After well over a year in the Navy, I finally had to learn to talk like a sailor. I had the obscenities down pat, but I still needed to learn the lingo. So many everyday terms are different on a ship. Here are some good examples:

Forward: it's not the front anymore. Any time one is going toward the front of the vessel, even if they're walking backwards, they are going "forward".

Bow: the front of the ship. If a sailor tells another to go to the "very front of the ship" They're going to get drug tested.

Aft: it's not the back anymore. See "forward".

Stern: the back end of the ship. See "bow".

Deck: it's not a floor. Floors are in buildings. Well-seasoned sailors will never say the word "floor" again. Even in buildings.

Bulkhead: Vessels don't have walls. They have bulkheads.

Overhead: in a room, one has a ceiling. On a ship, it's called an overhead. The lamp hangs out of the overhead.

Space: no, it's not the final frontier. It's what a room is called on a ship. Some good examples - berthing space, engineering spaces.

Then there are the terms a lot of people already know. The head is the bathroom. The galley is the kitchen. The mess deck is the dining room.

I had plenty of help learning all this new information. I had very able instructors...the crew of Skipjack. What a bunch these guys were! Sadly, many of the names are lost to the mists of time that constantly reduce the visibility in my memory to zero.

I was given a tour of the boat from bow to stern. Not such a good idea, I thought, since I was wearing my dress whites. At least I wouldn't get lost. The layout was pretty simple. There are only so many curves they can throw you on a sub. She was 252 feet long. Thirty-two feet wide at her widest point. Since her hull was round, she drew well over twenty feet under normal conditions. She was broken up into five compartments, the first of which I had essentially fallen into.

The very first compartment was the Torpedo Room. When Skipjack was designed and constructed, there was such a thing as a good fast sub. But, there was no such thing as a real, honest to goodness "guided" torpedo. Even if they could home in on a target to some extent, they still had to be aimed at the target. Having the Torpedo Room in the bow was still a must. It was essentially one level. There was a dry bilge storage area for the "fish" that wouldn't fit in the racks, and other odds and ends. Above was an area similar to a loft, called the Mezzanine. It was a small berthing area. The business end held six torpedo tubes, in two horizontal rows of three.

Next was the Operations Compartment. It had three levels. The bottom level was berthing, the heads, the Goat Locker, and the ELT (Engineering Lab Technician) lab. Below the deck was a dry bilge for food storage. The middle level was the Mess Deck, and the Galley on the starboard side, the Wardroom on the port side, and the Wardroom Pantry stuck just about in the middle. The upper level held the Radio Room in the port aft corner, with the Nav ET/IC shop just forward. The Yeoman's Office was in the aft starboard corner, with the Ship's Office just forward from it. The Control Room took up the rest. The Control Room was about the size of the average living room. On the port side, starting aft, was the ESM (Electronic Surveillance Measures) station, BPCP (Ballast Plant Control Panel), the elevated seat for the Diving Officer Of the Watch, and finally the stations for the Helmsman and Planesman. On the starboard side was the Sonar Shack (actually its own little cubicle), the Fire Control System, and the ladder to the bridge. Right in the middle of it all was the elevated periscope stand, also called the Band Stand, where the Officer Of the Deck sat. Directly in front of him were the wells where the two periscopes were stored.

Next was the Reactor Compartment. This is pretty much self-explanatory. The nuclear reactor was situated here. A heavily shielded passage led over the top to the next compartment. This was called the Reactor Tunnel. Next was the Machinery Space. It had two levels, Machinery Space Upper Level (MSUL) and Machinery Space Lower Level (MSLL). MSUL contained all kinds of wonderful things that, for me, amounted to PFM (Pure Fucking Magic). It also contained the ELT's sample sink. MSLL held the Feed Station, the Reefer Units, The Diesel Generator, and some other support systems. Next was the Engine Room. It too had two levels, Engine Room Upper Level (ERUL) and Engine Room Lower Level

(ERLL).ERUL held the Evaporator, Ship Service Turbine Generators, Main Engines, Reduction Gears, and Shaft Systems. It also held the all-important Maneuvering Room. ERLL held the AC Units, High Pressure Air Compressor, Main Seawater Systems, Main Condensers, and Lube Oil Systems. This diagram is available on several US military web sites.

So, how does one live on a submarine? There are all kinds of things people need to do. Everyone needs to eat, sleep, shower, go to the bathroom, do their laundry, get haircuts, all that fun stuff. Well, let's take it one piece at a time.

Eating: The mess deck and galley together measured about nine feet by twenty feet. If I remember correctly, the eating area had five tables, each accommodating between six and eight sailors, depending on their girth. We ate in shifts. First was the watch section relieving the watch. When they were finished, the folks they just relieved came down. After them it was open season for anyone quick enough to sit down before they closed up.

If we were in port, people in the duty section would be allowed to get simple items out of the galley on their own. Cold cuts, peanut butter, bread, pickles, hot peppers and condiments were readily available if someone didn't have a chance to eat, but was hungry at 0200. A quick sandwich before lying down for a few minutes of sleep could really hit the spot.

The funniest aspect of eating on the sub would have to be the BK runs. We had a Burger King on base. Sometimes a bunch of guys from the duty section would get together and set up a BK run. Technically, that wasn't supposed to happen. Therefore, it was critical to inform to Duty Officer when doing one. If he found out one was done without including him, they would crack down and outlaw them again for a while. I suppose the ultimate statement in favor of BK runs was when the cooks themselves placed orders.

A junior enlisted member would be drafted to make the run. Sometimes the runner would get dinner bought for him to make up for the chore. Other times it was just his tough luck. The worst part would be having several Chiefs and other senior Petty Officers each hand over a twenty dollar bill, and growl,

"And I'd better get the right change back, too."

What about sleeping? Only SSBN sailors are guaranteed their own rack all the time. Sharing racks is a fact of submarine life. The berthing assignment is set up so that three people share two racks. One of the people is always on watch, leaving two people left and two racks open. The expression used to describe this arrangement is "hot racking" or "hot bunking". The reason is that when one sailor rolls into the rack, it's still warm from the last guy vacating it. Hot racking is one of the biggest reasons why personal hygiene is so very important.

The size of the bunks is another oddity about a submarine. They are each a little bigger than a coffin. This similarity is so pronounced, it isn't uncommon for sailors to feel those confines in their sleep. The result is what's called a "coffin dream". In a coffin dream, the sailor dreams that he is being buried alive. Sadly, the first inclination in this instance is to wake up, and *sit* up. The bunk space is only marginally bigger in the vertical sense. So, a sailor wakes up, goes to sit bolt upright like anyone would normally do, and *WHACK*! They catch the overhead of the bunk space right in the forehead. If they weren't fully awake before, they certainly are *now*.

Getting into some of the bunks was quite a challenge. The first level of bunks weren't too bad. One just had to crawl around on the deck to get into them. The second level was easy. Just roll into them. It was the third level of bunks that was difficult. Imagine trying to get into a space the size of a coffin. At shoulder height. Sideways! The only way was to find something in the overhead to grab with both hands. Then swing your feet up like a gymnast, and poke them into the bunk. Now do a horizontal version of a pull-up to get the rest of your body in line with the bunk. Now grab the object you're holding with your left hand, with your right hand. At the same time, reach out with your left hand and try to grab the bunk. Now *quickly*, before you fall, swing and hoist yourself over and into the bunk. Now pick yourself up off the deck and try again. It takes a while before it can be done on the first try with any regularity.

Does that sound bad? Wait! It gets worse. Some of the racks were squeezed into places they weren't really intended. These bunks were actually smaller than a normal rack. I was assigned one of these on one of my patrols. This bunk was so small, I had to decide before going in whether I would sleep on my back or stomach. There literally wasn't enough room to turn over once I was in. I chose my back. There was no way I could possibly get in that bunk upside down.

That was one occasion when I essentially had my own rack. No one else had the patience to use that rack. It was all mine. Having a dedicated rack was rare for a junior enlisted member of the crew. At some points, depending on how many crew members went to sea, even Second Class Petty

Officers would have to hot bunk. On one very rare occasion, I had my own bunk for half a patrol. Halfway through, the berthing bill was changed, and my bunk was given to another junior member. That luxury felt so good, I couldn't begrudge him the same opportunity. I gave it up willingly, and went back to hot bunking.

As rare and peaceful as a period of sleep can be, it can never last forever. No sleep was ever enough, and the time to get up for watch always came too soon. It was the unfortunate duty of the Messenger of the Watch, a very junior crewman, to gather up the watch bill and berthing bill. He would go from rack to rack, hunting down the men for the next watch, and waking them up. Finding the proper people in a dimly lit berthing compartment, when each of them could be in two different locations, was never easy. Woe be to the Messenger who roused the wrong person! An unhealthy portion of abuse was waiting for him if he hesitantly pulled back the wrong curtain, and shined in his flashlight, only to find his target was in another rack. Even if he had the *right* person, contempt and abuse would usually follow. My brother encouraged me to be polite to the Messenger of the Watch, even under the worst conditions. I did my best. No matter how rotten I felt, I always tried my best to not call him names, and always say thank you.

For a while, we had a problem with crew members being roused, and then going right back to sleep. Standing watch was bad enough, without being relieved late. By the end of watch, all one wanted to do was get a bite to eat, and maybe get a little closer to the rack. The Captain quickly found a solution. When a crewmember was awake, he had to be awake enough to sign his initials on the watch bill. If those initials were present, a late reliever was in for trouble. No excuses!

There was one rule that was always in effect when it came to sleep. Keep it *quiet*. Woe be to the man who showed indiscretion and woke his shipmates by dropping something or speaking loudly. I was once one of those offenders, and under the worst possible conditions. I woke up a Chief! I went into the Goat Locker to ask a Chief a question. That question quickly turned into a conversation. In my enthusiasm, my voice got louder. Suddenly, the face of our Reactor Division Chief poked out from behind one of the bunk curtains. His face was half "ugly sleep face", half intense irritation. He looked a lot like Freddy Kruger. I was quickly ordered to keep it down. I kept it down.

Speaking of "ugly sleep face", we used to have ugly sleep face contests. The first few people arriving at the mess deck would rate the sailors coming in according to severity of ugly sleep face. We had a few favorites whose arrival was always awaited with anticipation. But one particular crewman almost always came in first. He had a cleft pallet, however, which gave him an unfair advantage.

Taking a shower on a submarine was a very rare treat on the old diesel boats. They only had the fresh water they carried with them, and the ability to produce more was very limited. There was water to service the batteries, cook, and clean, with little left over. Sailors were allowed to clean themselves, maintaining basic hygiene. But, an honest to goodness shower was rare. That didn't apply on nuclear boats. Even older nuclear boats had facilities to produce larger quantities of fresh water. The endless flow of nuclear steam made things like electricity, propulsion, and heat secondary concerns. Skipjack had a water distillation plant that was standard for any boat with an S5W reactor plant. It was called the 8K. The name came from the fact it could produce eight thousand gallons of fresh water per day.

The limitation for showers now became the number of available shower stalls versus the number of crewmen. I can't recall if we had two or three small, cramped stainless steel shower stalls. The showerhead was always too low, except for the shortest of crewmen. Each stall was equipped with a small squeegee, used after every shower to wipe down the walls of the stall. This had to be done after every shower. It kept the stalls much cleaner.

Showers on a submarine are showers in name only. Yes, there is plenty of fresh water. But, most of it is held in reserve for the propulsion system. There is a big difference between the shower taken on a sub, and the shower taken in one's home (also known as a "Hollywood" shower). In a Hollywood shower, the water is left on the entire time. One might even let the hot water pound on their head for a few minutes. Not so on a submarine. A boat shower is very different. First turn the water on, and adjust it to the temperature desired. Wet down the entire body, head to toe. Turn the water off using the slide valve in the showerhead. Soap up the entire body, head to toe. Then turn the water back on, and rinse off completely but quickly. Turn the water off again.

A sailor could conceivably take two showers a day, but the water use would have to be kept to an absolute minimum. Taking Hollywood showers on the boat, even in port, was strictly forbidden. Even taking too long with a boat shower could make someone a target. If someone was seen to be habitually indiscreet, they were punished…with a medal.

Yes, a medal. The offender was required to constantly wear a large, heavy brass medal around their neck, conspicuously labeled:

WATER BUFFALO

They would often be required to wear the cumbersome medal until they found some careless soul deserving it more.

What about going to the bathroom? Surely something that regular (pardon the pun) couldn't be complex. When, dear reader, will you catch on? Nothing is easy on a submarine. The only easy part about bathrooms on a submarine is keeping them clean. They too are stainless steel. The commodes and urinals, two of each, were piped directly into the sanitary tanks. There were no water traps or baffles of any kind. The only barrier is a hefty ball valve at the bottom of each fixture. This comes into play later. So, if someone were to open up one of these key valves, and leave it open, the boat would soon smell very smelly. This too comes into play later.

The procedure is very specific.

1) Run a little water into the commode (or urinal) with the flush valve. The water level should look like your throne at home.

2) Commence the doing of business.

3) Complete the paperwork.

4) Open the ball valve to send the browns to the Souper Boal. Open the flush valve for a second or two to complete the process.

5) Close the all-important ball valve

The sanitary tanks are emptied by pressurizing them with air. Remember, we're under water. That means more pressure is required. The tanks are pressurized, and the outlet valves are opened. Those valves are shut before the tanks are completely empty. If we emptied them entirely, we would burp the tanks, and large bubbles of air would shoot to the surface. This is scarily similar to farting in a bathtub, but on a much larger scale. Our location would be instantly marked by a giant sub-fart. So, the outlet valves are shut, and we're left with a steel tank filled with a little bit of waste, and a large quantity of highly compressed air. That air has to go somewhere before the tanks can be used again. Obviously, it can't go outboard. You can see this coming…can't you? That's right. It has to be vented *inboard*. This is done gradually, through a small valve. If someone opened one of the large valves, it would happen much quicker. But, then we'd all have ruptured ear drums. The Navy wouldn't want anything to distract us from that wonderful smell! By the way, this task is almost always carried out right before or during meals. That's a no shitter!! Well…okay. *That* pun was intended.

The most perilous time during the emptying of these tanks is when the tanks are pressurized. This horrible event has happened countless times. It almost happened to me. All the precautions in the world can be thought of and taken. It'll still happen. Someone will go into the head to do their business when that tank is pressurized. When they open that ball valve…*FOOM*! They are lifted from their seat, probably into the overhead, by a Propulsive Pillar of Poo! To add insult to smelly injury, the offender is then made to clean up the mess.

Now, how about laundry? With all the working and sweating going on, there must be a lot of dirty laundry. There is. So, how do we do our laundry? It's simple. We don't. Well, on shorter assignments we don't. But on the longer patrols, we do. The most junior, non-qual member of the crew is designated the "Laundry Queen". His task, for the most part, is nothing but washing and drying laundry. He then folds it, and puts it either in a designated spot, or in the crew members' bunks. One thing that makes this task a little easier is the uniform we wear while underway. We wear overalls. Everyone wears the same dark blue overalls, with stenciled names. The only distinction of rank is collar insignia. Of course, we don't call them overalls. That's way too boring for a place as colorful as a submarine. We call them "Poopy Suits". Why poopy suits? It's simple. If one is going to use the commode, and the sleeves aren't taken care of in the proper fashion, they end up being poopy! Get it? I knew you would.

What about haircuts? Are they really necessary at sea? Yup. But, almost every boat crew is blessed with at least one member who can give a decent haircut. Ours was a Reactor Operator named Simms. Every once in a while he would set up shop in the crew's head. If anyone showed up, he would cut their hair. Sometimes nobody showed. Sometimes there was a crowd waiting for their turn. Some boat barbers would charge a couple of bucks per head. I don't recall Simms charging anything.

What is a typical day like on a submarine? That's a trick question. There is no such thing. But, I can give some rough examples. Let's break it up into two categories: in port, and at sea. Each will have two sub-categories: good day and bad day.

At sea – good day:

0000 to 0600: Stand watch. Minimal work. No drills.

0600 to 0620: Breakfast. It could be Lunch, Dinner, or Mid-rats depending on when the watch ended. This time I got off watch at 6AM. So, it's breakfast.

0620 to 1145: Work, maintenance, studying.

1145 to 1200: Showering and other personal hygiene.

1200 to 1330: More studying, training, or maybe a little bit of a movie.

1330 to 1800: Sleep, with no drills or other interruptions. At 1800, get up again for watch and start it all over.

At sea – bad day:

0000 to 0610: Stand watch. Red hats are coming aft. Drills. Behind on work. Relieved late.

0610 to 0615: Wolf down breakfast.

0615 to 0700: Start studying and trying to figure out how to get caught up.

0700 to 0745: Reactor scram drill. The red hats are still at it. I'm in the off going watch section, so I have to respond as part of the Casualty Assistance Team.

0745 to 0845: Resume studying.

0845 to 1000: Get called aft because I'm behind in my work.

1000 to 1100: Fire Drill. Fucking red hatted bastards!! I don't have to go aft this time. I'm *already* aft. Lucky me.

1100 to 1200: Finish up enough work to stop and go back to studying.

1200 to 1330: Get a checkout and research look-ups.

1330 to 1430: Study for next checkout.

1430 to 1500: APD alarm. Put on EAB mask. Sit for thirty minutes in complete unproductive disgust.

1500 to 1630: Mutter imaginative array of obscenities when APD alarm is declared "spurious". Get called aft to assist in maintenance.

1630 to 1800: Sleep. Maybe. At 1800, get up for watch and start it all over.

The bad days far outnumbered the good days, especially on a boat older than most of its crew. There was always something to fix.

Okay, now for the in port days.

In port – good day:

0530: Get up. Get ready for work. Shower, shave, brush teeth, try to make myself look somewhat human.

0600: Walk down to boat. Stop at Burger King for some breakfast.

0715: Quarters on boat.

0730: Start work and/or quals.

1200: Stop for lunch.

1225: Back to the grindstone.

1630: End of the workday. Depart boat, clean up, change into civilian clothes.

1700: Determine location for eating and drinking and more drinking.

1730 to 0530: This part is usually pretty hazy, and the main reason it's so difficult to make myself look somewhat human the next morning.

In port – bad day:

0530: Get up. Get ready for work. Shower, shave, brush teeth, try to make myself look somewhat human.

0600: Walk down to boat. Stop at Burger King for some breakfast.

0700: Relieve the duty section, and assume the duty. Relieve the previous Shutdown Roving Watch and Shutdown Reactor Operator Watch.

0715: Quarters on boat.

0730: If not on watch, start work and/or quals.

1200: Stop for lunch.

1225: Back to the grindstone or watch.

1700: Stop for dinner.

1725: Back to the grindstone or watch.

2000: Go topside for a little fresh air, and maybe a phone call home.

2015: Back to the grindstone or watch.

0000: The work is probably done for the most part. Time to dedicate all efforts to quals.

0500: Revile. Not that it matters. You're awake already on account of not sleeping in the first place. Check the status of the boat to ensure it's ready for the oncoming duty section. Clean up any work sites and take out the trash.

0600: Time for breakfast. The fat pills are delivered about this time as well. You'll learn about fat pills later.

0700: Hand over the duty to the oncoming duty section. (SPECIAL NOTE: This is where an alternate scenario can come into play. If one is ahead in their quals, already qualified, and worked extra hard the previous night, they might be allowed to leave the boat. They have the rest of the day off. This extremely rare event is called "day after duty". I only recall having day after duty on two occasions.)

0715: Quarters on boat.

0730: Start work and/or quals.

1200: Stop for lunch.

1225: Back to the grind stone.

1630: End of the workday. Depart boat, clean up, change into civilian clothes.

1730 to 0530: This part is now *extremely* hazy, since one has now gone over thirty four hours without any rest. We will now continue to go longer without rest, for the simple reason that having endured this torture, we are now more determined than ever to eat and drink and drink some more.

Duty was stood every third day, on average. Day after duty was very rare. Being the oldest boat on the east coast, Skipjack had plenty of broken equipment to repair or replace. I was also "Mr. Dink" much of the time. Put these factors all together, and one can see that I had this type of day much more often than not. You'll learn about being "dink" later.

Many of these aspects of submarine life were complicated further by events or conditions. For example:

Emptying the sanitary tanks, or, "blowing sans". We spent a good deal of our time in the north Atlantic. Some of this was during the winter months. The contents of our sanitary tanks would often freeze during these periods. The Auxiliaryman who ended up with the nasty job of blowing sans would have to open the ball valve on each commode, take a broom handle, and break up and stir the "poo" to ensure it would be blown overboard.

Sleeping. When we surfaced in the middle of Narragansett Bay, during Hurricane Gloria, we stayed on the surface long enough for me to eat and then go to bed. I was sleeping in the Mezzanine on that patrol. I crawled into the rack and somehow managed to wedge myself in so I could eventually fall asleep and not fall out during the extreme rolls we were taking. I had fallen fast asleep. Suddenly, the boat took a severe roll to starboard. Before I could react, I was spit out of my rack, and ended up in the far corner of the space, piled up on top of my own head. One of the Senior Chiefs from COMSUBRON2 was riding us for that patrol. He poked his head out from behind his bunk curtain, and whispered,

"Son…are you okay?"

I nodded a groggy "yes" to him with a convincing grunt. I got back into my rack to try again. I fell asleep again. Apparently, this was just the moment Mother Nature was waiting for. Another severe heel to starboard, and I was rolled out of my bunk again. This time my reflexes were a little quicker. Instead of being flung across the berthing compartment, I was rolled out sort of like a jellyroll, and unrolled a little at a time as I hung on to the edge of my rack for dear life by one hand.

Showering. When we surfaced in Hurricane Gloria, we were in sea state six. When we surfaced off the coast of Scotland, we were in sea state seven. There wasn't even a storm! That was their normal conditions. I had always read about how the German U-boats were beaten up so much in the north Atlantic during their patrols in World War Two. Now I believed it! It was absolutely insane! Sadly, I got off watch and decided to take a shower before eating. I had bruises all over me from the inside of the shower stall taking exception to me having the nerve of actually trying to shower in this kind of weather. I finally staggered up for my meal. The others looked at me with a look of shock and sympathy.

There was one occasion when we had a rare opportunity to see what life was like in the old days. We were out for our ORSE work-up (see Chapter 12 – May the ORSE be with you.) Our 8K still had broken down. We barely had enough water for the plant, cleaning, cooking and drinking. I actually got my butt reamed for turning on the drinking fountain, and letting it run while waiting for the water to get cold. The end result of the breakdown was that we had no water for showers. We all went without showers for a little over a week. This wouldn't have been so bad, if it wasn't for the intense drill schedule we had to run for training. Here is the average day during that week:

1) Go on watch.

2) Run a wide array of drills, most involving running around like a lunatic in a 140 degree engine room. Make sure you are literally soaked to the skin in sweat.

3) After your drill watch, stop at a bilge funnel to pour the sweat out of your shoes. This is not an exaggeration.

4) Go down to the head. Take off your poopy suit, wrap it around a pipe, and wring it out.

5) Put it back on. Go back up to the mess deck and sit down with thirty other guys who just did the same thing.

6) Eat lunch.

7) Go back down to your rack. Take off your still sopping wet poopy suit, and climb into a rack just vacated by someone else who did what you just did, a few hours ago.

That's what submarine life was like in 1944. Okay all you nostalgic "Diesel Boats Forever" sailors. Yes, you have a point. Duty watches were easier when you were in port. I know, more of the crew could hit the beach at one time. There was no reactor to baby sit. Life was just simpler back then. But, you were all packed into an oily tin like a bunch of smoked oysters. How do you like your nice nuclear generated shower now?

The oddities and inconveniences of submarine life became routine. There are elements of military life, sea going life in particular, that simply can't be avoided. We need to keep the boat clean. It isn't just about health. As pissed off as someone can be regarding cleaning a bathroom, that clean bathroom is proven to have a positive impact on morale. The term for cleaning in the military is just a cruel, cruel hoax. It's called Field Day. The first time I heard that term in the Navy, I got all excited. I know what that is! It's time for a fun break. It's time for a trip. We're getting out of the stuffy classroom and going to a farm or a museum!

The other guys were amazed to see me so happy. Then they told me what the term really meant. Oh, heartless life! As I went through the shore based time of my naval service, it became a sad fact of life that only the junior enlisted men actually had to do field day. The senior enlisted and officers just sat back and watched, or even better, just left. My first field day on Skipjack was an eye opening experience. Everything started out as always. I buckled down and tried to get the ordeal over with as quickly as possible. Time went on, and I stood up to stretch and take a break. I looked around, and couldn't believe my eyes!

Everyone was cleaning. No. You don't understand. *EVERYONE!* Along with the junior people were the officers, chiefs, even the *Captain*! Now granted, the Skipper wasn't cleaning the head or the bilge. But, he found a dirty place and kneeled down right next to the blue shirts and scrubbed. It was then that I realized the biggest difference between a sub crew and a surface ship crew. The phrase, "we're all in this together" really meant something.

Another oddity of submarine life is the way certain parts of the boat are lighted, depending on the local time of day. The berthing areas are always lit with red lights, or "rigged for red". Every other compartment is lit with white lights, or "rigged for white". If it's daytime on the surface, the Control Room is rigged for white. If it's after sundown, it's rigged for red. This is to preserve the OOD's night vision. Multilayer blackout curtains separate the Control Room from every other space. If outside light is minimal, the Control Room is "rigged for black" for about an hour before coming to periscope depth. This is to give the OOD's eyes the maximum opportunity to acclimate to darkness. This condition is just outright eerie! All lights are turned off. The only illumination is the instruments and gages themselves. When rigged for red, the OOD wears red goggles in case he's called away suddenly to another area. One of the odd effects of wearing these red goggles is that many red objects are difficult to make out. Red writing on white paper is invisible! I'm not joking. I didn't believe it either. I was in the Control Room during a rig for red period, talking to one of the guys just relieved from Helmsman watch. He told me about how red writing can't be seen under those conditions. I immediately called him out for trying to fool me. He said,

"Really? You think I'm shitting you?"

"That's right. I may have been born at night, but not *last* night."

"Okay…watch this!"

He took out a lined notebook with plain white paper. He found a red pen near the plotting table. In very plain printing, he wrote on the pad,

HEY ASSHOLE

He turned around and held the paper up to the OOD. The OOD looked, looked closer and then shrugged.

"Just making a point, sir."

He ripped off the page, balled it up and threw it away. I was now a believer. That wasn't the only odd facet of submarine life revolving around light. Any time a white light was going to be turned on in a red-lit space, or totally dark space, they would announce,

"Watch your eyes! Bright light!"

I forgot to do this once. I made many people very unhappy. To this day, I make this announcement when turning on a light in a dark room.

One part of submarine life that is quite anti-climactic, is the act of submerging. Sadly the "oooogah-oooogah" of the klaxon is long gone. It was replaced by a very irritating electronic siren that goes more like "raaaah-raaaah". Life will never be the same. First, the announcement is made,

"All compartments rig for dive."

Everyone at their stations consults a list of requirements, and ensures all conditions are met. A few minutes later,

"All compartments report status on rig for dive"

Everyone in the Engineering Spaces calls Maneuvering, and reports their space rigged for dive. Maneuvering calls the Control Room along with everybody else to report their condition. In the Control Room a large status board showing all hull openings is checked. This board is called the "Christmas Tree". Each opening is represented by a circle, if it's open, or a horizontal line if it's shut. The desired configuration is all horizontal lines, or a "straight board".

If the requirement for a straight board is met, the boat can dive. The OOD gives the order to dive. The announcement is made, the alarm is sounded, and the main vents are opened. Elsewhere in the boat, all that is noticed is a faint rushing sound and an almost un-noticeable down angle. As the boat sinks deeper and deeper into the water, the OOD calls off various steps watched for.

"Foredeck awash...aft deck awash...scope under."

He turns to the Chief of The Watch, sitting at the Ballast Plant Control Panel,

"Cycle the main vents and trim for ahead one third."

"Cycle the main vents and trim for ahead one third, aye sir."

When the boat is completely dived, and the scope is lowered, the announcement is made,

"All compartments report conditions on the dive."

Everyone goes through their spaces with a fine tooth comb. Every single pipe, flange, and hull connection of any kind is scrutinized with a flashlight. All critical components are checked, and the reports come in. Unless something strange turns up, it's on to bigger and better things. That's it. It's over. Nothing to see here! Everyone go back to your homes!

Chapter 6 -
Techno-jargon makes me horny.

"Incomprehensible jargon is the hallmark of a profession."

-Kingman Brewster

"Westfield Ground...Cessna 94513...public parking ramp...ready to taxi with ATIS for northbound departure."

"Roger 513...you are cleared to taxi to runway 3-3...contact Westfield Tower."

"513."

"Westfield Tower...Cessna 94513...ready for takeoff on runway 3-3…requesting left turn on departure."

"Roger 513...you are cleared for takeoff on runway 3-3...no hesitation."

"513 rolling."

The only thing more spine tingly than flying is talking about flying. All those neat sounding words have a meaning. To the unknowing, I could have been an astronaut talking to mission control. But in reality, I was just making simple statements containing important information. I was only using terminology required by the industry and regulatory bodies governing that industry. The same situation applies to the submarine community. But, now that the reader is being immersed in that environment, they need to know how to understand what's being said. One never knows...they could suddenly find themselves dropped into a submarine, needing to know that a CPA does *not*, in fact, do their taxes. Here is a brief list of important terms along with their meanings:

AEA: Auxiliary Electrician Aft, the Electrician on watch aft who travels through the engineering spaces, carrying out routine and minor duties. This is typically a junior member of the crew.

AEF: Auxiliary Electrician Forward, the counterpart of the AEA who stands watch in the forward portion of the boat. This may or may not be an actual Electrician.

APD: Airborne Particulate Detector, this boxy component constantly samples the air in the submarine, looking for radioactive particulate. If it finds any, an alarm goes off.

Bearing: A bearing is a specific direction relative to the boat. Imagine a huge compass suspended above the boat. 000 degrees is dead ahead. 180 degrees is dead astern. 90 degrees is directly off the starboard side. 270 degrees is directly off the port side. So, a contact bearing 315 would be 45 degrees to the left of dead ahead.

Biologics: Natural sources for sounds picked up by sonar. Good examples would be dolphins, whales, schools of fish, and schools of mating shrimp.

Boundary Layer: A horizontal layer of water having a different temperature, density and salinity than the water around it. This layer of water will often cause sound waves to reflect in different directions. A submarine can often hide beneath one of these layers because it will deflect active sonar away from the submarine.

Convergence Zone: An area of water with very specific density and salinity characteristics that alter how sound waves travel through the ocean. This can make an object appear closer or in a different position.

CPA: Closest Point of Approach, as two objects move in relation to each other, each going in its own direction, there will be a point at which they are closest together. Then they will get further apart. See? Not *one* Form 1040 in sight.

DCA: Damage Control Assistant, the officer in charge of all damage control efforts. This is typically a midlevel officer.

DSRV: Deep Submergence Rescue Vehicle, this is a cigar shaped vessel design to be lowered onto the hull of a stranded submarine. An air tight seal is made, and crew members from the submarine can be brought to the surface in small groups.

ELT: Engineering Lab Technician, a specially trained crew member responsible for taking radiation surveys throughout the boat, and maintaining proper chemistry in the Primary and Secondary Coolant. This person is always a nuclear Machinist.

Master: A type of contact that has been located by two or more methods, i.e. sonar and radar, or radar and visual.

NBOA: Narragansett Bay Operating Area, the area of ocean extending from Narragansett Bay into Long Island Sound. This is a popular area for local operations.

PD: Periscope Depth, the depth at which the periscope or other masts can be raised for use. For most submarines, this is roughly sixty feet.

Port: Left.

Plot: The radar display used for surface navigation. This is the stereotypical round screen with the radial line going round and round, that we all see on TV and the movies. This display has two knobs that can be turned to determine the bearing and distance to the contact. This area is equipped with a microphone allowing direct communication with the Bridge.

Propulsor: This is the latest thing in propulsion, especially for submarines. It is essentially a traditional propeller fitted inside a tube. Noise decreases and efficiency increases.

Romeo: A contact detected by radar.

SCRAM: An automatic shutdown of the reactor, achieved by quickly driving the control rods into the reactor core. Though usually initiated by safety systems, it can be done manually. Legend has it SCRAM stands for Safety Control Rod Axe Man. The term dates back to the Manhattan Project. Supposedly, a man was located in the framework above the nuclear pile, equipped with an axe. He would use this axe to cut the rope from which the control rod was suspended, allowing the rod to drop back into the pile, thus stopping the reaction.

Sierra: A contact detected by sonar.

Starboard: Right.

Target Angle: The relative angle *we* present to a contact. If we were directly in front of them, our target angle would be 000. If they were faced directly away from us, our target angle would be 180. If we were directly off their port beam, our target angle would be 270.

Time: the minutes after the hour at which a particular event will occur. Used in a sentence: X event will happen at time 23. (23 minutes past the hour)

TMA: Target Motion Analysis, this is the process of collecting consecutive sonar bearings to determine the speed, direction, and course of the target.

Transient: A distinctly man made sound, one that cannot be replicated by a natural source.

TDU: Trash Disposal Unit, this is essentially a tube running out the bottom of the sub. It has a huge ball valve at each end. The trash is compacted into burlap bags the same diameter as the tube, and weighted down with disc shaped steel weights. The bottom valve is carefully checked shut. The upper ball valve is opened. The bag of trash is dropped into the tube. The upper ball valve is shut and carefully checked. The bottom ball valve is opened, and the weighted bag drops to the ocean floor.

Turns: RPMs, if a specific speed is required, a specific number of RPMs will be called for. The number of RPMs required for one knot of speed is a known characteristic of the vessel. If that number is ten RPM, and fifteen knots is called for, the OOD would call for 150 RPM, or "turns for fifteen knots".

Victor: A contact detected visually. This should not be confused with the class of Soviet submarine.

So, with this new found knowledge, the reader could understand this dialogue:

"Bridge, Plot...radar contact bearing 340, range 30,000 yards. Designating this contact Romeo 1." (first radar contact of the patrol)

"Bridge, aye."

"Plot, Bridge...visual contact on Romeo 1. Contact is visually identified as an unloaded tanker. Designate Romeo 1 as Master 1."

"Bridge, Plot...Master 1 is now at 335, range 27,000 yards. CPA for Master 1 is 5,000 yards at time 37, at current course and speed. She'll pass astern of us."

"Bridge, aye."

Or this one:

"Con, Sonar...contact bearing 045, we're having a problem classifying at the moment. Designating this contact Sierra 5." (fifth sonar contact of the patrol)

"Con, aye. Is the contact biologics?"

"Con, Sonar... it really doesn't sound like it."

"Con, Sonar...Transient. Transient. On the bearing of Sierra 5. Sounds like steam flow noise."

"Sonar, Con...do you have a range to Sierra 5 yet?"

"Con, Sonar...negative, but it's sounding more and more like a submerged contact."

"Sonar, Con...is the contact in a convergence zone?"

"Con, Sonar...I doubt it, sir. Not much of a boundary layer around here."

"Diving Officer, let's get the towed array straightened out. We'll do some TMA and find out who this guy is. New course 025."

"New course 025, aye sir."

"Con, Sonar…we've got some more data. Sierra 5 is definitely a submerged contact, ahead of us, moving right to left. Still working on a range."

Wasn't that easy? The next time you're watching Hunt For Red October, or some other movie or TV show about subs, you'll probably be the only one in the room who knows what they're talking about. Then you could say something like,

"They'd better sweep the baffles to make sure he doesn't have friends around."

That's okay. Don't worry, you'll learn about baffles later.

Chapter 7 –

Only as good as her crew.

Another Disclaimer

So many people from this period in my life have taken up residence in my fragile little memory. Some sit right at the front. Some only appear as glimpses of faint haunting faces when I hear a particular sound, song, or figure of speech. They are all important, regardless of status. I would love to give each person their due moment of dubious fame. But, as I said before, a memoir is by essence an exercise in memory. If I have left anyone out, or attached the wrong face with the wrong memory, please forgive me. It only means you have remembered me better than I've remembered you.

People always say that it takes a special type of person to volunteer for submarine duty. But, that quality is very difficult to quantify. The Silent Service has always been a closed society, a black world existing only in shadows and rumors. This can only make any attempts at speculation that much more haphazard.

Another wrench in the works is the fact that few people realize what submarine duty actually entails. I think the reason for that is so few people actually realize what a submarine is. Isn't that really the important part? Would anyone really care what a lion tamer is, if no one knew that a lion is a carnivorous beast that, as a species, has gobbled up people like potato chips? One doesn't need to know all the dirty little secrets about where we go, what we do, or who we do it to. We do it all in submarines. What is a submarine? It's really very simple. In fact, I can tell you how to construct a submarine of your very own. It goes something like this...

First, get a hold of a big steel tube. Now cram it full of high pressure hydraulics, high pressure air, high voltage AC, high voltage DC, fuel oil, and several large steel cylinders of compressed oxygen. Got any room left over? Sure you do. Fill most of it with tons and tons of high explosives. There are no gas stations where you're going, so power it with a nuclear reactor. Finished? Good. Now take out your new creation, and sink it in salt water. Don't be a weeney! Take it down a good thousand feet or so. What do you mean that doesn't sound like a very safe thing to do? Sub sailors do this every day!

It is that danger that's responsible for the biggest difference between a submarine crew and virtually *any* other military unit. The military runs on one very basic principle:

Someone tells you to do something, and you *do it*.

Without obedience, military operations would be complete anarchy. Unit integrity would be non-existent. Authority would be based solely on intimidation. But, you need some people to *think*, and some people to *do*. It's accepted that those people doing the thinking have been exhaustively trained to do it properly. It's equally accepted that those in the doing position know what they're doing. And, it works incredibly well. In most circumstances.

That's where the submarine is different. Now, I'm not saying submarine sailors aren't exhaustively trained. Many can't make through the basic schools required just to set foot on one. The point is this: if someone has a bad day in an F-15, they might die. If someone in a tank has a bad day, a few people might die. On a surface ship, many people might die. But on a submarine,

They all die.

One person making a mistake can kill every one of them. Can the Captain be the one making that mistake?

Yes.

The one characteristic setting sub crews apart is their need to constantly watch out for each other. Don't let them make that mistake. That's why, on a submarine, you don't blindly obey an order. You question it, even if only mentally. You think about it. Does it make sense? What are the consequences? If you honestly feel it's a bad idea, you say so. The submarine is one of those extremely rare places where a sailor can respectfully refuse to carry out an order. If there is a valid reason for doing so, there will be no repercussions. But if you end up being wrong…*GODHELP YOU.*

This incident will illustrate what I'm trying to say. During one of our patrols, we ran a set of drills. This time, I was in the group of people conducting the drills. This group is called the "drill monitors". After the drill watch is over, everyone meets in the Wardroom to discuss how things went in a "drill critique".

During this drill critique, the captain was addressing the EWS on watch. During one of the drills, the EOOW gave an order that probably wasn't the brightest thing to do. The EWS carried the order out dutifully. Should he have been complimented on his rigid adhesion to duty under such stressful conditions? One would think so. And, they would be very wrong. The Captain instead said,

"How could you let him *do that*?"

If you see someone doing something wrong, you tell them. Even if they're an officer. Even if they're the Skipper. Isn't staying alive that important?

Oddballs, geniuses, country bumpkins, wise-asses. Loud mouths, human dormice, grumblers and peacemakers. Academy graduates and inner city gang kids. These were the people who made up the lifeblood of U.S.S. Skipjack SSN585. She was an engineering marvel in her day. Yet without her crew she was only a conglomeration of steel, rubber, plastic, and Uranium. She would go to untold places and break records with reckless abandon. Without her crew, she would never leave the pier. Yet, she was only as good as her crew. We were the limiting factor, the weak link. This motley assortment of souls is what made her swim and breathe. This is the human definition of the boat's crew. The Department of Defense, however, took a more clinical approach. To them, we were only a machine within a machine. Even our little group was broken up into pieces, parts, and cogs like any vast army, into units, sub-units, and sub-sub-units.

The crew was divided up into "Departments". These were further broken up into "Divisions". I was in the Engineering Department. Since I was a Machinist (in the nautical perspective), I was in Machinery Division. This was usually shortened to "M Div". There was also an E Div for the Electricians, and a RC Div for the Reactor Operators. The Operations Department was for the guys up forward. They had divisions for Sonar, Weapons, Fire Control, and such. M Div's rough equivalent up forward was Auxiliary Division, also known as A Gang.

Each one of these divisions was led by a Division Officer. There were officers for M Div, E Div, RC Div, Weapons (usually shortened to Weps), CRA (Chem Radcon Assistant), Supply, Navigation (usually called Nav), and the Radio area. He was called the Communicator.

These officers cycled through these different positions, from one division to the next, in order to gain as much experience as possible. Among these officers were:

Lt. Cahill

Lt. Deegan

Ltj.g. Thorpe

Lt. McGuire

Ltj.g. Roth

Ltj.g. Wallis

Mr. Wallis was always our supply officer. He was also one of extremely few Supply Corps Officers to qualify as Diving Officer of the Watch. Supply Officers weren't required to qualify on watches normally stood by Line Officers, so the overwhelming majority of them didn't bother. Not Mr. Wallis. He insisted on being qualified on the Diving Officer station, and being rotated into the watch bill. Sadly, it was the only station regulations allowed him to stand. Even though enlisted men gave even small compliments to officers begrudgingly, he commanded a substantial amount of respect for his "no slacking here" attitude.

Mr. McGuire will always have a special place in my memory. Being from New Hampshire, he was an avid Red Sox fan. As any Sox fan will remember, our heroes made it into the World Series in 1986. My duty section had the overnight duty, and was watching "The Game Of Doom" that night on the little TV in our mess deck. It was that infamous day of the even more infamous "Bill Buckner incident". At that pivotal moment when that ground ball rolled between Mr. Buckner's legs, Mr. McGuire turned away from the TV, leaned against the bulkhead, and started pounding his fist on the cheap, fake Navy paneling. I'm not sure, but I think he might have been crying.

Mr. Thorpe was the only person to catch me on the verge of falling asleep on watch. Let's face it, Engine Room Lower Level was *designed* to put someone to sleep. First off, imagine you're sleep deprived to begin with. Now go into a space that's warm. There's machinery all around you, humming away. There's a comfortable bench locker for you to sit on. That's where I was. The magic was starting to take effect. I was right on the edge of nodding off, when I heard a voice,

"Do you want to get woken up, or *written* up?"

It was Mr. Thorpe, poking his head out from the Shaft Lube Oil bay. He was making his hourly round as EOOW. I was much more awake from there on out.

The junior officers all had to qualify as Officer Of the Deck, or OOD. While standing this watch, a curious device could be seen hanging around their neck. On a nylon cord hung a thin, flat device around six inches in diameter that looked like a circular slide rule. A few thin plastic discs were stacked upon each other, each disc getting smaller. Each disc had numbers and graduations around their perimeters. The effect was that a number could be located on one disc, and related to a number on another disc, making rapid calculations possible. It was used to convert heights into distances. It was called the "Whiz Wheel". The one worn by the OOD was labeled "OOD Whiz Wheel". The student OOD was called the JOOD, or Junior Officer Of the Deck. Appropriately, his was called the "JOOD Whiz Wheel".

Each time we went to periscope depth, increments were called out by the OOD, and the JOOD's fingers would be fumbling and flying around this little white plastic wheel.

For senior officers, there was obviously the Captain. He is always called CO, Captain, Skipper, Old Man, or some variation thereof. Directly below him was the Executive Officer (always referred to as the XO). Below him were the Engineer and Navigator. The relationship between the Captain and the XO is a peculiar one. It's an involuntary game of Good Cop-Bad Cop. The XO's duty is to enforce the Captain's rules, regulations, and principles. The end result is that the XO is always forced into the role of Jerk, Meanie, Prick or any other names one can think of. Now that he has his Bad Cop to keep everything in order, the Skipper can go around smiling, patting the boys on the shoulder, asking how they're doing, and being the all-around nice guy.

Our Captain was Commander Mendes. Technically, he wasn't the Captain when I first reported aboard. We had a change of command ceremony shortly after I arrived. Commander Eller relinquished command in one of the longest, most boring ceremonies I've ever known. Our first XO was Commander Ulriche. Mr. Ulriche was probably the best XO I ever had. Yeah, he had to be the prick. But, everyone knew what his roll was. I always got the impression he was genuinely liked by the crew. Our next XO was a miserable man named Lieutenant Commander

Forbes. It was said that his initials cryptically stood for "Field-day – Every-day".

Mr. Forbes found himself in one of the most unfair predicaments found in military service. One of the most serious offenses any Officer of the Line can commit is grounding his vessel. Running a naval vessel aground, *any* vessel, *any* ground has severe and instant repercussions. It is the instant kiss of death to any naval career. If a vessel is run aground, the Captain is instantly relieved of his command, and will never command a naval vessel of any kind again. Circumstances are of no consideration. Exceptions to this are extremely rare. The Navigator suffers the same fate, as does the Officer Of the Deck who has the con at the time of the incident. Other officers may be removed as well, depending on circumstances. This is one of those instances where one can delegate authority, but not responsibility. Whether or not the officers were directly responsible for the accident, they are blamed and punished, because of their position of responsibility.

Back in the early 1980s, the U.S.S. Kamehameha, one of our ballistic missile submarines, was grounded. Mr. Forbes was the Navigator. He was instantly relieved. It was made clear to him that no matter how well he served, he would never have his own command. Considering the fact that he may have had absolutely nothing to do with the accident, but was receiving the blame anyway, his pissy attitude was understandable…to a point. It is my opinion that he far surpassed that point.

Our Engineer was Lt. Commander Ted Riles. Almost everyone called him "Eng". He resembled Graham Chapman of Monty Python fame. He was a very talented Engineer. His only flaw was that he was just a little arrogant at times. I will always remember Mr. Riles for one interesting episode. We were in the Bahamas, conducting a combat exercise. We were spending a lot of time at PD, checking for signals and targets, and receiving instructions in radio messages.

Mr. Riles had the con, and stood at the bandstand, the periscope glued to his eyes. Suddenly, the control room heard,

"Oh…shit!"

Everyone in the Control Room turned to see Mr. Riles frozen at the periscope, his mouth hanging open. He began to stutter.

"Uh…ah…ah…um…uh…"

The Chief of the Watch, Diving Officer, Helmsman, and Planesman all sat staring at him. They were cocked and ready to carry out any instruction given. Now, if only he would give them one! Just when the tension became unbearable, and the Chief of the Watch was about to physically shake the Engineer, Mr. Riles blurted out,

"EMERGENCY DEEP!!"

That's what everyone was waiting to hear! All over the boat, anyone not strapped down reached for something to hold on to. All planes were pushed to full down position. The boat sank like a stone, plummeting down at a thirty degree angle. Later on, we found out the issue was a huge painted wooden barrel. It was just floating along on its merry way, completely oblivious to the fact it was about to shear off our Search Periscope.

The Navigator was Lt. Commander Boris Sweeney. He was a tall, slim man with a sparse but bushy mustache, and conspicuous nose. He was soft spoken, with an esoteric sense of humor. I'll always remember one particular incident involving Mr. Sweeney.

For some reason, he had to come up to the barracks to see one of the crew. I was going back to my room at the same time, and ended up riding up with him in the elevator. I turned to look at him and noticed his Dolphins weren't the usual design we were accustomed to. I asked him why they were different. He explained that they were special "deep water" Dolphins. The only vessel I could think of fitting that description was our highly classified nuclear powered research sub, NR-1.

I asked him if that was the vessel responsible for his special status. He turned to me with sincere surprise on his face, and said,

"What? That skimmer?"

Now I was really confused. "Skimmer" was the derogatory term sub sailors used to refer to surface vessels. NR-1 was the deepest diving submarine I'd ever heard of. I voiced my complete confusion. Mr. Sweeney looked at me with a wry smile,

"It's all a matter of perspective, Petty Officer Smith. I sat on the bottom of the Pacific Ocean in Trieste (a very famous deep submergence vehicle), over 28,000 feet down. Compared to that, NR-1 *is* a skimmer."

I quickly learned the rumors about submariners were completely true. It truly was a different lot of people who would volunteer for duty on a ship designed to sink. It didn't take long to realize that submariners are, as a group impeccably insane. The longer I ponder this concept, the truer it becomes. It's extremely dangerous. It's extremely stressful. It's extremely demanding. It takes a special type of person to deal with those conditions, and there was no group more special than Skipjack. Some names and faces will be in the forefront of my memory forever.

M Div:

MMC(SS) Quince Jardin:

Chief Jardin was my Division Chief. I recall him as being average height and build, with thinning hair. He had a thin moustache that looked good on him. I seriously doubt I had any positive effect on the hair issue. Like everyone else in my division, he endured his association with me with tolerance and a sense of humor. A resignation to his fate probably helped as well. One of the most endearing qualities about him was his habit of dressing someone down, in true Navy tradition and vocabulary, and ending his rant with,

"I hope you take this in the kind, constructive manner in which it was intended."

Or,

"Have a nice day."

As I look back on some of the mistakes I made, it's a wonder he lasted as long as he did. Some of the M Div guys will remember him staring mutely at me, wide eyed and silent, slowly shaking his head. It was he who was responsible for my Bluenose initiation being so interesting. Prior to the fateful day, he caught me looking over his shoulder as he made notes about the event. During my initiation, I was charged with…

SPYING AGAINST THE COURT OF BOREALIS REX!!

Oh, yay! This is going to go well!

Some of my interactions with Chief Quince made it into the "Attaboy Book", a hardbound volume of handwritten notes about boneheaded things the crewmembers did. Sadly, I was probably personally responsible for his departure. He left the boat due to an ulcer. That *had* to be on account of me.

MM1(SS) Jonny Mains:

Jonny was a short wiry powerhouse. He played semi-pro soccer before joining the Navy, and was looking forward to taking it back up when he ended this chapter of his life. He was very intelligent, with a quick wit, and excellent aptitude for his naval profession. He was one of the first people I spoke to upon reporting aboard. My brother warned me about what these events could be like. A person's sensibilities, sense of humor, and quick thinking could be tested with a single verbal exchange. A fine example was my brother's experience when he reported aboard U.S.S. Tullibee. He was introduced to one of the engineering Chiefs. The man shook his hand, welcomed him aboard, and asked,

"How long is your dick?"

"What??"

"I *said*, how long is your dick?"

"In what state?"

"Flaccid.", the Chief responded.

So Steve told him. As the Chief walked away, he lamented,

"Goddam coners *still* got us beat!"

Jonny was no different. As soon as I was introduced, he said,

"You suck dick?"

"Not that I…know of. No."

As he turned and walked away,

"Hetero-trash!"

His harsh callused exterior was only a cover for his harsh callused interior, but I figured he had to be a good guy. He put up with me. If I remember correctly, he was right on the edge of being discharged when I was pulled off the boat.

MM2(SS) Harry Mills:

This guy had to be one of the nicest people a person could ask to meet. This poor guy probably found himself on the receiving end of my stupidity more often than anybody else. He was smart, quick thinking, and easy going. That's a great combination to have in a submarine crewman. I recall him having a strong New England accent, which somehow made him seem even more easy going. He had a wife and a pre-school aged daughter when I knew him, and surprisingly, she was instrumental in one of the funniest events I'll ever remember with Harry.

One night, we were in port, shut down, and tied up. Harry and I were in the same duty section. It was about 0130. I had the Shutdown Roving Watch, and Harry was trying to finish up a repair on the Diesel. I don't recall exactly what the repair was, but it involved removing one of the pistons from its cylinder. It was now time to put the piston back in, and *that* was a problem. The ring compressor he was using was very old and beat up. It couldn't really compress the piston rings properly, but it was the only one we had. This was the predicament in which I found him as I got to his location in the Engineering Spaces. I came around the corner of the compartment, and there he was. He was taking up the entire passage. He was half lying in the passageway, and the other half of him was somehow wedged inside the access panel of the diesel. He was wrestling with this heavy, awkward diesel piston and the almost useless ring compressor. In between grunts and curses, I could hear his muffled voice,

"Little Bunny Foo-foo, hopping through…the…forest, scooping up the field…mice…and boppin' 'em…on the…head."

I froze in my tracks! Obviously, poor Harry had finally beaten me to the finish line at the Looney Bin. He was just getting to the part about the Good Fairy when he finally extricated himself from the diesel's crankcase compartment. He half rolled to reposition himself for another try, and saw me standing there. I can only guess what the expression on my face said.

"What?"

He looked at me as if this was completely normal behavior, and I should be the strange one for not joining in.

"Harry. What on Earth are you singing?"

"Little Bunny Foo-foo."

"Little Bunny...*WHAT*?"

"Foo-foo. You've never heard of Little Bunny Foo-foo?"

"No..."

"Do you have kids? No, wait. No, you don't have kids. *That's* why you've never heard of Little Bunny Foo-foo. If you had kids you'd know. My daughter is in pre-school now. She just learned the song. We've been singing it a lot."

I continued to stare, just taking this all in at the usual speed 0130 allowed. Finally, he figured out how to bring this to a less painful end. He performed the song for me, complete with appropriate hand gestures. Apparently, these were crucial to any proper rendition. Wow. I was missing out on some major stuff by not having kids. I half climbed, half leapt over Harry to continue on my way. I wanted to help, but it was against the rules, and I had already been caught making animal noises over the Engineering Announcing System.

I checked on him two more times during my watch. The next time, he was still singing, but frustration had replaced the absent-minded lilt. I asked him if I could help. He declined, reminding me how much of a stickler Eng was for regulations. It was forbidden for the SRW to do physical work. The condition of the plant wasn't the first priority. It was the *only* priority. I reluctantly moved on.

Now it was 0300. I went on my tour again, clip board and pen in hand. As I got closer to Harry's location, I could hear faint clanging and shouting. When I got to the diesel again, a sorry sight met my eyes. Harry's uniform shirt was tossed over a nearby valve. The T-shirt remaining was covered in grease. He was once again halfway inside the diesel, but something was different. Any sense of musical tune was long gone. He was *screaming* the words of Little Bunny Foo-foo, who had apparently given up bopping the mice on the head in favor of dismembering them with a pair of rusty pliers.

I couldn't take it anymore. I offered my help again, and wouldn't be denied. Screw the rules. Revile was at 0530. If he finished this soon, he could still get some sleep. Apparently what he was now doing was using the ring compressor to squish the rings, and a screwdriver to push in what the compressor couldn't. It would have to be better having another pair of hands now. Harry finally relented. I squeezed into position next to him, reaching in with the screwdriver. I could barely see what was happening. We made three attempts, each just falling short. Finally, Harry said,

"It's pretty cramped here, and you're just in the way."

That is something a submariner is accustomed to hearing. They will take it with no offense…unless it happens during group sex. I felt terrible as I got up to continue my rounds. I tried my best. I knew it, and Harry knew it. 0400 finally came around. My relief showed, and I went forward to get some rest. I found out later he had in fact reinstalled the piston. But, not in time to get any sleep. When Chief Jardin came aboard for quarters, he took one look at Mills,

"Harry, get the hell out of here. Get some sleep."

MM2(SS) Tim Blodget:

Tim was a hoot. He was a soft spoken man with an extremely acute, but subtle, sense of humor. His forte was asking the too obvious question at exactly the worst possible moment. He was very good at his job. When I left, Tim was still only a Second Class, but he was starting his quals for Engineering Watch Supervisor (EWS…pronounced Ee – Whiz).

MM2(SS) Bobby Porter:

If I had to describe Bobby in as few words as possible, I would say "highly educated Droopy Dog". He just had that super easygoing nature about him. Beneath that was a quick mind that was always working. His wit was as quick as his intellect, but that didn't always show up. Often he would make a witty comment, but I could often figure out what he was going to say before he was finished saying it. He went through some tough times with our Division Officer, but I heard he made it to Master Chief before he retired. I wouldn't be the least bit surprised.

MM3(SS) Tom Pilsbury:

Tom was a "good ol' boy". There was no other way to describe him. Apparently, he got off to a rocky start, because he acquired an interesting nickname: "Brainstem". This was short for "Brainstem, and no others." It was a play on the unique terminology used in military transfer orders. Few people called him Tom, Petty Officer Pilsbury, or even Pilsbury. It was always,

"Brainstem, where did you put that wrench?" or "Brainstem! What were you thinking?" or "Where's Brainstem? Anyone seen Brainstem?"

I refused to call him Brainstem, especially to his face. First, I felt it was demeaning. Second, I didn't think I was even up to Brainstem's level yet. Tom had a typical nickname for me, however. In true naval tradition, he called me "Nub". That was a popular nickname for a new member of the crew. There was just one problem. At one point, Tom got busted. He was reduced in rank after a Captain's Mast. I now outranked him. Right after it happened, he came to me and said,

"Don't you *ever* call me nub."

I had always felt that he and I were in the same boat. That sentiment was reduced a little that day. The thought of calling him that had never crossed my mind. Why would I subject him to something that made me so unhappy?

He got me good one time, though. We were getting ready for a big drill set during one of our patrols. He and I were talking in Engine Room Lower Level. He was telling me about a drill he had to run involving Shaft Lube Oil. The casualty was a leak in the pump housing. He told me that his first reaction was to grab a rag and press it over the spot of the leak. This had apparently impressed the drill monitors quite a bit! I remembered his advice. Sure enough, during my drill watch, we had a leak in the Shaft Lube Oil pump. I ran, grabbed a rag, and pressed it over the spot of the simulated leak. The Engineer was there observing everyone's actions. He saw me do that, and *flipped out*.

"Smith!! What the fuck are you doing? What's *that* supposed to achieve?"

I tried to stammer out a mumbled explanation.

""What's the discharge pressure of that pump? Think! What is the discharge pressure of a Shaft Lube Oil pump? You'd better be able to answer that!"

My mind raced as he stared. The number came to mind. I blurted it out.

"You think you can stop that kind of pressure with a rag? A *rag*? Really?"

The humiliation and sense of betrayal was burned into my psyche forever. The little voice in my head said,

"Don't you *ever* forget that. *Never!*"

At some point, Tom must have turned the corner. The records I had access to indicated he was promoted twice more before he was discharged. I'd like to think that is an indication of the progress he made. I'd also like to think he was able to grow enough to make that progress.

MM2(SS) Henry Tillman:

Henry was like one of the paper dolls all the girls had when they were little. One could change its appearance by swapping out different one-piece combinations of clothing. Now he's in a bathing suit. Now he's in a tuxedo. Now he looks like a farmer. Henry could be wearing his uniform at first. Now take that away and put him in cut-off coveralls and a straw hat. Make him barefoot. Give him a fishing pole and a hay stem to chew on. He wouldn't change a bit! Henry was as back woods as the day is long. He was a simple man with simple roots, who in some obscure way, fit in where ever he went.

I'll always remember Henry, his wife, and I driving off somewhere to try and find the federal building that was issuing passports. We would possibly need them for an upcoming patrol. What a goat rope that was! The three of us wandering around with their toddler, on a wild goose chase, is forever in my memory. The wild goose eventually ran out of steam, and we caught it.

MM1(SS) Bart Dietrich:

This guy was the classic man's man. He had the best of everything. Good looks, pretty girl friend, intelligence, and easy going nature. Every once in a while he would catch a little ribbing for being just a little too "homey", like the time he tried to get me and two other junior guys to sing the classic summer camp "Chicken pot pie" song with him. He was best known for his ability to get seasick, it seemed almost on a whim. Seasickness is no laughing matter. As I was to learn later, it can incapacitate a man. But some guys were just ridiculous. I'm not talking about guys barfing over a few slight rolls. I'm talking about guys who would barf as soon as we stationed the Maneuvering Watch. Come on, guys!! We're not even moving yet!

MM2(SS) Ron Rodrigues:

Ron was always one of the brightest people in our division. He was very quick thinking. That came in handy on a number of occasions. Technically he was very competent, and exacting. But, he did have his drawbacks. His extremely sharp wit came with an equally sharp tongue to match. He wasn't the least bit hesitant to use either, on virtually anyone. He had the habit of holding court with some of the other crewmen whom he found to be like-minded. Those around them would be picked apart like road kill by their lofty condemnations. He ended up leaving the boat, and the Navy, under "less than optimum" conditions. Well, what do you know about that. I've learned over the years that's a common pattern.

MM3(SS) Izzy "Digger" Dias:

I didn't get to know Izzy very well. I left shortly after he reported aboard. From what I saw, he seemed like a good guy. I knew he was going to have some abuse to live down. His nick name was the same as a popular toddler's toy promoted by frequent commercials on TV. It was accompanied by a very distinctive jingle, which was sung repeatedly on board. I'd be willing to bet he never wanted to see that commercial again as long as he lived.

MM1(SS) Steve Champlain:

Steve was one of our ELTs. I'll always remember him for one of the most interesting exchanges I've ever had. It also perfectly illustrated one of the advantages of being part of a submarine crew. I had a question, and was told he was the best person to ask. I finally found him in Machinery Space Lower Level.

"Hey, Petty Officer Champlain..."

"What did you say?"

"I've got a question, and I was told..."

"Did you call me Petty Officer Champlain?"

He went on to explain, in his finely crafted southern drawl, exactly where I went wrong,

"Look, y'all can call me Champlain. Or y'all can call me Steve. Or y'all can call me Fat Freddy. But don't call me *Petty Officer* Champlain."

MM2(SS) Nick Norinson:

Nick was another of our ELTs. He played a major part in one of the best practical jokes ever played, upon one of the most obnoxious people to ever set foot on the boat.

MM1(SS) Noino Caramon:

Noino was from the Philippines. He was slight in stature, and very quiet. With his round metal rimmed Navy issue glasses, he was a dead ringer for a quiet dignified Japanese gentleman. He was extremely intelligent and competent. While out on patrol, he was teaching himself to speak and read Russian, in *Cyrillic,* Russia's unique alphabet! Once, on a patrol, we had a key piece of equipment break. The part was made of Teflon. Noino took a solid block of Teflon, and carved an exact duplicate…*by hand.* Noino was always completely composed and unflappable. I only witnessed one incident when Noino blew his cool. I was the reason. Surprise, surprise.

One of the evolutions I needed to complete for my Engine Room Supervisor quals was "locking the shaft". Locking the shaft was accomplished by slowly reducing the shaft RPMs with the throttle valves, and tweaking the steam flow between forward and reverse until the shaft stopped revolving completely. At that point, the jacking gear could be engaged. Unless the jacking gear motor was started, the shaft would remain immovable.

Noino and I went back to the Jacking Gear Station. He donned sound powered phones, and I stood by at the jacking gear lever. Noino communicated directly with the Throttleman, coaching him through the process of slowing down the shaft. A constant flow of information was what the Throttleman needed. RPMs of one or two wouldn't show on the tachometer in Maneuvering. Noino talked him down slower and slower,

"Shaft is slow ahead. Slow ahead. Slow ahead. Still slowing. Shaft is slowing. No. Shaft is slow astern. (The Throttleman had over-compensated.) Shaft is faster astern."

Noino patiently talked him down like a passenger trying to land a plane. Finally, we got back to the point that the shaft was almost motionless. Finally, the moment arrived,

"The shaft is stopped."

CLUNK!

I threw the lever as soon as I heard those words leave Noino's mouth. He went absolutely ballistic!!

"WHAT ARE YOU DOING!! WHAT ARE YOU DOING!! WHATAREYOU DOING!!"

Poor Noino's eyes were bugging out so far I thought they'd push his glasses off his nose. He was so spun up, it seemed as though there were two of him standing there. Seeing him so angry would have been comical, if it didn't mean I had obviously done something very, very bad. This calm, quiet slight man was in a condition I had never witnessed before, never mind even contemplated. After a few minutes, he calmed down. He seemed to return to his usual serene demeanor. He took a deep breath, and apologized for becoming so angry. Then he explained what I did wrong.

The purpose of the jacking gear is to turn the shaft very, very slowly. It's used when the propulsion system is shut down, either for an emergency, or an in port period. Keeping the shaft moving keeps the bearings from wearing unevenly. In an emergency, the purpose is to lock the shaft and keep it from turning. The system works by taking a motor that turns at several hundred RPM, and attaching it to a machine that reduces the speed from shaft revolutions per minute to shaft "minutes per revolution". This machine is usually engaged after the shaft is completely stopped.

If the system is engaged during an emergency, the chances of the shaft moving are much higher. If the system was engaged, and the shaft turned, the "gearing down" effect from motor to shaft would become a "gearing up" effect between shaft and motor. The end result is that the motor would be spun up many times over its maximum over speed rating, and disintegrate.

To make sure this doesn't happen, the man engaging the lever for the jacking gear waits until the ERS says the shaft is stopped three times. Noino should have said,

"The shaft is stopped...the shaft is stopped...the shaft is stopped."

before I threw the lever. Luckily for me, the shaft really was stopped.

MM2(SS) Glen Casey:

Glen was a pleasure to be around, and serve with. He was one of the most easy going people I ever met. Everything flowed easily for him, regardless of the situation. As far as I could tell, stress just flowed off this man's back, like water off a duck. He had a good sense of humor, liberally applied on a regular basis. This even extended to his racial origin.

Glen was a great example of the wide variety of people making up a submarine crew. We came from all walks of life, and all environments. The standard was based upon intelligence, reliability, and resistance to extreme stress. Where a person came from had absolutely no bearing on their qualifications. One of his parents was black, and one was white. Occasionally he would be teased about his "mixed" origin. Regardless of the race of the person poking at him, his response was the same,

"Well...God made my mother, then he made my father. Then he finished screwing around and made me. I'm perfect."

I only saw Glen truly angry once. It was during an exchange between himself and the next subject of discussion...Tom Reynolds.

MM3(SS) Tom Reynolds:

Tom, Tom, Tom. What to say about Tom. We met at Knowles Atomic Power Laboratory, and got transferred to Skipjack together. He was extremely intelligent. He was tenacious. When he set out to do something, his ability to reason it through and work 'til the end was nothing short of amazing. I'm sure his IQ was at least genius level. During our time together on Skipjack, not only did he breeze through quals in comparison to me, he also taught himself to play the piano. He just bought a book...bought a keyboard...and went to work. One day he called me into his room. To demonstrate his progress, he sat down and played "Somewhere over the Rainbow". He played it beginning to end. A few days later, it was "Fur Elise".

Sadly, he was as socially inept as he was brilliant. It was painful to watch at times. Sometimes it seemed that he was truly at a loss for what to do or say. Other times it seemed that his actions were deliberate. I sometimes wondered if he had decided to say or do things to screw with peoples' minds, or if he simply gave up and decided to begin the free fall to his social doom. Here are some examples:

1) Chief Jardin brought Tom and I back into shaft alley to do some cleaning. The area was very difficult to access, explaining why it had been so long since it was last properly cleaned. The area was a mess. The Chief's instructions were clear,

"Get everything out of there. The oil, water, grease, dirt, dust. I want it all out of there."

Tom held up a finger to get the Chief's attention,

"What about the smegma?" (A fifty cent word for slimy dirt.)

"The what?"

"The smegma."

"The...smegma."

"Yes. The smegma. Do you want me to get the smegma?"

"Yes, Tom. While you're down there, you might as well get the smegma."

Chief Jardin just shook his head and walked away, mumbling something about life being too short.

2) Engine Room Upper Level was where the steam turbines and most of the Main and Auxiliary Steam Systems were located. Included in this mind boggling maze were the steam inlet valves for the Ship Service Turbine Generators. These were big, heavy valves with large hand wheels that, when put in motion, seemed to spin forever. Provided the

plant was shut down, it wasn't odd for a bored Machinist to absent mindedly spin one of these valves just on a lark. One day, Tom found himself doing just that. There was just one little problem...it had a Caution tag hanging on it. The tag indicated that the valve was involved with some kind of maintenance, and could only be operated after getting special permission. Yet there he was, spinning it open, spinning it closed, back and forth, over and over.

Chief Jardin saw him doing that, and became a little perturbed. He went to Tom and said,

"Tom, if you're willing to just play with a device with a Caution tag on it, how do I know you won't do the same to a device that's Danger tagged, while I'm working on it?"

Tom looked him right in the eye as he delivered his response,

"You don't."

The situation degraded rapidly from then on.

But by far, the exchange between him and Glen served as a snapshot of how his mind worked.

3) We were in port, tied up, and shut down. We were in a brief maintenance period between patrols. Everything was, for the most part, relaxed and running smoothly. Glen was the Shutdown Roving Watch, while Tom and I were just trying to look more useful than ballast. Not an easy thing for a non-qual to do.

We had divers over the side working on a hull fitting. Their operation had progressed to the point that they needed a gasket cut for the flange they were about to use. They asked where they could have it done, and were directed back aft.

When most people think of divers, they imagine people on vacation petting fish. Or perhaps an underwater cameraman. The most rugged prospect might be a safety diver for a movie shoot. Navy divers aren't like that. A Navy diver is essentially an underwater construction worker. They're in excellent physical shape, highly motivated, and very technically minded. Imagine a Navy SEAL without the guns and explosives. That's a Navy diver. Not the type of person one would piss off just to see what happened.

These two divers were brought back to the engine room with their gasket pattern. Glen went and broke out the gasket material. Being the SRW, he wasn't allowed to do the job. Either Tom or I would have that honor. That's when it happened. Glen turned to Tom,

"Tom, would you cut this gasket for these guys?"

"Why?"

"*What?*"

"Why?"

"Because it needs to be done, and I can't do it."

"Do I have to?"

"What! Yes, you *have* to. Come on, these guys are waiting."

"But...I'll get dirty."

"I don't care. You need to do it."

"I'd rather not."

"JUST CUT THE FUCKING GASKET!!"

The expressions on the two divers' faces indicated *they* would be more than happy to cut the gasket themselves. However, they would be using Tom as the gasket material.

Anyone on the boat who didn't see the end coming simply wasn't paying attention. Tom was standing watch in Engine Room Lower Level. For whatever reason, he found himself in a position encountered by virtually every watch stander to ever set foot on a ship: he got behind on his logs. There are all kinds of reasons why a sailor could get behind on his logs. He could be working. He could be studying. He could get caught up in an evolution that goes bad. It really doesn't matter. The end result is the same. There's an hour on the log sheet not filled in. It *has* to be filled in. Unless the world has come to an end, and it has been properly documented, there is absolutely no acceptable reason for an hour of logs to be blank.

There's only one thing to do. The unfortunate victim must quickly fill in the numbers with no one else seeing. No one else is the wiser. No one can prove when the numbers were written down. There is a name for this activity. It's called either "blowing off" or "radioing" your logs. That practice is just as frowned upon as leaving them blank. A watch stander can get in an extremely large, smelly pile of trouble if caught radioing his logs. Only a completely heartless psychopath can do it without feeling bad about it. But, each watch stander will encounter this nasty situation once in their career.

This is what happened to Tom. But, it wasn't what he did. It was what he said when he was caught. Chief Wilson was Engineering Watch Supervisor that day when Tom was in ERLL. He was making his rounds, and like so many others, went down the aft ladder into ERLL instead of coming down the forward ladder. Some people do this because the watch can't see him coming. Wilson popped his head out of the Shaft Lube Oil bay, and found himself staring at Tom radioing his logs.

Tom knew he was caught. The Chief quietly asked,

"Why do you do that?"

At that point, Tom could have begged for mercy. He could have made up any excuse, claiming he had never done it before, and would never do it again. He could have said anything other than what he chose to say,

"Do what?"

That was the beginning of a very quick, very painful process culminating in the discharge of Tom from the Navy. I don't know where he is now. But, I sincerely hope he built a new life on all the positive characteristics he possesses, while shedding the self-destructive ones.

E Div:

EMC(SS) Art Wilson:

Chief Wilson was probably the best candidate for "submarine poster child of the year". His hair was always cut to spec. He had a tightly cropped moustache that was groomed to exacting standards. His uniform was spotless, even on patrols. He had a quiet, confident demeanor that usually served to quiet down any flustered environment. If he wasn't in the position he was, he probably would have been elected God.

EM2(SS) Carl Firenze:

Carl was a riot. Always quick with a joke or a good story, he was always a welcome addition to any group. The best way to describe Carl would be to say he was half Harrison Ford and half Zorba the Greek, with a New York/New Jersey accent. I'll always remember him for three special stories he told.

1) We were sitting in Engine Room Upper Level one day, during one of the few slack, quiet times. We were discussing muscle cars. I can't recall whether this was his own car to which he was referring, or that of a friend, but I'll always remember how he chose to describe the enormous size of the engine,

    "A house fly could fly in the carburetor, fly out the exhaust pipe still alive, and say WHAT THE FUCK WAS THAT??"

2) One day while browsing through the "Attaboy Book" he came across an entry he had written himself. It involved the basic electricity checkout for one of the new machinists in A Gang. This poor kid was really having a hard time grasping the idea Carl was trying to get across. Carl asked a very simple question,

    "What drives the Turbine Generators?"

    "The generators."

"No, the generators are driven by something. What is that?"

"The generators."

"No! I'll give you a hint. The generators are driven by steam turbines. What drives the turbines?"

"The generators."

"*NO!*"

"Air?"

"(SIGH) Just give me your qual card."

3) We went down to the Bahamas to do a TRE (Tactical Readiness Exercise). It would involve firing a live torpedo at a target, and participating in some war games with the Brits and some local surface units. The exercise finished up just in time for lunch. As I went past the Control Room to the ladder down to the Mess, I could hear Captain Mendes talking to the skipper of one of the British frigates. The Fire Control Tracking Party was just wrapping things up. Carl was in the FCTP, and we asked him how things went. He face was very long. That should have been our first clue.

"They sank us. (He made a whistling noise, and mimed an ASROC arcing through the air.) Boom."

Poor Carl seemed inconsolable. We told him it wasn't as if we had really died. It didn't matter. Every once in a while, he would arc his finger through the air…and go boom.

EM3(SS) Mike Jeeves:

Mike was from New Jersey. He was a tall slim guy with a mop of dark hair and a moustache that seemed to have a mind of its own. He was one of the more junior electricians, which put him a rung or two higher up the ladder than myself. He was very happy-go-lucky, and a great guy to go drinking with. He always seemed to find the fun. He had a girlfriend back in Jersey he reminisced about often. Mike played a major role in one of the more humorous events during that frustrating period at the end of my enlistment.

EM3(SS) Nate Garner:

Nate arrived on Skipjack a while after I did. We spent a lot of time together, with me ending up in Engine Room Lower Level, and him as Auxiliary Electrician Aft. He was comfortably average in virtually every way, with the exception of one thing: he was prematurely grey. Now, I started getting grey hair when I was twenty two years old. But Nate was a little younger than me, and he was "salt and pepper". He caught a lot of ribbing for that. The one thing I'll always remember about Nate was our dependents' cruise. Every once in a while, a Navy vessel will be allowed to bring family members out for a brief cruise. It gives the families a chance to see what their son/brother/father/husband does for a living, and where all those tax dollars go. Nate's family came aboard, along with his sister. Let's be clear here. She was hot. Very, very hot. Nate was getting a little defensive and protective of his extremely hot sister in this submarine full of horny submariners. It was clear the stress was starting to take its toll. By the end of the day, he looked like a rooster who had to escort a flock of hens through a field of foxes, one at a time. Oh, did I mention she was hot?

EM2(SS) Virgil Deene:

Virgil arrived on board about halfway through my tour on Skipjack. If I had to compare him to a well-known person, it would be the character Dietrich on the TV show Barney Miller. He was quiet, quirky, and just a little off. We spent a lot of time talking, and I noticed a peculiar habit he had. Any time someone sneezed, he would say "Salud", instead of "Gesundheit" or "Bless you". Finally I couldn't stand it anymore. I sneezed, and received my obligatory "Salud". I told him I'd never heard that before, and asked him why he said that. He explained that it was what Spanish people would say when someone sneezed. Some of his in-laws were Spanish, and it got him in the habit. I let it go soon after. It wasn't until later that I was reminded of it, when Virgilwas talking to his wife on the phone. He was blabbing away, speaking in fluent Spanish. Apparently, some of his in-laws were *very* Spanish! He later explained that he married a Spanish woman who spoke no English. After that, I gave him a hearty "Salud" any time he sneezed.

EM1(SS) Ernie Jiles:

Ernie was a big man. Not necessarily hulking, just tall. He was from the inner city. It was obvious his life there was not an easy one. He had plenty of scars, and gang related symbols literally burned into his dark skin. And...the man was a walking encyclopedia of all things electric on U.S.S. Skipjack. He was abrasive at times, there is no denying that. But, his good points outweighed his faults, and it was very good to have him around.

EMC(SS) Gerry Cole:

Chief Cole was a typical Chief. Almost middle aged, slightly thinning hair, highly experienced, and pear shaped.

The one event featuring Chief Cole that will always be burned into my memory, involves a drill gone wrong. Now, I don't recall what the drill was for. It could have been for anything, fire, flooding, it isn't important. What *was* important was the fact things were starting to go wrong. It's okay. It happens. Some of the scenarios can be a little over the top. We're reminded that the important part is our learning from them, and that's why we run them in the first place.

Chief Cole was the EWS for this watch. Everything was normal. Then the drill happened. Then the drill went wrong. Then the Casualty Assistance Team came aft. Then another Chief asked Cole what he needed. That's when it happened. Chief Cole flapped his hands in consternation and yelled,

"I...NEED...HELP!!"

The only thought that came to everyone's minds was how amazingly similar he looked to a penguin trying to take flight! The drill finally ended. The watch ended. The day ended. The hand flapping, sadly, did *not*. For the next few days, someone would routinely ask a shipmate if they needed anything. The reply had become the stuff of legend. Hands would flap in desperation,

"I...NEED...HELP!!"

RC Div:

ET2(SS) Kenny Adair:

Kenny was quiet, reserved, conservative, and dignified...usually. He was always good for an interesting story. If I remember correctly, he spent some time in the

Middle East teaching either Iranians or Iraqis to fly Bell UH-1s. He had some very disturbing, yet funny tales to tell about those times he spent living there. He smoked, and the ritual he went through to take out and light a cigarette was pretty funny. It wasn't a *ritual*, per se, but he did the same things every time. It was very distinctive. Some of the other crew members would do impressions of Kenny lighting a cigarette. It was always good for a laugh.

ET2(SS) Connor Andrews:

Connor was best known for "Connor's Rules of Life". These numbered perhaps six or seven, and were permanently inscribed somewhere on the boat. I have no idea or recollection where, which is now unimportant since Skipjack is now "razor blades" (the term used to describe a submarine that has been scrapped).

The two "rules of life" that was recited to me over and over by concerned shipmates were,

"Rule number one: don't sweat the small shit. Rule number two: it's *all* small shit."

ET1(SS) Manny Mitchell:

Manny was just an all-around good guy. He was smart, competent, and easy going. I was intensely jealous of him because he had a jacket from his previous boat that had a patch showing Mickey Mouse from the Sorcerer's Apprentice. It was the scene showing him up on the peak, waving the magic wand. In hind sight, I can't recall for the life of me why I was so envious. Maybe it was just a really cool patch. There was a period when Manny and I hung out quite a lot. I'll always recall this one restaurant we went to in Old Saybrook. It was called The White House. Yes, *that*

White House. Their matchbooks featured the Presidential Seal. This was it bit odd, since it was a very traditional Hungarian restaurant. I never did figure out the connection. It didn't really matter, because the food was absolutely out of this world. It was my first time tasting paprikash. It's very similar to goulash but with more meat, and if one could imagine it happening, *more paprika*! If I ever run across that restaurant again, I'm sorry. No one else will have any say regarding our dinner plans.

ET2(SS) Dana Mota:

First off, Dana did, hands down...the best impression of Kenny lighting a cigarette! He was hilarious. He was the one non-machinist I spent most of my duty time with. It was he who used to announce the "coffee pot low level alarm". It was he who made the unfortunate request resulting in my being caught making animal noises over the X60J sound powered phone circuit. Dana was always a pleasure to be around. He always seemed naturally light hearted.

The Forward Guys:

MS3(SS) DioneAngilante:

Dione, like many other Navy cooks at the time, was from the Philippines. He was a competent cook in general. But, when it came to Philippine food he was the man. He rocked! He made the best pork adobo on the planet. His lumpia were outrageous. I always looked forward to his meals. A popular song on the radio at the time was paraphrased in his honor. What was even better, I learned the proper names for much of this regional food. Why would this be so handy? When I became a civilian and began working at Monsanto, we had co-ops from local universities working at our site. Some of them were from that region of the world. Some of them were pretty. Some of them were *very* pretty, although I wished one in particular would shave her legs a little more often than she did.

It made them happy being so far from home, to hear someone say things familiar to them. I'll always remember this one day, when one of these girls came back to the office with her lunch. I watched her open it up. Inside were some very nice spring rolls. Well, that's what we call them *here*. Without really thinking, I blurted out,

"Lumpia!"

She spun around.

"You know what they are?"

That started a very nice conversation with a very pretty girl. Thank you, Dione. Thank you very much.

MM1(SS) Bob Erie:

Bob was a big man. No, let me start over. Bob was an enormous man. Sorry, I'm still falling a little short. Okay, one last try. Bob was a huge, heavy, hulking monster of a man. That's better. He was one of the senior machinists in Auxiliary division. He was very experienced, very strong, and very surly. He wasn't a hard person to be around, but his attitude could be purely rotten at times. He was particularly nasty to non-quals. After a while, I think I figured out why. It was his weight. He could barely fit through the hatches. He had to buy civilian shirts because the Navy didn't make shirts big enough. God only knows what his home life was like. I suspected this was all taking a huge toll on his self-esteem. People often wondered why he was allowed to stay in the Navy, or why he wasn't required to go into some kind of weight loss program. The answer was simple. He was an extremely talented and experienced machinist. Having him in that condition was better than not having him at all.

A while after I left the boat, I ran across Bob again. I couldn't believe my eyes! After I left, Bob and another heavy crew member were sent away to a "fat farm". Apparently it worked extremely well. I almost didn't recognize him. In fact, it was his voice I'd recognized before his actual appearance. I commented on this to some of the Skipjack guys I still saw once in a while at the barracks.

They told me his mental transformation was even more impressive. He was a completely different person. He was pleasant, engaging, patient, and much kinder to the non-quals when he ruthlessly abused them.

YN2(SS) Brian Reed:

There are some people in a submarine's crew who you simply don't piss off. Here are some good examples:

The Yeoman: the Yeoman handles all of your important papers. He takes care of crucial things like your leave papers, promotions, and very often, your pay record. Want to have your leave disappear, or go without pay for a month? Piss off your Yeoman.

The Corpsman: while the Yeoman can hurt you mentally, the Corpsman can hurt you literally. The Corpsman has your shot record. Remember all those inoculations you received in the first few months of naval service? Those are very important. So important, in fact, that if your shot record vanishes, you have to get them all over again. *All* of them. Usually, for the sake of expediency, all in the same day. I guarantee you, if you go out of your way to piss off your Corpsman, your shot record will promptly vanish. Oops. Sorry. No idea where it could have gone.

Brian Reed was probably one of the few Yeoman who would give you a good hard slap before messing with you on a professional level. He was as meticulous as he was easy going. How do I know he was so patient and understanding? It's easy. I never missed a payday, and my leave always happened on time. If anyone would have driven him nuts, it would have been me.

Here's another indication of what a good guy he was: he let me borrow his Quadrophenia cassette. He also didn't mind too much when I thought I'd lost it. That alone is reason enough to make my life a living hell.

QM3(SS) Chuck Dante:

Chuck was one of the junior Quartermasters on the boat. He was very easy going, considering the duties he had. Quartermasters worked for the Navigator. The Navigator's job is very high profile. If a submarine isn't aware of its location, bad things can happen. That pressure, much like "poo", rolls downhill. A QM's job is not easy.

It was Chuck who taught me the "Submarine Cheer". In fine military tradition, many different occupations and/or individual units have their own cheer. Submariners seized upon this aspect of military service, and bent to the task. The result, now decades old, did not disappoint.

The Submarine Cheer:

Submarines once, submarines twice!

Holy jumping Jesus Christ!

We go up, we go down!

We don't ever fuck around!

Rat shit, bat shit, dirty old twat!

Thirty one douche-bags tied in a knot!

Oooogah, oooogah! Dive, dive!

And all you skimmers…fuck you!!

QM Dante was also responsible for the Falco 80s hit "Rock me Amadeus" being transformed into its much more artful form, "Bake me Angilante."

Chuck was always good to have around. He was good for a laugh, or story, or some kind of distraction from what we were doing at the time, which entailed being locked up in a big sailing sewer pipe.

ST1(SS) Ned Montecello:

Ned was good at his job. There's no denying that. But, like so many other people who are good at their job, he would occasionally do something incredibly inept. This can be very frustrating, as I know from personal experience. It can be especially so if one is working in a high stress environment, where that stress is released by making fun of people who do inept things. I hope that made sense, because I think I just wrote the literary equivalent of the Mobius Strip.

The first thought that pops into a person's mind when they've done something inept is,

"Look, I know I just did something impressively stupid. Can we just acknowledge it and move on? I'd like to think we all know I'm not that stupid all the time. Right? *RIGHT?* Oh, nuts...they're not letting this go."

That's why Ned's incident was so classic. This is the one event I'll always remember him for. We were on patrol just outside Narragansett Bay. We were tooling along, everything going as it should. Well, not *everything*. The Crew's Berthing compartment was a little stuffy. One of the guys got up and turned on the ventilation fan. Ah...that's better.

Aha. What's this? That's new. Ned watched as a new contact lit up on the sonar display. He looked it over, and picked up his microphone,

"Con, Sonar. Contact bearing 287, range unknown. Sounds like a merchantman making way on a four blade screw. Designating this contact Sierra Three."

"Sonar, Con. Very well. Keep me posted on Sierra Three's movements, and any new information."

"Con, Sonar. Aye, sir."

Ned continued to scrutinize his new playmate. Definitely a four blader. But, he couldn't figure out any blade rate information. How fast was this guy going? And, he was just sitting there in the same position. No target motion meant he was on the same course, at the same speed. But the sound didn't match what his speed should be. Back to the microphone,

"Con, Sonar. Sierra Three appears to be on a parallel course. Her speed appears to be the same as well. I'm continuing to analyze."

"Very well, Sonar."

The OOD decided to come up to PD and have a look. It would appear they were alone.

"Sonar, Con. Tell me about Sierra Three."

"Con, Sonar. They're still there. Same course, same speed."

"Sonar, Con. Is it possible the target is in a convergence zone?"

"Con, Sonar. Negative. It's a good solid contact. I think this one's close, sir."

The OOD sighed. A few minutes later, another ST came up so Ned could take a quick break and take a leak. He sat down, and looked at the display. Well, *that's* not good!

"Con, Sonar. I'm picking up a harmonic. Definitely us. It sounds like it might be a ventilator or something."

"Very well, Sonar."

The OOD ordered the Auxiliary Electrician Forward to start looking for the culprit. Meanwhile, Ned came back to Sonar. His relief rushed back to his card game. The AEF found the noisy fan. He turned off the fan.

"Con, Sonar! Sierra Three just vanished!!"

"What?"

"Sierra Three is gone, sir. She just disappeared! Like poof, gone."

"Sonar, Con. Are you sure?"

"Con, Sonar. I'm absolutely positive, sir."

The AEF walked back into the Control Room.

"Found it, sir. It was the fan in Berthing."

The OOD was silent for a moment. No...it couldn't be. That's just stupid. There's no way. The little voice in his head just wouldn't shut up.

"How many blades on that fan?"

"Four, sir."

"Are you sure?"

"Yes, sir. They all have four. They're all the same type of fan."

"*MONTECELLOOOH!!!*"

And the rest is...well, you know.

By the way, Ned was later assigned to NUSC (Naval Undersea Systems Command). They don't assign idiots to NUSC.

ICC(SS) Steve Morrison:

Chief Morrison was one cool guy. The one thing I'll always remember Morrison for was his great talent as a singer/songwriter. He almost always brought his guitar with him on patrols. I remember one day, a small group of us was sitting in the Torpedo Room. Steve had his guitar. I mentioned to him that I loved writing songs. He decided to play and sing one he wrote for his ex-wife. It was a very well written piece about how sorry he was that things didn't work out, how it was mostly his fault, and so on. But here's the kicker. He sounded exactly like Gordon Lightfoot. I'm not saying he *could* sound like him. He naturally *did* sound like him.

It wasn't much of a surprise then, to find out he did some Lightfoot covers during his bar gigs. One went over particularly well. He always played "The Wreck of The Edmund Fitzgerald" during his sets. One night, he had a man come to him and hand him a fifty dollar bill. He didn't care if anyone else wanted to hear it again. The fifty was his if he played it again. I'm pretty sure he played it again.

Chapter 8-
You non-qual puke.

Either you're qualified...or you're not.

—Submariner's adage

Knowles Atomic Power Laboratory gave all of us a taste of what qualifying would be like when we got to the fleet. As we would all find out, that taste would be like judging a chili cook-off by chewing one uncooked bean from every pot. Yes, technically it did illustrate the basic process of qualification. Try holding a gun in your hand, and comparing it to actually being a crack shot. As we would find out, there were some major differences between quals at S1C, and quals on the boat.

First, at S1C all they wanted us to do was study and qualify. Our very existence was focused on that one single goal. There was nothing else on our plate, nothing else to distract us. After all, they didn't want anything distracting us from that crucial objective. Not so, on a submarine. On a submarine, one is expected to qualify. That's only the *beginning.* Not so fast! Where are you going with that manual? Back aft, buddy. There's work to do. We were expected to keep up on the schedule to qualify, and stand instructional watches, and perform maintenance, and clean. If S1C was like that, it would be like going to class at the site, going home and taking apart your lawn mower, cleaning your house, studying some more, getting a couple of hours of sleep, and going back the next day. That's okay. You'll get caught up on your days off. Wrong! No days off, at least not at sea. In port you could get time off if everything was fixed, and you were caught up on your quals.

Second, at S1C all one needed to do is qualify on the engineering portion of the site. Also, we weren't required to pass quals for Engine Room Supervisor. On the boat, we had to qualify for all of our watch stations, Engine Room Supervisor, and...*and*... ship's quals. All those shiny Submarine Warfare pins aren't just given away. You don't get them in boxes of Crackerjack. In other words, we needed to know everything about our own jobs, as well as have a working knowledge of everyone else's jobs. *That* is ship's quals. I still recall the first time I was given my qual card for the U.S.S. Skipjack. It was a freakin' phone book! This was going to be very, *very* different. No, Toto. We're not at S1C anymore.

This fact was driven home with crystal clarity one morning a few days after I reported aboard. I'd finally decided how I was going to tackle this monster. I would have to start by qualifying Engine Room Lower Level, just like at S1C. I picked out which system I would get a checkout on first. I located the Manual that included that system, poured myself a cup of coffee, sat down in the mess deck, and began to read. Maybe this wouldn't be so bad after all.

"Smith! What the fuck are you doing?"

Startled out of my studies, I spun around to see Chief Jardin, my division chief, staring down at me.

"Oh, hi Chief. I'm starting work on the Main Condensate System."

"So, while everybody else is back aft working, you're taking a break and reading?"

"Well...studying, really..."

His thumb jerked in the direction of the engineering spaces.

"Get back there."

No checkouts for me that day. As I recall, not the next day either. But, I did find the next couple of days very interesting. And frightening. And...very, *very* daunting.

We were given a thorough tour of the engineering spaces. Much of it was vaguely familiar. Back in Nuke School, a model was on display just down the hall from the central foyer. It represented a typical S5W submarine reactor plant. The hull was made of transparent plastic, so the viewer could see the intended shape of the hull, and the structure of the propulsion plant within. The hull's diameter was about two feet, probably making it about 1/15th scale. Every single component and pipe was represented in that model. I spent many breaks and lunch periods just standing at that model, trying to form a mental picture of how it all fit together.

All that information was long since buried when I learned the S1C plant. Now here I was, having to re-learn all this information again. I asked myself, why couldn't they just take an old S5W boat out of service and use it as a floating prototype? Little did I know, they would eventually do exactly that. It would be long after I could have benefitted, and it would be at a time when newer plants were comprising a bigger and bigger part of our fleet. Los Angeles class fast attack boats and Ohio class ballistic missile boats were quickly replacing the older hulls.

I quickly acclimated to my new environment. The days fell into a mostly predictable routine. Quarters in the morning. Then work or study until lunch. Then work or study until dinner. If it was a good day, I'd be off the boat before dinner. Good days were rare. It was a constant struggle to fit qual checkouts into the day when so much work was waiting to be done. It didn't help that M Div was understaffed.

The process of getting checkouts felt more and more like an old familiar routine. That was one aspect of submarine life that seemed to be a constant. That was virtually identical to that of S1C. Only the level of complexity had changed. Now there were many other systems to affect our operations. I quickly realized this was because our hull at S1C completely lacked a forward half, with all its systems that would interact with ours.

It was at this point that my social strategy paid off. The military in general, and submarines in particular, is full of rivalries. The Machinists Mates didn't mesh with the Electronics Technicians. We both flung grief at the Electricians Mates. The "Nukes" in the aft of the boat didn't get along with the "Coners" in the forward half. There was always some form of grief between the "Fuckin' Nukes" and the "Coner Motherfuckers". We had one saving grace. We all hated the Skimmers more than we hated each other. Perhaps hate is too strong a word. We didn't really hate each other. Maybe these phrases would clear it up:

"You nukes are our chauffeurs. That's your only purpose."

"Oh, yeah? Like taking hot showers? Watch your tone."

"If it wasn't for us cooks, all your asses would starve!"

"Right! Gotta have our fair share of *shit* to eat!"

But at the end of the day, the drinking parties still included everybody. I remained diplomatically neutral. They were all saints, or all demons, depending on who I was listening to at the time. The end result was that I got along with everybody, even if the assessment was that I was *okay* as far as nukes were concerned, or flange heads were concerned, or blue shirts were concerned.

This critical status became very important when it came to quals. Why? It often saved me from joining that dubious group of unfortunates:

THE DINKS!

It's spelled "d-i-n-k". But it's slang for "delinquent", as in "delinquent in qualifications". That means a non-qual is behind the curve for the length of time they've been on the boat. A new crew member has one year to become qualified in every category required. During that year, one is expected to have acquired a certain number of signatures at any given point. If someone does not have that number of sigs, they are delinquent. Or dink. They can be dink in a particular watch station, as in,

"I can't go out this weekend. I'm dink in Engine Room Upper Level."

or,

"Where are you going? You're not qualified Lookout, you dink puke!"

Almost everybody is dink at some point. Some people are never dink, although those are the people with no girlfriends, drinking buddies, or bad habits. In other words, they don't really count anyway. Then there are those who are excessively dink. The slang term is "dink life". That means if they *can* be dink in it, they *are* dink in it. Often one of us would say,

"Don't even ask me about parties this weekend. I'm dink life!"

Being a dink was a sorry fate. Liberty was suspended. Instead of going home, the dink would stay several more hours for study and checkouts. If they had the weekend off, it was spent on the boat. Incentive was strong to get off the dink list. That was where my friendly nature came in handy.

I can't possibly count the times I was looking at a ruined weekend. My depression had returned with a vengeance. As soon as I learned something, I'd forget it. Checkouts became quite a challenge. Often I would research a look-up, only to forget it before I made it back to give the answer. I had to learn and re-learn information several times before I could retain it. I was dink *a lot*. Just when it looked like things were hopeless, someone would come over to me and say,

"You dink? What do you need? Gimme your card. Now, you have to get this checkout first thing Monday! Have a good weekend."

It didn't matter if I was a nuke. It didn't matter if I was a flange head. It paid off to be good to everyone, no matter who they were. It all came back.

But, on the U.S.S. Skipjack, it wasn't good enough to not be dink. The ultimate status was being *qualified*. If one wasn't qualified, they were a non-qual. Non-quals were second class citizens. Non-quals weren't allowed to watch movies. Non-quals weren't allowed to read anything except training manuals.

Holidays were no exception. During one of the holiday seasons, we were headed out on a patrol. Another boat was supposed to go. They were reassigned at the last minute for a high profile mission, rare for a submarine. Reassignments, like poop, roll downhill. Now here we were steaming out to our dive point, preparing to spend Christmas away from family. Such was the fate of a service member. And, it was always last minute. Sailing dates for submarines are *always* classified, even for routine patrols.

Christmas Eve of 1985 was spent submerged off the coast of Maine as we headed up the Canadian coast for our destination. Spirits were low. Submarines had been tasked for missions like this for decades. We all knew that. The odds of getting plucked out of port like this were high. We knew that, as well. These things couldn't be predicted, even in the best of times. All those elements meant nothing as we watched all our carefully made plans go down the tubes. But, I was given a gift to lighten the mood. Christmas eve was a traditional time to receive gifts. That must have been why that time was chosen to deliver mine. My gift?

A letter of instruction from the Captain.

I had been dink too long. I had managed to attract the attention of the Captain. My "dinkness" had become unacceptable. Hand delivered to me was an official letter from the Captain detailing my dereliction of progress in qualifications. If I didn't improve my performance to meet the prescribed guidelines, I would be subject to disciplinary action. I was officially dink life and then some. I was depressed, away from home, on a mission of unknown consequence. My parents were traveling to see me, and I wouldn't even be there. I guess that wasn't bad enough. Merry Fucking Christmas.

Half a step up the ladder from being dink, was being a "non-qual". On the U.S.S. Skipjack, the only difference in treatment was that a non-qual wasn't required to stay after hours for dink study. All other restrictions remained the same. We had a small, but passable, paperback library in a metal rack in the mess deck. Non-quals couldn't touch them. No reading leisure materials until you're qualified. If you have time to read, it'd better be a procedure or manual. We had an old beat up VCR. The selection of movies constantly changed as requests and donations rotated through the boat. No movies for non-quals. One guy would actually look around the mess deck to see if any non-quals were with viewing range. If any were, they were quickly ordered out in no uncertain words. If you have time to watch a movie, you should be putting that time toward a system checkout.

Sleep quickly took lowest priority. On multiple occasions, I fell asleep with my head stuck in a manual. I recall one particular time when I was studying in the torpedo room. We were at sea, times were quiet, and I had some precious free time. I laid down (what on Earth was I thinking!) on the deck with a manual, and began to read. It was comfortable. It was quiet. I could concentrate. I read for a while, then noticed how good everything felt. It was like a warm feeling of well-being. I moved my head to make myself a little more comfortable. I heard the rustling of paper. I bolted awake. *That's* why everything felt so good! I was *sleeping*! I must have woken up with one of those cliché "Huh?" sounds, because the Torpedoman on watch turned and looked down at me.

"Good morning."

I looked around.

"How long was I out?"

"About an hour."

"An *hour*? Why didn't you wake me up?"

He stared at me for a moment, and then said,

"Would you *want* me to wake you up?"

He had a good point. I let the subject go, and went back to my reading.

There was one unproductive habit that stayed with me since S1C. I rethought and re-rethought everything. My depression has reached a new pinnacle. If I learned something, I soon forgot it. These two anchors insured my qualification process would be torturous. Just do the math. If it takes three times longer to retain what one has learned, and they rethink and over analyze everything before they act on it, they're going to be slower than everybody else. Unfortunately, I only had the same year as everybody else. This was going to be interesting

My six months at S1C only made things more complicated. If I couldn't remember something from the Skipjack, my brain filled it in with something from S1C. I recall one instance when that little glitch made for a very interesting conversation. I was going for my checkout in one of the crucial systems involving the reactor. I went to my fellow machinist, Harry. It wasn't common, but sometimes people were qualified to give checkouts in systems outside their work area. This was one of those times. As hard as I studied, I still found myself in a situation where the answer I needed was eluding me. I concentrated as hard as I could. Finally, an answer came. I finally remembered. I gave Harry my answer. He stood in silence for a few seconds. Then he said,

"You went to S1C, didn't you?"

I was a little taken back. I never told him that. How did he know? I told him he was correct, and asked him how he knew.

"Only someone from S1C could give an answer as *fucked up* as that one!"

He told me later that he too had qualified at S1C. That system at S1C was unlike anything developed for any other power plant.

My studies continued. So did my qualification process. Ever so slowly, my qual card filled up with signatures. It seemed to take forever, but I continued to compile and retain information. Finally, the great moment arrived. It was time for my Qualification Board. Hopefully, I would pass. Hopefully I would reach that goal sought by every man to be assigned to a submarine. I would be one of those envied men walking around with silver Dolphins on their chest. Also, I would have the designation of "(SS)" after my rank, telling the entire world I was qualified in submarines. I would no longer be a non-qual. I would be a full-fledged submariner. I would be an accepted member of the crew. It was time to earn my Dolphins.

I walked into the Wardroom. This was it. Waiting for me was the Engineer, Lieutenant Commander Riles, Chief Jardin, another Chief from "coner land", and a senior Petty Officer. For a few hours, they grilled me on everything from the reactor plant, to what the boat's emergency call sign was. I recited, demonstrated, drew, and reasoned my way through a maze of demands and questions. On the other side of the mine field...my Dolphins. Finally it was over. I was dismissed. I waited outside the Wardroom while they discussed my fate. Everyone who walked by the Wardroom door knew what was going on, and wished me luck.

After what seemed to be an eternity, the Petty Officer finally called me back in. I was asked to sit down. The first thing that entered my mind was that cliché preamble to any bad news,

"Are you sitting down?"

Finally they told me. My performance wasn't stellar by any sense. But...they were more than confident to declare me "Qualified in Submarines". We all stood, and they shook my hand and congratulated me. The wave of relief that swept over me would have taken out Disney World, Papa Gino's, and the little adult entertainment store on the corner across the street. I made it. I was qualified. No more non-qual. I was now one of them. It was now time for the fun to begin...*for them*!

I'm not sure if this tradition is exclusive to the submarine community, exclusive to the Department of the Navy, or just a military tradition in general. When someone gets their dolphins, they get them "tacked on". Here's how it works. A newly designated submariner is walking around after the ceremony. Someone who hasn't had the honor yet walks up, shakes their hand, congratulates them, and then punches the recipient in the chest in the area of the dolphins. Thus they "tack" them in place, ensuring they "stick". This usually involves a soft or subtle tap on the chest, or at the most, a quick charlie-horse type punch. One of the proudest moments of my life was when I stood before the Captain and crew, listening to Commander Mendes read the accompanying citation, and then pinning the silver Dolphins to my chest. I then saluted him. He returned the salute, and shook my hand. Then, with a huge grin on his face, he gave me a playful tap on the chest. *He* had to be the first.

That was the beginning of a very interesting day. All day, it seemed as if every time I turned a corner there was someone there waiting for the honor. Usually it was the light but firm tap along with the handshake. That wasn't always the case. There were some who seemed as if they really didn't trust the process. Among them were Steve Jones, and Bob Erie. Sadly, they both got me early in the day. Both viewed the tacking of Dolphins as being the same as defending one's daughter from a Hell's Angels gynecological exam.

Steve got me first. I was walking around a corner. He was coming the other way. Apparently he had *very* good reflexes. I didn't even realize he was there when he launched his shot. He was one of the boat's designated divers, so he was in excellent shape. Good aim, too! He got me square on the Dolphins. The sad part was, the cheap thing they used for the award was very flimsy. His shot flattened the device, and the thin brass backings for the pins. The end result was both pins were driven directly into my chest. I'm pretty sure that's the effect he was looking for.

Over the next several hours, those pins were relocated and reinserted many, many times. That softened me up nicely for Bob. People knew what happened when *he* tacked on a pair of Dolphins. A couple of guys would come up behind the poor soul to prop him up. Bob was as strong as he was hulking. He was officially told to "tone it down a bit" when they thought he had collapsed someone's lung. When he was through with me, the pins were actually stuck in my chest. I had to reach down and pull them back out.

The day continued from there. The assault on my poor, innocent Dolphins continued unabated. But, it was all worth it. I need to set the scene for this next event. The Navy has a tradition where the Commanding Officer of any vessel is formally announced when he arrives or departs any other vessel. Every time our Captain arrived, the topside watch would go to his 1MC microphone and say,

"Skipjack...arriving!

Any time he left, the watch would inform the boat and crew,

"Skipjack...departing!"

If the CO from the Tautog came to the boat, it was,

"Tautog...arriving!"

You get the picture. After a while it just blends in with the background unless it's someone really different or high ranking. At the end of that day, I tied up my loose ends, shook a few more hands, gathered my stuff, and prepared to leave the boat to go on leave. I was walking down the pier when I looked up and saw the Captain coming the other way. At the prerequisite distance I saluted.

"Good afternoon, sir."

He returned my salute. But instead of giving the usual response of "good afternoon", he smiled broadly and said,

"MM3(SS) Smith...departing!"

I had arrived! I was finally a recognized member of the crew in full standing. I was officially a member of the group. I was officially one of *them*. As I dropped my salute, I gave him a hearty,

"Yes...*sir*!"

The next day, I departed for Florida to see my parents. The battered area of my chest was already starting to bruise that night. By the time I got on the plane, my chest looked like a raw steak. Countless small scabs covered the spots where the pins had been driven into my chest over and over. It was all worth it. The entire area was nicely counter shaded in a deep purple and blue. I'll always remember my Mom's response when I got home and took off my shirt to change into lighter clothes. My Dad shouted a question to me back in the spare bedroom. I was shirtless when I walked out to answer him. My Dad's eyes widened, by my Mom's reaction was priceless,

"Oh, my God!! What...*happened*?"

I told them that was part of my good news, and described the events of the previous day. My Mom listened with growing horror, and my Dad with swelling pride. His son had gone to the "dark side". Just like him.

As my time in Florida passed, the bruised area slowly shrank. It also turned a strange array of hues that I didn't even know could appear naturally on human skin. Yellows, oranges and greens all made their appearance. My Mom would check the progress each day, each time threatening to take me to the hospital at nearby Patrick Air Force Base. I didn't care. I knew I would be returning to an entirely different world, as an entirely different person.

Qualified in Submarines.

Chapter 9-
Puss rockets and sail rabbit.

An army marches not on its legs, but on its stomach.

- *Napoleon*

In the United States Navy, submarine duty has always been an all-volunteer service. Even during wartime, when life expectancy was short, each and every man to set foot on a sub was a volunteer. Not one, not even one, was forced into submarine duty, from the Captain to the cook. Not all navies can make that statement. As of last inquiry, the Royal Navy can assign personnel to submarine duty, whether they like it or not, if it suits the needs of the Ministry of Defense. Granted, the overwhelming majority of personnel *are* volunteers. And, those assigned to it usually *chose* to stay when their opportunity to move on arrived. But, there's just something about a submarine force made up entirely of people who made the active choice to be there.

Now having said that, not everyone is crazy enough to go into that sort of duty simply because it was a childhood dream. Every single nation to field submarines has "sweetened the pot", so to say, to entice more to join. This enticement usually takes the form of higher pay, better living accommodations, more R&R, promoted reputations of mystique, elite status, and the allure of women who enjoy a "dangerous man".

But, there's one way to make this duty appealing that is essentially a no-brainer. It's logistically easy. It's relatively inexpensive compared to other options. And, it's the second quickest way to a man's heart...

Better food.

The submarine services of the world's navies have always gotten the best food. In the Soviet/Russian Navy, submariners are supplied with caviar. Not just the commissioned officers, but the entire crew. In navies allowing alcohol at sea, the submariners get better rations of rum, beer, wine, and vodka. The U.S. Navy's endeavors in the food category are a prime example of how this lure is shined up, sprayed with fish oil, and dropped into the drink.

American sub sailors do indeed get the best food. Notice I specifically said "food". I didn't say we always got the best cooks. We can lament that fact at a later point. But, the food! I will always remember the food (and most of the cooks) very fondly. Let us reflect on the food:

Steak: yes, I said steak. Real steak. Not steakums, soy, or snouts. This was the real deal. And, they were usually cooked as close to order as possible.

Shrimp: nice and big, usually served fried. In large bowls that seemed bottomless.

Sea Scallops: these things were huge. They weren't always the most tender, but they were always very tasty. They were usually broiled in butter, and served in the same large bowls.

French Fries: these were always good. Usually nice and crunchy, they were always a nice side to whatever else was on the menu.

Hot Italian Sausage: these things were absolutely incredible. I know that government food is always bought from the lowest bidder. That didn't matter. These things were wonderful, packed with spices and fennel seeds.

Lobster: no, it's not a myth. I saw lobster served at least twice on our boat. Notice I said "saw". I never managed to get any. There was always some strange circumstance that precluded me from having any lobster. That was a bit of a put-off. I always wanted to have some just so I could say I had it. The only consolation was that it was frozen rock lobster. It was always served with all the proper fixings, but it wasn't real Maine lobster.

Pastries: always excellent! We often had one cook designated as a dedicated baker. One of these guys was gifted. He would turn out homemade jelly rolls and donuts that would rival any professional bakery.

There were some items that were good, but not great:

Turkey: this was usually canned turkey loaf. When served with gravy this was pretty good. Not like homemade, it was closer to what you'd get at a Howard Johnson's.

Cornbread Stuffing: this was a little dry. It almost always needed something to moisten it up. But, it was a good recipe. Sadly, any good recipe can be ruined by modifying it for military use.

Bread: at sea, we always made our own bread. This was one of the few things that were hit or miss. It was either properly baked, or half baked. If it was half baked, we would put it in the toaster to finish it up. If we wanted toast, we would run it through twice. It usually it worked out pretty well.

Rabbit: we ate *a lot* of rabbit! It was served a number of ways. It was always a little dry, probably because it was frozen. God only knows how *long* it was frozen. The first several times I had it, I thought it was chicken. Finally, one day I remarked,

"Man, this is the strangest chicken I ever saw."

A couple of the guys looked at me.

"That's because it's not chicken"

"What the hell is it? It tastes like chicken."

"Hold it up on its side and imagine it hopping across your plate...what do you see?"

It took a few seconds, but I finally got it.

"It's a rabbit! It's a fucking *rabbit*!"

"Very good."

I reflected that it would have been easier if he had told me to imagine it hopping along with a basket.

Breaded Veal Patties: let's face it. You can only do so much with a deep frozen breaded veal patty. It was passable. It depended mostly on what sauce was served with it.

Omelets: these were essentially a culinary miracle. Our supply of fresh eggs always ran out after about a week and a half. From there on, it was powdered eggs. Our cooks discovered that one could pour out a puddle of powdered egg, and let it partially cook. Then they would pour in the filling. They would take a large spatula, and fold one half of the thin layer of egg over onto the other. Let it sit for a few more seconds, then onto the plate. This was a prime example of making a silk purse out of a sow's ear.

Now let's talk about the things that were plain old bad. Even submarines had bad food once in a while. I looked it up. It's actually a very important military tradition. Here are the worst offenders. In the interest of the good cooks that always tried their best, I want to state that these bad items weren't always that bad:

Pizza: we always had pizza for mid-rats on Saturday night. It was one of those things we looked forward to during the endless cycle of days upon days at sea. Sadly, it was usually just plain old bad. The dough was undercooked, or burned. The sauce was bland. The toppings were either freeze dried, or over processed to the point of being unidentifiable. But, it was pizza. Even bad pizza reminded us of home.

French Toast: this was actually a piece of bread with scrambled eggs pressed into it. This was one of the foods that convinced me that some kind of curse existed in the galley. The food gods were just in a nasty mood on some days.

Bacon: how the fuck do you screw up *bacon*? The Navy found a way. I really think this is actually a social experiment of some sort. I think it would actually take a great deal of concentration to make this happen. Here is the way they served bacon...burned into charcoal at one end, and *raw* at the other end. Both ends were inedible, with nothing useful in the middle. If Gordon Ramsey was presented with this bacon in Hell's Kitchen, he would've simply had a stroke on the spot, and received his change of orders to the real Hell's Kitchen

Cottage Cheese: this was useless. It was freeze dried, and had to be reconstituted. It was like chewing kitty litter.

Jalapeño Cornbread: *WHAT?* Well, it might have worked out if the cook had drained the peppers first.

Then there were the errors resulting from sheer stupidity or laziness. Several times we were served pancakes or French toast with corn syrup instead of maple syrup. One of our mess attendants almost got lynched over that one. One of the cooks rolled out of his rack to the sounds of a riot, and dug through the dry bilge and presented a can of maple syrup. Shortening was once presented in place of butter.

Sometimes the culinary failure had nothing to do with the cooks, nothing to do with the food, and everything to do with plain simple bad luck. The shad would run up the Thames River every year. The river would just be packed with shad journeying upstream to spawn. Not quite as spectacular as salmon, but still a wonder of nature. As anyone would know, not all these fish made it. Many died along the way, and the river was littered by dead and dying fish. All around the boat were fish floating, or trying to swim upside down or in circles, as they lived out their last moments of life.

It never failed! What would they serve for dinner after watching a day of this carnage?

FILLET OF PERCH!

I'm sorry, but that was just so wrong on so many levels. Every one of us had a mental image of one of the cooks coming topside. He looks around. He can't believe his eyes! Holy smoke!! He's got to get the other cooks up here. Don't forget the nets! I don't care how well that fillet is prepared. It's not perch any more. It's shad, fresh from the river.

The one meal that held no pattern, no expectations of any kind was mid-rats. Mid-rats is the midnight meal, served to those coming off the mid-watch. It could be anything. It could be soup, cold cuts, pizza, canned ravioli, anything. It was literally the luck of the draw, based on what struck the cooks' fancy, or what was closest to the front of the fridge.

Some of my most distinct memories of submarine life revolve around food. Here is a selection:

1) Okay, let's face it. I'm "different". There are many reasons for that. The biggest reason is family influence. My Mom's side of the family is from England and Northern Ireland. Northern Ireland is under the realm of The Crown. So, needless to say, I had a very strong British influence in my family. One of the big treats in my family was a French fry sandwich. It's called a "chip sandwich" over in any place with a U.K. influence. It is virtually unknown outside of that community. I literally grew up with them.

This one day, we were out on patrol. Things were following the usual routine. I had gotten off watch, and came forward to the mess deck for lunch. I don't recall what the main dish was, but the side was French fries. We had bread that came out quite good, and butter that hadn't yet spoiled. And French fries! What more could a displaced Brit ask for? I soon set about the critical business of constructing a French fry sandwich.

I gathered a goodly amount of fries. Two good slices of "boat-made" bread. Where's the butter? There it is. I put the bread on my plate. I carefully spread the butter. Any Irishman will tell you, *every* part of the bread *must* have butter! Then the most important part...placing the fries. I carefully placed the fries on the bread. It's a lot like making a brick wall. Everything needs to fit together, and every space must be filled. With great concentration I worked.

Something odd was going on in the back of my mind. As I worked, it became more and more pronounced. I wasn't sure what it was. It wasn't important. There were French fry sandwiches to make, don't you know! I continued my work, watching this beautiful creation take shape. I was close to the end, when the strange change in the atmosphere became too strong to ignore. I stopped. I listened. I realized what the change was. As I worked, the conversation in the mess deck slowly died away. The room was now completely silent. The hum of the blowers and the vibration of the straining shaft were the only sounds. A few faint words of conversation drifted down from the Control Room. I slowly looked around.

Every man in that room was staring intently at me. That's why they weren't talking. Each one of them was staring at me in mute, astonished amazement. I looked around at the room full of staring faces. Some actually looked a little concerned. They had seen people go nuts before. It was never like this! I was getting a little defensive.

"What!"

One of them tentatively asked me,

"Smitty...what are you doing?"

"I'm making a French fry sandwich. Why?"

Now, one would think clarification would be like a soothing balm at this point. It's okay. Smitty's not going mad. He's just making a French fry sandwich. A *what*?

"What the fuck is a French fry sandwich?"

I explained the family tradition. Surely *that* would clear everything up. It's like people in the northern central states eating a bull's...you know...junk! A French fry sandwich would surely pale in significance to that! Well, I was wrong. It had absolutely no soothing influence on the alarmed group of men that surrounded me.

A restrained buzz of conversation erupted in the mess deck. It reminded me of the unsettled buzz that preceded the burning of a witch in all those old black and white movies.

"What's wrong with you guys? You've never heard of a French fry sandwich?"

That didn't help one little bit! I might as well have asked them if they had never seen someone conjuring up demons before. Wow! This was a really protected, isolated lot! I went into damage control mode,

"Try it! They're good!"

Apparently this satisfied the angry mob with flaming torches.

2) Once while we were out on patrol, one of the senior cooks made some very nice blueberry cheese cake. Our supply officer was standing Diving Officer of the Watch,

and had been relieved late. Oops!! No more cheese cake. It was quickly devoured by enthusiastic officers and enlisted men. Mr. Wallis came down to have dinner, and heard about the cheese cake. He was delighted! He *loved* blueberry cheese cake! Then he was given the terrible news. He flipped out. He ranted. He raved. He blustered. Someone had better produce a piece of blueberry cheese cake, rectus extractus, in a hurry! This slight was not going to be tolerated! He was their boss, and they couldn't save him a piece of fucking *cheese cake*? The cook knew dire measures were called for. Technically, there *was* cheese cake. Lots of it! But, it was now in a form Mr. Wallis would probably find very unpalatable. What to do?

The cook finally found a solution. It was a long shot. He took a one pound block of butter. He spread a liberal layer of leftover blueberry sauce over it. With his heart in his mouth, he put it on the table before the furious Mr. Wallis. A palpable silence hung over the wardroom. Larry Coikos, the senior cook, wasn't going to stick around any longer. He bolted for the door. Just as he touched the door knob, he heard Mr. Wallis' voice,

"Petty Officer Coikos!"

He froze at the door. A ball of icy lead formed in his stomach. He was busted, in more ways than one.

"Yes...uh...sir?"

"That is the..."

Coikos' heart sank. It could have worked. It was all he could do! He had no other choice!

"...best..."

What? It worked? It worked! Now if everyone could just keep their mouths shut!!

"...cheese cake I've ever had. Keep up the good work."

Disaster was averted.

3) Back in 1986, we on operations in Narragansett Bay. No one could tell me why this had to happen, but we had to surface. We *had* to. We couldn't just come to periscope depth. We couldn't put up a radio mast. We *had* to surface. This event was rare enough at it is. But, this was worse. Why? Hurricane Gloria was raging at full strength at the time. The worst part of the storm was right over the NBOA. Can it get worse? Sure. It had to happen at lunch time. Can it get worse? Of course! They had to serve lunch! Really?

I had just rolled out of the rack. I was going on watch, and amazingly enough, was hungry. I went up to the mess deck, expecting to be disappointed. Of course they wouldn't be serving lunch under these conditions. Maybe I could grab a snack before I went aft. I got to the mess deck. They were serving lunch!! No one was eating, but they were serving lunch. I was delighted! The cooks saw my face light up. They both had a look on their faces that said, *really*!

I sat down. That's actually a mis-statement. I sat on the opposite bench, and braced myself against the table behind me. I held myself with my knees by wedging them up against the table before me. I put my silverware in my shirt pocket. Between forty five degree rolls, the mess attendant ran into the galley, grabbed me a plate of food, and ran it out to me. I held the plate in one hand, matching the rolling motion of the boat to keep the food from falling off. At the end of each roll, I would grab a bite of food. I needed something to drink. Milk had long since run out. Cold drinks were limited to varying flavors of bug juice. Again between rolls, he ran in, poured a cup of bug juice, and ran out to hand it to me. With my silverware in my pocket, I grabbed the cup. At the right moment, I guzzled it down. He leaned out the galley door, and I threw the cup back to him and thanked him. He held up the cup to ask if I wanted more.

"What? I'm not going to make you do that again!"

I was one of six people on the entire boat to eat lunch.

4) This tale involves what would have to be one of the most bizarre events I can recall. It was midweek. We were tied up in port, and shut down. My section had the duty. It was one of those days that was so full and hectic, no one had a chance to sleep. If that chance ever came, we were too spun up to relax enough to sleep, anyway. So, we eventually ended up sitting around in the mess deck around 0200. We knew the cooks had put out an impromptu mid-rats spread. Why not check it out?

The men began to drift forward as they finished up whatever task was at hand. Soon a very distinct odor began to drift through the boat. It wasn't a good odor. The first thought I had was that someone was blowing the Sanitary Tanks. That process produced a similar odor. But, there was something a little different this time. I shrugged to myself. I'd find out in due time. I started forward myself. I noticed with some uneasiness that the odor became stronger as I got closer to the mess deck. By the time I slid down the ladder rails from Ops Upper Level to Ops Middle Level, I realized the smell was coming straight from the mess deck. This was *not* a good sign!

I walked in, and discovered the source of the nauseating odor. There on one of the mess tables, was a large stainless steel bin often used for cooking soups and sauces. In it was a substance I could only describe as looking like a mixture of sewage and vomit. A thick layer of clear grease covered the surface. There was a large ladle stuck in this diabolical stew. I was struck by an odd compulsion. I reached for the ladle,

"SMITTY! NO!!"

The man sitting closest to me tried to stop me. It was too late. I stirred the stuff. The layer of grease parted, and released a fresh poof of this horrible odor into the room. Now I realized what happened earlier. The smell began when the first person made the mistake of moving that ladle. Now the room stunk all over again. The guys looked at me with an expression of sheer hatred. I could feel my face flushing hotly.

"Guys, I'm sorry! I'm so *sorry*..."

They couldn't stay mad for long. After all, a few of them had made the same mistake. I asked myself why someone hadn't just taken the ladle out. That way no one could stir it at all. I quickly answered my own question. Would I want to smell that again? Then the ladle would be waving around in the air. And, where would we put it?

I gave the pot a wide berth, went to the cold cuts, and made a sandwich. When the odor subsided a little more, I'd be able to eat it. Finally things were back to normal. We sat there eating. We heard footsteps as the last man, an electrician, came down the ladder. His face screwed up the way I'm sure mine had a few minutes before. We all pointed to the pot. His hand began to move toward the ladle.

He never had a chance!

5) I was known on the boat for my ability to eat. The quantities of food that disappeared from my plate were the stuff of legend. One of the newer crew members, a young addition to Seaman Gang fresh from Sub School, gave me a nickname that said it all...Munchie. It was a regular occasion for Seaman Gaines to see me first thing in the morning, and say,

"Hey, Munchie! How's it going"

But this one incident really brought the point home for everyone. We were having lunch. The main course was the sea scallops described earlier. The first fresh bowl came out to the table. One of the guys got it first, and scooped a few onto his plate. I reached out and took it next. Proclaiming my love for them, I proceeded to empty almost all the remaining scallops onto my plate.

"Hey, Smitty...leaving any of those for us?"

I looked down. My plate was full! I felt terrible. I mumbled an apology, and started to wrangle the scallops back into the bowl.

"Whoa, whoa, whoa!!! We don't want them *now*. They've already touched your plate!"

I stammered a muted protest. Nothing doing. I had taken them. I couldn't give them back. My actions could not be undone, and I would simply have to live with myself and the terrible slight I had delivered to my friends. The table was permeated with a dark cloud of mock disgust. When the next bowl arrived, one of the guys leapt into action,

"Keep the bowl away from *him*! In fact, Glen, just hand me your plate and tell me how many you want. Smitty's not getting his hands on any more scallops!"

The bowl wouldn't even be sent to the person sitting across from me! Apparently, my poor fellow diners had been scarred for life. It took a little while before they would trust me alone with a bowl again.

6) This story involves more of a principle than an actual event. There is one very sad fact about food on a submarine. It is plainly expressed by these three statements:

a) The morale of the crew hinges on the quality of the food.

b) The quality of the food hinges on the morale of the cooks.

c) The morale of the cooks hinges on absolutely nothing at all.

The most thankless job on a submarine is that of the cooks. If the food is bad, they hear about it. If it's good, the guys just bitch less. The cooks never hear positive feedback, not to mention a compliment. There was one saying that was heard during meals. It got a laugh, but it was discouraging none the less.

"Aaah...just like Mom used to make. Gee, how Dad used to beat Mom so after dinner time."

Fitting in with my strategy of being nice to everyone, because they might be nice to me later, I decided to take a different tack.

I was walking out of the mess deck one day. I stopped at the open doorway of the galley,

"That was good, guys. Thank you."

All the cooks in that tiny galley spun around and looked at me as if I was stark raving mad. One of them looked like he was about to poke a bear,

"Really?"

"Yeah, I mean...it wasn't perfect. But, I thought it was good. I liked it."

Another cook asked a question he most certainly was not accustomed to asking,

"What would have made it better?"

"It could have done with a little less salt. Try not so much salt next time."

They nodded their approval. I went aft to take the watch. I had no idea what impact that had. I just figured if someone hears about all the bad, they deserve to hear about the good, as well. After that, every once in a while the cooks would stop me on my way out. They wanted to know what I thought of the meal. If it needed something, I'd tell them. If it didn't, I'd tell them it was perfect. If I knew something was beyond repair, like the French toast, I'd simply ask a question,

"Why do the eggs end up like that? Do they have to be that way?"

Everyone else just told them the French toast sucked.

But, one incident really drove home what had actually happened. We were in port. It was a typical work day. I had gotten relieved late from the SRW watch. Everyone else was walking out. Lunch that day was steak and sautéed mushrooms. I was walking past the galley to sit down. The head cook had set aside a nice steak for me. He took some mushrooms, and sautéed them on the spot where all the steaks had been cooking. Before I even had a chance to say anything, he walked over and plunked that plate down before me. I didn't know what to say. It was such a kind gesture.

The last story doesn't even include food. It does, however, include drinking. No, it's not a drinking story. Well, technically it is a "drinking" story. I should just cut through the confusion, and just tell the story.

Engine Room Lower Level is known as "The Hole". It's an undesirable place to work. It's hot. It's noisy. It's where the junior Machinists start out. One reason is that it's the simplest watch station for Machinists. The other is that senior watch standers don't like it, so they're not going to do it. But, there is one thing making The Hole not so bad. One of the air conditioning vents is situated so that it's perfect for holding a polyethylene bottle, or "poly" bottle of water. That water gets nice and cold after sitting there for a while. After a couple of hours laboring in the heat and noise, nothing beats a drink of ice cold water. It was a common event for the ERLL watch to call the ERUL watch to the ladder, and toss him up an empty poly bottle. The ERUL watch would fill it from the drinking fountain, go back to the ladder, and drop it down to the expectant ERLL watch. He would then pop it into the AC vent at the bottom of the ladder.

One day I was on watch in The Hole. On my way down the ladder, I peeked in that AC vent. The poly bottle was there. I reached in and grabbed it. It was full. It was cold. Perfect! I situated myself, filled out the initial conditions at the top of my log sheet, and went about doing my job. Things started out bad. I found myself working harder than I expected, sooner than I expected. I sat there huffing, puffing, and streaming with sweat. It was time to get that bottle. I drank almost the entire bottle, which would hold a bit over a pint. I decided to have it refilled later.

I continued on with my watch. About an hour later, one of the ELTs came down the ladder. He looked around with a confused look on his face. Finally, he walked over to me.

"Hey, Smitty…have you seen my sample?"

"Where did you last leave it?"

"I forgot some stuff down here, so I went back for it. I was at the top of the ladder, so I think I stuck it in the AC vent. But, it's not there anymore. Did you see it?"

I quickly put two and two together, and it equaled barf. I knew it was too good to be true! A full bottle of cold water just waiting for me? I should have known! He had stuck his sample bottle, *also a poly bottle*, in the vent while he went back for his stuff. He then went right past it, out of sight and out of mind, back to the lab. When the time came to run the tests, he remembered where he had put it.

"I know exactly where your sample is."

He breathed a sigh of relief.

"Where is it?"

"It's in my stomach!"

He looked at me with an expression of shock and disbelief. He shook his head. I nodded mine. He visibly deflated as he too realized what had happened.

"You drank my sample…you drank my Secondary Coolant sample."

I reached into the vent and handed him the poly bottle. He hefted it in his hand, feeling how light it was.

"You drank my *entire* Secondary Coolant sample!"

"Not quite all of it. There's a little left in there, as you'll notice. But you'll need to take another one.

The ELT turned and flew up the ladder! I heard hectic, jumbled conversation, then loud raucous laughter and shouting. Chief Jardin walked to the ladder and looked down at me. He just sadly shook his head. The ELT returned with a fresh bottle, took another coolant sample, gave me a sheepish smile, and left.

At the end of my watch, Chief Jardin was waiting for me at the top of the ladder. He gave me the bad news. In all the time he had been in submarine duty, he'd never seen or heard of someone drinking Secondary Coolant, never mind an *entire bottle*. I started to explain that there was, in fact, a little left in the bottom. My feeble attempts of salvaging any dignity from this event were swept aside. The result? Consuming that much Secondary Coolant would most surely be fatal.

He was lying. It only gave me the shits for about a day and a half. Oh, and most importantly, I did not need two friends and a Ouija Board to write this book.

One of the interesting aspects of military life is the names we give to things. This is something that will never change. For example:

1) In Viet Nam, one of the rations eaten in the field was a can of beans and chopped up hotdog. Did they call them beans and hotdog? Of course not! Why would you want to say that when you can say "beans and motherfuckers"?

2) At KAPL, and on the boat, we wore radiation monitors called Thermoluminescent Dosimeters. This was shortened to TLD. They were small, black and cylindrical plastic devices worn on our belts. Would the Engineering Lab Technician ask you for your Thermoluminescent Dosimeter? No. Would he ask you for your TLD? Nope. He would come up to you and say,

"I need your Tiny Little Dick."

3) We used a waterless hand cleaner back in the engineering spaces. We were always dirty, so these tubes were lying all over the place. I don't recall what this substance was called. It wouldn't have made a difference. No one would have called it by its real name, anyway. Every single one of us called it "monkey cum".

It isn't hard to deduce that this lovable habit would extend to food, as well. For the reader's entertainment (and the faint possibility they could suddenly find themselves on a submarine, at meal time), I have included a glossary of terms used to describe varying articles of food.

<u>Pig Particles</u> or <u>Plastic Pig</u>: artificial bacon bits.

<u>Powdered Cow</u>: dried artificial coffee creamer.

Bug Juice: the military version of Kool-Aid. It was very acidic, and often used in a concentrated form to clean oil and grease off of metallic surfaces. It was virtually useless as a beverage.

Fat Pills: the base bakery's donuts that were delivered to each boat early in the morning.

Sail Rabbit: those deep frozen breaded veal patties. To this day I refer to a veal parm grinder as a "sail rabbit grinder".

Pieces-Parts: the canned turkey loaf used for traditional holiday dinners along with mashed potatoes, cornbread stuffing, gravy, etc.

Puss Rockets: the inglorious name given to those wonderful spicy Italian sausages. They only had one flaw: they were high in grease content. That grease would liquefy and become scalding hot when the sausage was cooked. When sticking a fork into one, the diner would invariably get hit by a spurt of searing hot grease.

Plastic Eggs: the modern day name for powdered eggs.

Horse Cock: cold cuts in general, and bologna in particular.

Dog: one of the prized pieces of equipment on any Navy vessel, regardless of type, is the ice cream machine. Grown men are like little boys when it comes to ice cream. The worst day can be turned around with a little bit of ice cream. Sadly, like any other piece of government issue equipment, the ice cream machine doesn't always live up to its title. Now, we're talking about soft ice cream a la Mr. Softee. Not hard ice cream one would find in an ice cream parlor. Our machine produced "ice cream". It was cold, semi-frozen, and sweet. The flavor was always chocolate. But, it never really got to that point of texture like civilian soft ice cream. It was always a little soft and runny. Its similarity to a runny dog turd was immediately recognized. Our soft ice cream would forever on be known simply as "Dog". It was still just as popular. It still possessed those magical qualities. We all squealed with equal delight when seeing it. Everything was just like usual:

Nothing could make a bad day good, or a good meal better, than a nice bowl of Dog.

Gedunk: this is a very versatile term that is used to label any sweet or pastry. It is also the slang term for the dessert course of a meal. It is also the slang term for a place where these items could be purchased and eaten; like a snack bar. Let's push the envelope and use this term in *multiple* conversations.

Sailor 1: Hey, Joe. What's for gedunk today?

Sailor 2: Dog.

or,

Sailor 1: Why so angry, Harry?

Sailor 2: My wife spent my entire paycheck on gedunk again! And the gas bill is overdue!

or,

Sailor 1: Freddy! Where you going?

Sailor 2: I'm going to the gedunk. I'm hungry.

I hope the reader found this little diversion useful and entertaining. It certainly brought back a lot of memories as

I wrote it. I'm actually surprised I could recall all this. I still use these terms today, although finding the proper context can be challenging. Master that daunting task. You can amaze your friends and family, and be the life of the party.

Chapter 10-
Mother may I...

The single biggest problem in communication is the illusion that it has taken place.

-George Bernard Shaw

Talking is so easy. Granted, it takes a few years to really get it right. But after that it gets pretty simple. Just open your mouth, and words come out. They may not come out exactly as you intended. They may not be tactfully timed. They may not even be directed at the correct person. But the act of talking, in and of itself, is pretty easy.

Not so easy on a submarine. Oh, no. It's totally different there. A submarine is an extreme environment. I'm not talking about extreme in the same way a sports drink is extreme. Not the way jumping the Grand Canyon on a rocket powered skateboard is extreme. It's more like the "if-anyone-makes-a-serious-mistake-we'll-all-die" type of extreme. On a submarine, everyone is constantly that one mistake away from being dead.

That is why talking on a submarine is so carefully controlled. I say one thing. You think I said something else. You do something other than what I intended. And, there we are. All dead. To keep people from getting dead in large numbers, and more importantly, keep billion dollar submarines from sinking to the ocean floor, very specific rules are followed regarding talking.

We've all seen it. We're watching a World War Two submarine movie. All sorts of exciting things are happening. People are racing all over the place and...and...saying the same things over and over again. Is it bad acting? Is it bad script writing? No. What you are seeing is absolutely correct. And that, is what brings us to speaking rule number one:

THE VERBATIM REPEATBACK.

It's actually a pretty simple concept. If someone tells you something; something to do, something to say, something to tell others to do, you repeat it back word for word to show you've heard and understood it.

For submariners, it's second nature. We don't even realize we're doing it. For outsiders, it is absolutely *bizarre*. I've taken the liberty of constructing a little scene to show exactly what verbatim repeat back is, and how it works. It involves a simple and routine task: the switching out of a feed pump.

Cast of characters:

The Engineering Officer of the Watch, or EOOW (pronounced Ee-yow)

The Throttleman of the Watch

The Machinery Space Lower Level Watch (MSLL)

Scene: Maneuvering Room -

Camera is rolling...Action!!

EOOW: Throttleman, to Machinery Space Lower Level. Start number three Main Feed Pump, secure number two Main Feed Pump.

Throttleman: To Machinery Space Lower Level, start number three Main Feed Pump, secure number two Main Feed Pump. Throttleman, aye.

The Throttleman reaches down and picks up the sound powered phone next to him, turns the dial to MSLL, and turns the crank on the side half a turn very quickly.

Scene: Machinery Space Lower Level -

WOOP! The Machinery Space Lower Level Watch hears his sound powered phone "ring". He walks over and answers it.

MSLL: Machinery Space Lower Level.

Throttleman: Machinery Space Lower Level, Maneuvering. Start number three Main Feed Pump, secure number two Main Feed Pump.

MSLL: Start number three Main Feed Pump, secure number two Main Feed Pump. Machinery Space Lower Level, aye.

The MSLL watch walks over to the Feed Station panel. He turns the switch for 3MFP to "run". He checks the discharge pressure. It looks good. He turns the switch for 2MFP to "off". Then he picks up the sound powered phone at the panel, turns the dial to MAN, and turns the crank on the side half a turn very quickly.

Scene: Maneuvering Room -

WOOP! The Throttleman hears his sound powered phone "ring". He reaches down and answers it.

Throttleman: Maneuvering.

MSLL: Maneuvering, Machinery Space Lower Level. Number three Main Feed Pump is running, number two Main Feed Pump is secured.

Throttleman: Number three Main Feed Pump is running, number two Main Feed Pump is secured. Maneuvering, aye.

The Throttleman hangs up his phone, and turns to the EOOW.

Throttleman: Sir, from Machinery Space Lower Level. Number three Main Feed Pump is running, number two Main Feed Pump is secured.

EOOW: Very well, Throttleman.

All that, just to start one pump and turn off another right next to it. All orders are handled in that fashion. It's deadly serious. Those who fail to carry out the repeat back are chastised. So...the act is carried out regardless of what is said...

Morning broke in typical fashion aboard U.S.S. Skipjack. Those in the duty section actually able to sleep awoke to the revile announcement. Final touches were applied to overnight watch logs. Breakfast was cooked and served. Sailors straggled in for morning quarters and duty section relief. The Duty Officer turned over the boat to his successor. In this instance, the new Duty Officer was Lt. Cahill. He took the Duty Keys from the departing DO, turned to the nearest Petty Officer and said,

"Petty Officer Jones, pass the word over the 1MC... I am the Duty Officer."

Steve Jones had a particularly strong, deep, voice. It was quite impressive to hear his voice booming from every 1MC speaker on the boat,

"I AM THE DUTY OFFICER!"

I was back in Engine Room Upper Level at the time. Eyes widened. That was *unusual*. Then the laughter echoed through the boat, from end to end. I immediately dropped to my knees and bowed deeply, chanting,

"Oh, Duty Officer! Oh, Duty Officer! Oh, Duty Officer!"

Soon the others followed my lead and fell into sequence.

"Oh, Duty Officer! Oh, Duty Officer! Oh, Duty Officer!"

The laughter finally died away, and a sheepish Lt. Cahill was heard over the 1MC,

"Uh...Lt. Cahill is the Duty Officer."

But, Steve did exactly what he was told! Mr. Cahill had no one to blame but himself.

Now let's talk about speaking rule number two:

NUMBERS.

Numbers are funny things. They could quite possibly be the single *biggest* source of misunderstandings known to mankind. Just to review, misunderstandings can be catastrophic on a submarine. The biggest issue with numbers is that so damn many of them sound alike.

Anything ending in a "teen" or "ty" is essentially an accident waiting to happen. The difference between fif-"ty" and fif-"teen" can be fatal, depending on the context and circumstances. So...how do we avoid constant accidents, injuries, fatalities, and even worse...embarrassment? It's very easy.

Don't say fifty. Say five-zero. Don't say fifteen. Say one-five. Problem solved. It doesn't matter how much noise there is, or how bad the confusion, it's perfectly clear. Throw in the constant use of the phonetic alphabet, and we've got everything pretty much covered.

So, we've covered the fanatical lengths to which submariners will go, to ensure clear and fully understood communications. Does anything ever go wrong? Oh, of course. Gratefully, it's usually due to stupidity and/or frivolity. And so it was this time...

We were in port. Tied up. Shut down. Quiet. It was one of those nights that just seemed to go on forever-r-r-r. I was standing Shutdown Roving Watch. A friend of mine was standing Shutdown Reactor Watch. On a quiet night, the midnight watch was the worst, like a coma one is forced to stay awake through. We needed something to break the monotony. Replacing our Navy issue coffee with fine Columbian Supremo only went so far. It tasted much better. It had more caffeine. It gave me a chuckle to hear my watch mate announce over the 7MC system,

"Coffee pot low level alarm!"

But, we still needed something else. Something better. Something new and different. It was then that my talent for doing animal calls came in handy. One night I was making my hourly rounds to take the logs. I took my usual route through Engine Room Upper Level, Engine Room Lower Level, Machinery Space Upper Level, and Machinery Space Lower Level. I could walk that route in my sleep. At some points I probably have.

Suddenly I heard the voice of the SRO over the 7MC (the announcing system specifically serving the engineering spaces).

"And the cow says..."

I stopped in my tracks. What did he say? I stood there for a few seconds. Nothing more came over the speaker. Maybe I was imagining things. The unique combination of sounds in an industrial environment can be misleading at times. I continued along my route.

"And the cow says..."

I knew it! I wasn't hearing things. But what on earth did it mean? Finally it dawned on me. I went to the nearest X60J phone, picked it up, and did the best cow call of my life.

(Now would be a good time to share some useful information. We had a few different sound powered phone circuits on the boat. X1J was for the entire boat, bow to stern. X60J was for the engineering spaces. There was a speaker on the bulkhead in Maneuvering that monitored all traffic on the X60J circuit. Anything said over that circuit would be overheard by those in Maneuvering, especially the Engineering Officer of the Watch. For that reason, it was known as the "White Rat".)

Moooooo! I could hear the SRO's laughter faintly in the distance. That was the start of a very happy tradition. Over the months, the in-port shutdown periods got slightly more entertaining. During the overnight watch periods, the animal call requests came in. Cows, pigs, sheep, and roosters checked in over the White Rat on a somewhat regular basis, and we would both laugh our sleep deprived asses off.

Then came that awful night when it came to an end. I can remember it like it was yesterday. It was a typically quiet shut down period. We were in port, and it was a dull, quiet overnight watch. I was making my rounds, and had made it as far as Machinery Space Lower Level. I had just checked the reefer and chiller readings when I heard my cue. I chuckled, and figured I would call back when I got to the feed station around the corner. A few minutes later, at the feed station, I serenaded the Maneuvering Room with yet another high quality cow call from Smith Animal Noises Productions, Inc.

A few seconds later, I heard something unexpected and unpleasant,

"Shutdown Roving Watch, report to Maneuvering...*immediately*."

It wasn't the voice of my SRO. It was the voice of the Engineering Duty Officer, Lieutenant Deegan!

Like a man walking to his execution, I trudged up to Maneuvering. Mr. Deegan was going through the day's reactor logs. I cleared my throat,

"Permission to enter Maneuvering."

He looked up,

"Granted..."

In the same fashion one would inquire about a dead raccoon stuffed in someone's trousers, he asked,

"Was that you making cow noises over the X60J?"

I hesitated, and he looked back up at me. There was no weaseling out of this one. (Ironically, I never did make weasel noises over the X60J.)

"Uh...yes, sir."

"What does the Internal Communications Manual say about making animal noises over the X60J?'

"I don't know if it specifically mentions that, sir."

"I don't either. Do you think it's approved?"

"I would have to guess it's probably frowned upon, sir."

"As do I. Maybe you should reread the IC Manual, and transcribe it for me, in its entirety, just to confirm that you fully understand it."

"Oh...I don't think that would be necessary, sir."

"Are you sure? This seems like something that might happen again."

"I can definitely assure you, sir, it will *never* happen again."

"No more cow noises over the X60J?"

"No, sir"

"Any other animals?"

"Not a one, sir."

He turned, and without another word, strode back to the Wardroom.

Yes, they take this issue very seriously. I caught the heat for that one, kind of like The Beaver catching heat for one of Whitey's pranks. But, karma caught up with him.

Back in those days, the big rage was these little Casio Keyboards. They had enough keys to allow one to play something recognizable, yet they were small enough to take with you. Dana had one of those, and he absolutely *loved* it. He took that thing everywhere!

Well, one day he was standing SRO watch, and decided it would break the monotony if he brought it back aft with him. He sat there at the panel, occasionally tootling on this little keyboard between taking his logs and scanning the instruments.

Then he got an idea. A *wonderful* idea. He would hold the 7MC microphone down to the keyboard, and play that five note tune everyone knows from the movie Close Encounters of the Third Kind. Everyone in the engineering spaces would hear it, and they'd all have a good laugh. No harm, right? The only problem was, he didn't grab the 7MC mike. He grabbed the 1MC mike. It wasn't the engineering spaces that heard it. The *entire boat* heard it!

The Captain was heading up the ladder to leave the boat. Just as he got to the top step, this ethereal tune wafted through the boat. Witnesses say he stood bolt upright, stopped for a second, then went right back down the ladder. He found the Duty Officer and calmly said,

"That man is disqualified."

And left the boat.

The full ramifications of that simple phrase are lost on those not familiar with the submarine community. He has lost his qualification for SRO watch. But, he's on the watch bill. That means he's automatically delinquent on his quals. (Revisit Chapter 8- You non-qual puke for details.)

Dana never did *that* again!

So, one would think my experience with making animal sounds over the X60J would have turned me into an internal communications guru. Oh, you silly twisted reader! Don't you know? I never learn from my first mistake. We were sitting in the mess area, when the corpsman walked in. Known by the name all corpsmen are known by, "Doc" said,

"It's piss in the bottle time. Numbers ending in five and seven. Could one of you guys announce it?"

What he was saying was random urinalysis was being held for all personnel whose Social Security numbers ended in a five or a seven. No one moved. No one liked pee-in-the-bottle time. Finally, I said I would do it. I walked up to the Control Room, grabbed the 1MC mike, and said in my most professional voice,

"Random urinalysis for all personnel with Social Security numbers ending in five and seven is being held in the Crews Mess at this time."

Job done. I was very satisfied with myself. I was walking out of the Control Room when I heard a faint voice say,

"WHAT?"

I stopped. I thought about what I had said. Did I get the numbers wrong? What was the problem? I started walking again. A couple of guys walked past me into the Control Room. One of them casually asked,

"Smitty, why are we pissing in our dining room?"

It still didn't sink in. I went back to the Mess. Everyone was staring at me. Now I was really puzzled. What? What did I do? Why is everything becoming so weird? One of them said,

"Crew's Mess? Really? Crew's *Mess*? We're going to line up and pee in bottles in the *mess*? Are you sure about that?"

That's when it hit me. I was supposed to say Crew's *Head*, not Crew's *Mess*. Lining up and peeing in the bathroom made much more sense than lining up and peeing in the dining room. I was absolutely mortified! I ran back up to the Control Room, grabbed the mike and blurted,

"Correction! Crew's Head! Crew's *HEAD*! Sorry!"

I stood there. That didn't sound right at all. I keyed the mike again, and one of the guys said,

"Rich...just let it go. Just let it go. Why make it worse?"

Chapter 11-

Seaman Snerd, fetch me a bucket of steam.

"The gods are too fond of a joke"

-Aristotle

Some people may think the jury is still out regarding this issue. They're wrong. It's been pretty much carved in stone that the practical joke was invented in the military. It really isn't that difficult to imagine two Roman soldiers standing sentry duty on the frontier talking. One is older and battle hardened. The other is a new recruit fresh from Rome. It's his first real deployment. The older soldier is saying,

"No, really. General Balinius *does* like being called General Balls-in-anus. We all call him that."

The selection of pranks available to the industrious service member is virtually endless, as is the variety of circumstances in which they can be used. It begins as early as basic training. The most popular prank is the impossible item/action. An inexperienced person is sent to locate or carry out something impossible. They are usually sent to several different people and/or locations. Collaboration can be very involved. The chain of events is universal. It starts with an order to "go get me _____." or "I need you to _____." Each branch of the armed forces has its own specific stumpers. Here are some examples. First the nonexistent items:

Sky Hooks. They just don't exist, plain and simple. No such thing.

Relative Bearing Grease: Yes, it's true that a bearing requires lubrication. But, a relative bearing is a *direction*, not a mechanical device.

Chow Line: Line is a common term in the Navy. It means rope or cable of some kind. Chow line is where people line up for meals.

Waterline: See Chow Line. The waterline is the point on the side of the hull marking which part of the hull is under water. That portion of the hull is usually painted with special anti-fouling paint, which is normally a different color than the rest of the hull.

Bucket of Steam: This is physically impossible.

Bulkhead Remover: An interior wall on a ship is called a bulkhead. It cannot be removed by a cleaning product. At least not in my Navy.

Metric Crescent Wrench: Do I need to explain this? Really?? Okay, maybe some of you aren't mechanically inclined. A crescent wrench is a wrench with a movable jaw. This allows it to fit an infinite variety of fastener sizes within the range of the jaws. Why would one need a specific model for the metric system? Another variation is the Left Handed Pipe Wrench. No such thing.

The ID10T Form: You can see it coming, can't you? A raw service member can be sent to an incredible variety of locations in search of this elusive piece of paperwork.

When it's been determined that the victim has suffered long enough, the last person takes a blank sheet of paper. In very large printing, they write:

ID10T

Across the paper. At this point, if the victim hasn't figured out what happened, there is the option to send him to someone else for countersigning.

Machinists Mate Punch: This sounds like an actual tool, since many tools are referred to as punches.

Center punch...used to make a starting point for a drill bit.

Set punch...used for driving a pin or nail below the surface surrounding it.

Machinists Mate Punch...usually delivered by a very large machinists mate, to the unsuspecting arm of the person making the inquiry. This usually results in injury and crying, depending on the quality of the tool.

Okay, now let's talk about the impossible assignments:

Change the spark plugs on the diesel: Diesel engines don't use spark plugs. It's like changing the film in a digital camera. They got me with that one. No, really. They did.

Check the windings in the Vortex Generator: Most generators have a rotor, including windings. These windings do need to be examined on a regular basis. What's the problem? A Vortex Generator is a thin strip of metal on the wing of an aircraft. A vortex is a special type of air current. So, this little strip of metal works by causing the air to flow over the wing in a very specific way.

Sweep the baffles: The "baffles" is a region behind a submarine where the sonar is almost useless. Everyone in submarines knows this, including the bad guys. During the Cold War, the careful stalking of Soviet subs involved the proper use of their baffles. A submarine maneuvers to move that sonar blind spot into a location accessible to the sensors. This maneuver is called "sweeping the baffles". Any new member of the crew who doesn't know this critical fact will invariably grab a broom, and start searching for any baffles needing a good brush off.

Blow the DCA: This is a good one! You see...the DCA isn't a component. The DCA is a *person*! One can imagine the embarrassment resulting when a new sailor goes to the Officer Of the Deck, and requests permission to blow the DCA. This trick was extremely popular when the DCA, Lt. Cahill, was standing OOD. The scene was played out many times. A new member of the crew would walk into the Control Room,

"Uh...sir. Request permission to blow the DCA."

"What?"

"I need to blow the DCA for quals, sir."

"Again? Wow! They really should lighten up on you non-quals."

The Control Room would erupt in laughter as a look of pure horror spread over the face of the hapless dupe when he realized what he had really said. He would then walk away shaking his head, mumbling something about "killing" and "bastards".

The Mail Buoy: If you can pull this off, all the trouble is worth it!! Here's how it's done:

1) Find a new, young and gullible member of the crew, preferably one with some precious spare time.

2) Tell them they've been assigned to get the mail buoy. Explain how the only way vessels at sea can get their mail is via the mail buoy. This works on any ship, but it's incredibly ironic on a submarine. Explain the *extreme* importance of this assignment.

3) Dress the subject in as much safety equipment as humanly possible. In the incident I witnessed, they got him into a safety harness, life preserver, hardhat, and some rubber boots someone was able to locate.

4) Give them some kind of tool to snare the mail buoy as it floats by. We used a gaff. Explain how they *must* be ready. We only get one shot at this. They've got to get it on the first try. There is no second chance.

5) Place them at their station. In this case it was the bottom of the ladder going to the bridge. We explained how the submarine would surface, but only very briefly. He would then run quickly up the ladder to the top, lean over with his gaff, and snare the buoy as it drifted by.

6) Walk away. That's it, you're done. Human nature does the rest. Trust me. They *will not* leave that spot! Either they'll figure it out themselves, or someone will ask them what they're doing. The waves of laughter will eventually clue them in. The burning embarrassment and humiliation will insure the population of jokers is perpetuated.

I will always remember the occasion I saw this one pulled off. Everything went perfectly. They had the perfect person. They had the perfect situation. They had an entire Control Room full of people able to keep a straight face for a long time. He was dressed up, briefed, and stationed. He stood there for the remainder of that watch. At one point I was close to breaking out in laughter. Another guy turned to me and silently put a finger to his lips. I swallowed hard.

The watch was changed. Turnovers and briefings were given, and the next section settled into their routine. After a little while, the new OOD looked over to the ladder. A puzzled look crossed his face. He turned his attention to other matters, but returned his gaze to the mail buoy attendant. He stared for a few more minutes. Finally his curiosity got the better of him,

"Excuse me, Seaman. What are you doing?"

Our hero turned and looked. He proudly declared,

"Waiting for mail buoy, sir."

The OOD stared. He looked a little confused.

"What?"

"I'm waiting for the mail buoy, sir. When we surface I'm gonna go up and get it."

"You're *what*? What mail buoy?"

"The mail buoy. It has all our mail."

He stared at the officer with a look of contempt on his face. How could this guy not know about something so important? Was he not briefed?

"Seaman, there is no *mail buoy*!"

The transformation in this poor man was incredible. The best part was, it all happened in slow motion. As the laughter erupted, the chain of events was crystal clear. First came the instant of comprehension. Then the overwhelming embarrassment, and burning humiliation. Then...the *rage*. He was absolutely furious! He was going to get them back. If he couldn't, he'd get someone else. Someone else would be standing at the bottom of that ladder, and *he'd* be laughing!

I still remember the moment *I* got it. It was in the morning, and we were all standing in Engine Room Upper Level. Quarters had just finished, and we were figuring out what would go down for the rest of the day. Chief Jardin turned to me and casually said,

"Smith, grab the maintenance card for changing the spark plugs in the diesel. I'm going to need you to do that today."

Happily, I went to the cabinet that held the cards for all our equipment. I started flipping through the cards, looking for the section for the diesel. It would help if I knew the first few numbers of the designation. I leaned out into the aisle to ask for the numbers,

"Hey, Chief...what's the code...for...the..."

It dawned on me. That terrible truth. They were all looking, waiting for the other boot to drop. I met a collection of grinning faces, all saying "Gotcha!"

Cue the laughter. They got me good.

Then there were the pranks that were reserved for those who drew the contempt of their shipmates. It doesn't matter where one goes. There will always be those people who just can't get along, just can't lighten up, or just can't shut up. There are special behavioral modification techniques for these people. Would you like to know what they are? Why, sure you do!

The Grease Job: Several strong crew members subdue and pants the targeted individual. Another crewman then completely covers the offending party's ass and balls in thick, sticky industrial grease. Usually only one application is necessary.

The Wedding Job: This is similar to the Grease Job, but with much longer lasting after affects. If a crew member fails to properly protect the secret of his upcoming nuptials, he will fall prey to the Wedding Job. The mild form of the Wedding Job is when a few guys hold down the prospective groom, while another gives him a very large, very visible hickie. There he will stand, our hero waiting for his bride, with a huge hickie on his neck. Someone will have some explaining to do! The *full* Wedding Job is much more radical, and more permanent. In this operation, the victim is pantsed in the same manner as the Grease Job. But, this time the groom's balls are covered in Prussian Blue grease. Prussian Blue is a blue grease that permanently stains the skin blue. If not caught right away, it doesn't wash off. It *wears* off! So, our unlucky groom gets into bed on his wedding night, and the bride looks down to see her husband has blue balls. *Literally*, blue balls.

The Phone Job: Not so fast! Don't put that Prussian Blue away *just* yet. You're going to need it for this next prank. The sound powered phone handsets on submarines were black. Prussian Blue grease was virtually undetectable on them. Isn't that convenient! Tom, one of our mechanical operators, decided to play some pranks with the phones and Prussian Blue. He started with the Engineering Officer of the Watch. He went into the maneuvering room under the pretense of checking some logs. He sat down on the deck next to the EOOW's desk, reached up and grabbed the handset, and inconspicuously painted some Prussian Blue on the mouthpiece and earpiece.

Then he went back out to Engine Room Upper Level, dialed up the EOOW, and turned the crank. Mr. Thorpe picked up the phone, answered it, shrugged, and hung it back up. He now looked like a dancer from Moulin Rouge. Well, with *blue* lips. Tom got me with that one, too. But, it was at the very end of my watch. When I got off watch, I scrubbed my face and ear with Boraxo. It came off. I got to it before it soaked in. Mr. Thorpe wasn't so lucky. His didn't come off entirely. He had blue lips and a blue ear for well over a week.

The Powder Job: This is reserved for the shipmate who doesn't feel the necessity to bathe. Personal hygiene is extremely important on a submarine, and since we make our own fresh water, there's really no reason for someone to go without one shower a day. Since racks are shared on a regular basis, a stinky bunkmate is intolerable. But, sometimes a little extra hint is needed. It's all very simple. Wait until the subject goes to bed. Get bottles of Shower to Shower body powder, and take the tops off. When it's pretty good odds they've fallen asleep, two or three men sneak up to the rack. They pull the curtain open, dump the contents of the powder bottles all over the sleeping stink bomb, and close the curtain again. Again, usually one application will do.

The Mask Job: This is perfect for the new crew member who just can't seem to understand their lowly place in the crew. Again, wait until the subject goes to bed, preferably when the berthing compartment is rigged for red. The red lighting lends a dramatic effect. Wait for the person to fall asleep. Have a few guys grab some EAB (Emergency Air Breathing) masks. Find the air manifold nearest to the person's rack. Plug in the masks and put them on. When they're being used they make a very distinctive sound, very similar to Darth Vader. Pull the curtain open on the person's rack, and roughly shake them awake. The first thing they'll see is a bunch of EAB masked faces staring in at them, all hissing strangely. Then shout angrily,

"What the *fuck* are you doing in the rack? The boat is on *fire!*"

Trust me, it'll be worth it.

The EB Green Job: This was used most often on the Skipjack, for a number of reasons. First, the abundance of raw materials available. EB Green was a green duct tape that was always plentiful on the boat. It got its name from the fact it was originally used at Electric Boat, right up the Thames River from us, and it was a peculiar shade of green. This tape was extremely useful. It was strong, with an excellent adhesive. Once it was put somewhere, it was intended to be there forever. We actually repaired Freon leaks with it until we got back to port. Second, it was the perfect tool for the job. Lastly, once the lesson had been learned, it was easy to get the person out.

As useful as it was, it was equally famous for its ability to turn a troublesome crewmember into a green mummy. Now, no one willingly succumbs to a treatment like this. It always takes a few crewmen to assist in the procedure. But, once the victim is subdued they can quickly be wrapped up from ankles to neck. From there on, their fate can be pondered further, or just left to the next passerby.

Sometimes a man would be EB Greened for being a jackass. Sometimes it would be because he said the wrong thing, at the wrong time, to the wrong person. Sometimes they practically *dared* others to do it. Not surprisingly, sometimes it happened simply because people were bored. Why don't we look at some examples of these situations?

First, the jackass. Seaman Brent Gaines was quite a character. He was always fun to be around. But, when he first arrived on Skipjack he was a little hard to take. One day things just had to change. He was pounced upon, taped up, and then carried down into the berthing compartment. He was taped securely into the overhead, just outside the Goat Locker, with his face pointed toward the door. The guys rapped loudly on the door, and ran. A sleepy, irritated Chief came to the door. He looked around. Who was that? He looked left, looked right, and stood very still, listening intently. Then he finally looked up. He found himself eye to wide panicked eye with Brent. He couldn't speak due to the piece of EB Green over his mouth.

"What the hell are you doing up there?"

"Mmm mmm, mm mmm mmmmmm!!"

"Get down from there!"

"Mmmmmmmmmmm mm mmmmmm?"

Eventually they took pity on poor Brent. He was released unharmed, and became a normal Skipjack sailor.

Now the unfortunate, unwitting statement. We went out on this one patrol into the NBOA. It was nothing critical. We spent a lot of time there, doing what was formally called "providing services". That meant we were essentially playing "target" for someone, be it sub or ship or aircraft. This time it was different. We had U.S. Marine security at that time. For some reason, we had a Marine on board as a rider. There were a number of theories as to how he came to be there.

1) He was there because they wanted the security people to get a taste of what we went through. They wanted to see what made us so plain old loopy.

2) He won a raffle, and the prize was a week on a sub.

3) He lost a bet, and the loser had to spend a week on a sub.

4) He screwed his Commander's daughter, and the worst possible penalty was...yup, you guessed it. A week on a sub.

Anyway, he got along pretty well with us. He was a pretty cool guy with a lot of entertaining stories of what Marine life was like. He was sitting in the Torpedo Room with a group of guys, waiting to eat. We were telling him about our tradition of EB Greening people. He said the worst possible thing in a room full of bored submariners. I know it was probably absent minded. He probably regretted it as soon as the words left his lips,

"You don't EB Green a Marine."

Now, I have to give him credit. I heard it took about six guys to hold him down. But, his fate was sealed.

ZZZZZZZZZZZZZZZ!!

Round and round went the roll of EB Green! Soon he was fully wound up in green tape. Then they did something terrible. Some say they crossed the line with this action:

They left him there, and went to eat. He bawled like a calf as he watched everybody else eating. He repeatedly begged to be let out. He was hungry! They couldn't do that to him. After a few minutes, they cut him out and he sat down with them. He asked why they had done such a nasty thing.

"After what you said, what *else* could we do?"

He had to shrug and admit his mistake.

What about the idiot who dares someone to tape them up? Oh, they get special treatment. One of our new Torpedomen was sitting in the Torpedo Room. A Second Class held the watch, and a First Class was cleaning and inspecting pistols. For some unfathomable reason, he turned to the other two and said,

"You two don't have what it takes to tape me up."

The other two looked at each other. They each had a "did I just hear what I thought I heard" expression on their faces. Obviously, he was quickly taped up. Then they got a wonderful idea. They unbolted the ladder that led to the forward escape trunk. Then they turned it around, taped him to the ladder, and then bolted it back in place. The end result was that he was taped to the ladder...*upside down*. I arrived on the scene just as they were finishing up the taping job on him. Then I saw them unbolting the ladder. How could I leave now? This was obviously going to be one of those "I can't miss this" moments.

The deed was finally done. A small crowd had gathered by this time. There he was, taped to the ladder upside down, with the blood rushing to his head. He said,

"Okay. You guys made your point. I'll never say anything like that again. Just please get me down."

His head was turning the color of a plum. Maybe they should let him down. After all, they did make their point. Just as they were going over to cut him down, I said the worst possible thing,

"Anyone got a camera?"

A moment of silence passed. Then I felt hands patting me on the back as people scrambled for cameras. The poor guy looked at me, and quietly said,

"Smith. I am going to fucking *kill* you."

"Not like that you're not!"

I made very sure I was nowhere to be seen by the time he got out. He was too busy to stay mad at me for long. He was a non-qual like me. Now for the last reason someone could be EB Greened. Boredom. And in a way, I've saved the best for last. I should probably remind the reader of the closer knit, casual attitude usually present in a submarine crew. Also keep in mind the need for humor and comic relief in highly stressful environments.

Again, we were on patrol. One could probably figure out by this point, these actions would never be tolerated if the boat was in port. I was going into the Torpedo Room to study. Who should I see halfway through the process of being given a lovely green cocoon? Why...Mr. Wallis! This was a new one. I'd never seen a commissioned officer wearing that shade of green before. This ought to be good! Apparently, he walked into the Torpedo Room at just the wrong time. He was greeted with,

"Mr. Wallis! We're soooo happy to see you!"

He knew right away what was coming. He was protesting and threatening like a trooper as the tape was wound higher and higher up his body. Finally he was finished. The guys stood back to admire their handy work.

I didn't want to say it. It was stupid to say it. I don't know why I said it,

"Anyone got a camera?"

Mr. Wallis had the perfect answer ready to go,

"Alright, you guys! It was funny at first, but it's not anymore. I have work to do. Now, get me the hell out of this!"

The men sighed. He was right. They should let him go. They had already pushed the envelope of the blurred line between officer and enlisted. They would cut him out right away. Good thing Seaman Borque was there! It has always been very common for sailors to carry knives. They would practically die without them, much like women or coffee. But he was different. Yes, he carried a knife. It was the *type* of knife he carried that made him different.

Keep in mind, this was the mid-1980s. Rambo was very popular. Cutlery shops everywhere carried replica "Rambo" knives in their showcases. Seaman Borque couldn't resist the temptation. After all, the boat was the only place he could wear it without spurring 911 calls. So needless to say, when Mr. Wallis demanded to be cut out of all that tape, it was Borque to the rescue!

He pulled that huge knife out of its sheath with giddy relish. Mr. Wallis' eyes got very big. Everyone stepped back to give Borque plenty of room. He started at Wallis' feet. The knife went through the tape as if it wasn't even there. Apparently, having a knife like that wasn't worth it unless it was razor sharp. He kept slicing higher and higher up Wallis' legs. The blade was getting closer and closer to Mr. Wallis'...uh...stuff. Finally he panicked.

"Wait! Wait! Not so fast!!"

"I thought you wanted to be cut out right away. We don't *have* to cut you out. We could just leave you like that and carry you to the Ward Room."

Obviously, that alternative would never be lived down. Maybe he was hasty.

"All right. Just...be...careful!"

Mr. Wallis flinched as the cutting resumed. He was sweating by the time the knife made it up to his neck, but not so panicked. I suppose his heart, lungs, and jugular vein were less important than his...uh...stuff. Finally, he was free. He flew out of the Torpedo Room. Mr. Wallis knew better than to complain, and the Torpedomen knew better than to brag.

Seaman Borque was also the only crewmember I knew of, to pull a prank on an entire room. How could he pull off such a feat? He had one thing in his favor...it was a room of Midshipmen.

What is a Midshipman? It's easy. An Ensign is the lowest grade of commissioned officer. The classic phrase used to describe an Ensign is "lower than whale shit". A Midshipman is the only thing lower. They suffer their fate as "Middies" until they graduate from the Naval Academy at Annapolis. Then they get to climb *up* to the status of Ensign. They may not be the lowest form of life, but they do a great job of playing the part. They're not officers, but they *think* they are. This results in some awkward moments with the enlisted men.

The boat was heading out with a load of Middies for a Midshipman Run. Each year during the summer, each branch of the Navy hosts groups of Middies, in hopes of luring the new officers to their particular branch. The Marines, the aviators, the surface fleet, and the subs all get a crack at them for a week. It was our turn to host a group of Middies. The boat was transiting out to our dive point. Seaman Borque walked into the mess deck as the boat rocked unevenly in the moderate seas. All the Middies were looking a little green in the gills. Being the concerned gentleman that he was, he only wanted to *help*.

He went and fetched a piece of string and a large hex nut. He tied the nut and string onto a pipe in the overhead, near the front of the mess deck.

"Hey, guys. I've tied this nut into the overhead to act as an artificial horizon. Just watch this nut swinging. It'll keep you oriented and keep you from getting seasick."

A flood of thanks came from the Middies. Unfortunately, as Borque knew, the swinging nut had the exact opposite effect. Watching any oscillating object makes seasickness worse. In a *hurry*. The Middies dutifully watched the swinging nut. Finally, as if on cue, every one of them bolted out of the room. The small mob of Middies made a beeline for the head. They took turns calling his name... Bork!

As fate would have it, the best practical joke of all was played on a Middie. Midshipman Ciro was one of a kind. Thank God for that! He was tall, skinny as a bean pole, with a big angular nose. The only thing greater than his awkwardness was his arrogance. He may have been wearing a Middie uniform, but he was already an Admiral. He treated any and all enlisted men as obvious inferiors. Two people put an end to that.

One was Ernie. He was one of our senior electricians. He knew *everything* about the boat. He was highly respected by everyone. If the Captain had a question, he went to Ernie. The Middies were allowed to complete the first two phases of the ship's quals. If they succeeded, they were awarded silver Dolphins. Essentially, they were given a privilege after one week that should have taken a year of back breaking work. It was a PR move for the officers, but a terrible insult to the enlisted men.

Ciro went to Ernie for his electrical checkout for phase one and two. Ernie asked him the questions, and Ciro gave the correct answers. Ernie signed the qual card for phases one and two. Ciro just couldn't keep his mouth shut,

"Hey, sign off phases three and four while you're at it."

Ernie turned and looked hard at Ciro. Did he really say what he thought he did? He quietly said,

"I'm sorry. What did you say?"

"I said sign off three and four while you're at it."

"Oooh, you don't understand. The checkouts for three and four are much, much more difficult. Sit down, and I'll ask you the questions for three and four."

Ernie then proceeded to ask the questions for the checkouts. It was information an operator was expected to know after graduating from Nuke School, KAPL, and intense study of Skipjack. Ciro's head was spinning when it was over. He had a very lengthy list of look-ups to find answers for. He got up and started walking away. Ernie called after him,

"Now don't forget, Mr. Ciro. You need to get me those look-ups before you can do anything else on your qual card."

How he got those Dolphins, I'll never know.

The other thorn in Ciro's side was Senior Chief Hardington. He was another highly knowledgeable man. Chief Hardington was standing Chief of the Watch when Ciro came up looking for signatures. He walked over to the Senior Chief and said,

"Okay, Chief. This is how we're going to work this..."

Hardington's head spun around! Some people say it actually made it the entire 360 degrees. The veins stood out on his neck and forehead. He screamed at Ciro,

"What the fuck did you just say to me? Get the fuck out of my Control Room! Get the fuck *out*!!"

Visibly shaken, Ciro turned to look at the OOD for support. Strangely enough, the OOD hadn't heard a word. One would think he had suffered enough. Fate disagreed. Events had already been put in motion.

The plan was quickly formulated. One of the ELTs got into full sampling garb. Nick looked very impressive with the face shield, rubber gloves, apron, and radiac. He got a sample bucket and poly bottle. He filled the bottle with hot tap water. The Primary Sample Sink was located just aft of the hatch leading into the reactor tunnel. This was a major choke point for any traffic going forward or aft.

Ciro was paged back aft. Nick perched the cap on the top of the bottle. As soon as Ciro's dorky head was seen entering the reactor tunnel, Nick started walking toward him, making sure Ciro saw him leaving the sample sink. The location and garb made it obvious what had just happened. Surely, The ELT had just taken a sample of the highly radioactive Primary Coolant. Ciro came down the Reactor tunnel steps. Nick turned, pretending not to see him, and walked right into him. The cap came off the poly bottle, and he poured the entire contents onto Ciro. Nick, and two others nearby immediately freaked out. Beside themselves, they screamed at Ciro. He had been contaminated! That was primary coolant! He should have watched where he was going!! That shit will *kill* him!! While Nick and the others earned every shiny ounce of their Academy Awards, screaming and running in circles, Ciro just came apart at the seams. He dissolved in tears and ran screaming and crying out of the engineering spaces,

"I'm contaminated!! I'm contaminated!!"

He was almost humble the rest of the week. That still wasn't enough. He walked around that boat as if he was the Captain, flaunting his silver Dolphins. So...we stole them.

Now the Captain had to finally sit up and take notice. It was announced that if Ciro's coveted Dolphins didn't appear, no one would leave the boat upon our return. They turned up as mysteriously as they had disappeared.

At this point, one might think this is the extreme limit of what one might do to screw with someone else. Well...one would be sorely mistaken. There is one more deed that can be done that is worse still.

The Initiation!

The military is full of traditions involving the initiation of some poor unsuspecting slob or another. The Navy has elevated this event to the status of high art. Some are very simple, even impromptu affairs. Others are elaborately choreographed spectacles. Some of the more famous ones are:

1) The Shellback Initiation: held when the vessel crosses the Equator.

2) The Order of the Ditch: held when a vessel goes through the Panama Canal.

3) The Bluenose Initiation: held when a vessel crosses the Arctic Circle.

These initiations are closely guarded secrets in the submarine community. On some surface vessels, they are videotaped like a bad vacation. Some of these videos have been shown in the mass media. No such event will ever happen in the Submarine Service. However, some vague information can be revealed about what happens during a run-of-the-mill initiation. Some elements are universal. For example, the victim...I mean...initiate will:

1) Be required to consume some sort of absolutely vile substance. It is composed of all food grade products, so it's harmless.

2) Be required to endure some kind of physical discomfort. No one wants a medical emergency in the middle of a sensitive mission, so it's harmless.

3) Be required to endure some kind of verbal abuse, interrogation, and embarrassment. It's all good natured, and everyone endures it, regardless of rank. Yup, you guessed it...harmless.

But sometimes, it isn't the initiation that is so bad. For example, back in the mid-1980s I went through the Bluenose initiation. The initiation itself wasn't so bad. It was pretty much what I had heard and expected. Yes, I was completely covered in harmless gunk. I could deal with that. The problem was, I had been pulled off watch to be initiated. Before I could resume the watch, I had to shower and wash my hair. That's the problem.

You see, hours before the initiation, one of the crew who was already a Bluenose turned off the water heaters in the potable water tanks for the showers. These tanks are constantly surrounded by seawater. Because of this, the water in an unheated tank will quickly reach equilibrium with the outside water. The outside water was thirty seven degrees Fahrenheit. We had crossed the Arctic Circle, don't you know. We had to shower and wash our hair in thirty seven degree water. We had a lot to wash off. To make matters worse, we were only allowed to use gallon jugs of that crappy Navy dish soap! That all just makes the shower longer. I did manage to take my shower. I did wash all that gunk out of my hair. But, when I was done, I was on the verge of passing out.

Remember all those survivors from the Titanic? Recall how they all said the water was so cold it felt like knives were being stuck in all over their bodies. I can tell you from personal experience:

It ain't no joke!

I'd like to say at this point that all these experiences made me a better person. But...I won't. It isn't really true. Nor did it build any moral character. Or put hair on my chest. Most of that came much later in life. But, I will say one thing.

It sure broke the monotony.

Chapter 12 -
May the ORSE be with you.

Require rising standards of adequacy.

-Uncle Hymie

From the very outset, the U.S. Navy intended to train and evaluate its own nuclear oriented personnel. Hyman G. Rickover, aka Uncle Hymie, possessed the necessary clout, reputation, and sheer unpleasantness needed to ensure things went his way. As father of the nuclear Navy, his position with all rights and privileges pertaining thereto was cast in stone. Or, should we say, Uranium.

One step in segregating all things naval and nuclear into Admiral Rickover's exclusive domain was the formation of Naval Reactors, or NR. Naval Reactors was solely responsible for overseeing the construction, testing, evaluating, and operation of every nuclear propulsion plant in the U.S. Navy. It was also responsible for selecting, evaluating, training, and deploying personnel trained to operate those propulsion plants.

NR's requirements, procedures, and standards were *so strict* and *so exhaustive*, oversight and direction by the United States' ultimate authority on nuclear energy, the NRC, was deemed *unnecessary*. And, so it remains to this very day. For this very reason, U.S. Navy trained nuclear operators are considered the Gold Standard for control room operators in the civilian nuclear community, and a number of other industries.

There are a number of ways NR maintains this standard of excellence. One of the most important and arduous ways is called the Operational Reactor Safeguards Exam, or...ORSE. The utterance of the very word "ORSE" has been known to cause submariners to barf and/or wet themselves. The ORSE is by far the most exhaustive, arduous, physically demanding, mentally draining examination period a nuclear trained submarine watch stander can endure. Rumor has it that the first year of training for a U.S. Navy Nuc (pronounced "nuke") is just to ensure they can hear the word ORSE without having their head explode. That may be an exaggeration.

But, to be sure...the ORSE is very, very nasty. The ORSE itself lasts typically two days or so. It consists of:

1) written exams,

2) verbal exams,

3) thorough inspection of all training, operational, and maintenance records,

4) thorough inspection of virtually all equipment, and best of all

5) drills, drills, drills of virtually *every* kind imaginable.

Oh, yes. They're all there. Fires. Flooding. Airborne radiation, Chloride contamination. Reactor scrams (a scram is an emergency reactor shutdown initiated by automated safety circuitry). After a scram, comes a "Quick Recovery Startup" or a "Delayed Recovery Startup". Oh, if you can think of it, they've got a drill for it!

The end result of this two day sample of hell is very simple: it's determined if the command is capable of operating that reactor plant, taking it into battle, facing everything that could go wrong, and still keep it in one piece. Sounds pretty cut and dried, doesn't it? Well, it *is* simple...frighteningly simple. A failed ORSE can end a career. It can take a valued national asset out of operation. That's why they are just as important as they are intimidating.

The preparatory period is every bit as tortuous as the exam is monumental. It lasts typically two weeks. What happens during those two weeks is very simple. You spend every possible waking moment studying, taking test exams, cleaning, inspecting, affecting repairs, examining records, standing drills, running drills, assisting in drills, critiquing drills, or being critiqued. If it sounds as if there isn't much time left over for sleeping, that's because there isn't.

The effect on personnel during the workup and execution of an ORSE can be difficult to fathom. The average nuclear watch stander gets approximately ten to twelve hours of sleep *a WEEK,* during an average ORSE workup. That adds up to...oh, let's see...twenty-four hours of sleep in fourteen days. The crew is under constant stress, exertion, bombardment by extreme temperatures, unceasing pressure, strife, and calamity. During one ORSE workup period, my second, I lost eleven pounds in one week.

I endured two ORSEs during my tour of duty on Skipjack. As well as my second exam went, my first was every bit as tragic. I had reported on board a couple of months prior, and was starting my qualifications for Engine Room Lower Level (ERLL). My division was shorthanded. The Chief was trying to figure out who would stand watch in each position, ensuring an experienced person would be in each compartment. Things weren't working out. Finally, the Chief came to an ominous conclusion.

"Smith, you're standing Lower Level for the ORSE."

The first thing to come to my mind was the stories my brother told me about ORSEs he'd been through. His journey through the wonderful land of submarines began almost four years before mine. He also cut the trail for the Smith brothers' foray into naval nuclear propulsion. He was my Ghost of ORSEs Past. I looked back to his tales of how they did...that. Then they did *that!* Then they did *THAT!* Oh, not that! Really? *THAT?* Yes! *THAT!!*

I swallowed my fear, part of my lunch that threatened to come back up, and as I recall...a piece of gum I'd been chewing. All I could do was promise to do my very best under the conditions. I began my work on qualifying for ERLL in earnest. It was the starting point for anyone in Machinery Division. It was considered the simplest portion of the plant to master, and a good foundation for learning the systems, routines, and operations in the other three positions coming down the road. I can't let anything be simple.

For reasons already described, my qualification process was less than stellar. I *did* qualify. But, not by much. The process was fraught with errors, hesitation, second guessing, and any other obstacles a borderline insane person can throw into their own path. I was qualified in ERLL. As time went on, I gained experience on the watch station. But, I wasn't learning fast enough. I wasn't remembering what I was learning. Finally, the moment came. To this day, I can't decide if I was crushed...or relieved. The Chief came to me and said,

"Smith, I'm taking you off the ORSE watch bill. I'm not sure who'll be taking your place, but it sure won't be you. You're making too many rookie mistakes."

Of course, he was right. I *was* making too many rookie mistakes. In fact, I was making too many *stupid* mistakes. I was making stupid mistakes a stupid person wouldn't even make. Eventually, I did become competent in ERLL. It just took me longer. It was right about that time I realized I didn't learn like other people. I learned by watching. Sit me down. Tell me what we're going to do. Show me step by step, and let me watch. It might take a couple of times. I'll learn it, and I'll do it *exactly* like you do.

My qualifications continued, and I was starting on Engine Room Upper Level (ERUL). People weren't looking at me as if I was a total idiot...all the time. Then the ORSE came. I wasn't versed in much of the truly important facets of operations yet. There was only so much on which they could test me. I wasn't standing drill watches, but I still pitched in as part of the Casualty Assistance Team (CAT). The watch standers who stood the previous watch made up this team, and they carried out the instructions of the active watch standers, who were busy saving the day. I was still required to take written and oral exams. I went into the wardroom with another guy to take our oral exam. This is one event that will be burned into my psyche forever.

We went back into one of the staterooms. As I recall, the ORSE inspector, my division mate, my division officer, and I sat in this tiny stateroom. The ORSE man started asking us questions, alternating between the other watch stander and myself. We answered the questions as best as we could. Obviously, the other guy was having much better luck, having the added benefit of more experience and...a brain. As the exam progressed, I imagined I could feel the shame and disgust building up in the tiny room. It seemed to be emanating from the direction of my division officer.

Then came the last straw. The ORSE inspector asked me my last question:

"Do you believe a submarine's screw (propeller) is more efficient at a shallow depth, greater depth, or is there no difference?"

Before I go any further, think about it and get your answer. Got it? Okay.

My answer went something like this,

"Well, I know a screw at shallow depth is more inclined to cavitate (thrash the water creating noise and bubbles, instead of creating a propulsive force), such as a ship's screw, or the screw on a surfaced submarine. A submarine at depth would be operating in denser water. Denser water would make the screw more efficient. But, the denser water would be more difficult to push the submarine through.

I looked at my quiz mate occasionally as I spoke, looking for any visual clues that I was hanging myself.

"Keeping that in mind, I think one condition would offset the other, thus making things just about equal. Don't you think?"

I looked at the other Petty Officer as I finished. He looked at me with a wide gaping stare. The expression on his face clearly said *what the fuck are you asking me for!* The silence lasted about three seconds, then he softly said,

"I don't know, Richie...uh, Petty Officer Smith...I think he's asking you."

I turned to the inspector and authoritatively said,

"Yes. They're the same. That's my answer."

The silence in that little room was blaring. All three people sat there as if they had just watched someone casually pick up a passing sheep, and use it to wax their car.

Okay, reader. Now it's your turn. Which is it? Does the screw work better at shallow depth? Or deeper depth? Or are they the same? Here's a hint: I was very, very not correct. Here's another hint: Screws at shallow depth spend as much time boiling water for tea as they do trying to push a vessel. One more guess?

What?? Another ORSE!! How many more of these things must I endure? There's an easy answer. They happen once a year...just like sex with an old matronly bar tender. So I've heard. But this one was different. I was fully qualified this time. Qualified in Submarines, Engine Room Supervisor, the whole bit. I actually had a clue regarding what was happening. People didn't look at me like I was a complete idiot...it was more like I was a slightly deranged third cousin.

But, ORSE time came around again. The scars and bite marks from the last one had just faded. We were talking about who was going to do what, when I heard something I never expected;

"Smith, you're standing Upper Level for the ORSE."

I couldn't believe it. I was already standing Upper Level, had been for months. That was where competent watch standers spent most of their time. I had managed to construct a basic mental image of how the Engine Room was operated, although I still thought elves did part of it. But, the ORSE inspectors would get there long after the turbines were running, and the elves were sitting with their feet up. I actually had a chance. All I had to do was survive the workup. It would be different this time. As a watch stander, I would need all the practice I could get at drills and casualties. This would be unlike anything I had seen before.

It was truly two weeks of hell. I rolled out of the rack barely conscious. Then I had a quick bite to eat. Then I went on watch. The drills commenced, which were a lot like doing calisthenics for hours in a sauna. After watch we went to the drill critique, to see how badly we screwed up. When that was over, we supplied support as the Casualty Assistance Team. Then came time for studying, cleaning, and maintenance. Then we were briefed as Drill Monitors, and ran the drills for the next drill watch. Then we went to the drill critique for the drill watch we just ran, to tell them how badly *they* screwed up. Then it was time for a few minutes of sleep, hopefully not interrupted by another drill. Then, you guessed it...start it all over again.

Two weeks straight of that routine is an ORSE workup. Then the most wonderful, yet improbable thing happens. Everyone goes to bed. Everyone gets the chance to take a shower, have a meal, and *sleep.* A good twelve or so hours of quiet rest. Right before the ORSE team arrives, we surface and they come over by small boat transfer. Then the circus comes to town. Tests. Oral exams. Inspections. Records. Drills, drills, drills! Then we turn around and go back to port. They ride back with us, and we all talk it all through. Everyone seems happy, so we think we probably passed. We never assume we did. That would be blatantly tempting the jinx. I've said it before. Sailors have more superstitions than a pomegranate has pips. Right at the top of the list...*The Jinx.*

Of course, we find out later we scored average. Shouting, laughing, pats on the back greet the news. The Bull Nuc, a Senior Chief, tells me I did really well. But, we got an Average. Average is like the Stanley Cup. Above averages are rare. Below averages are rare as well. Failures are discussed in hushed conversations. We had one failure during the time I was at Groton. The boat's command was doing poorly from the beginning. Morale was low. They failed the ORSE. On the run back to port, they had a fire in their trim pump, a piece of vital lifesaving equipment. Not a *drill,* a *fire.* No one even rolled out of their rack.

When they got back, as soon as the boat tied up, the Captain stood up, walked away, and never looked back. Like I said, a bad ORSE can end a career. That boat now had no Captain. A bad ORSE can take a valued national asset out of operation.

ORSEs really, really suck. Repeat after me. ORSEs really, really suck.

Chapter 13-
So close to war...

"Think of it this way: Where can you go to sea in the most AWESOME piece of equipment ever built, have great chow, outstanding shipmates, piss off Ivan, and get PAID for it?"

-Attributed to a sub school instructor

To fully understand the nature of submarine warfare, and what sets it apart from the other aspects of war, one needs to understand the nature of warfare itself. It really isn't difficult. Consider this analogy:

Think of the world as a huge house. Let's say...a colonial. I'm just sentimental that way. Each room is a country. I'm one country, in the kitchen. You're another country in the guest bedroom. If I'm going to wage war on you, or you want to wage war on me, we need to move from the kitchen to the guest room. Or, vice versa.

So we move into our respective positions and start taking shots at each other. There's no huge surprise, so we pretty much know the other is coming. We can hear the creaking floor. We can see the enemy coming around the corner. We fight, and we go back to our respective rooms. For the most part, everything is out in the open. This is how surface naval battles, land engagements, and aerial warfare are conducted.

Submarine warfare is nothing like that. Let's say I'm preparing to go to war with you. I have to sneak into your room when you're not looking. Then I have to follow you around constantly, always just out of your sight. I constantly maneuver, ducking, bobbing, side-stepping to stay behind you or out of your peripheral vision. This can go on indefinitely. Then the order to go to war arrives. I just reach out, put a gun to the back of your head, and blow your brains out. I was already there the entire time. You simply didn't know it, or realize it soon enough. Now, it doesn't go perfectly every time. The enemy steps on the creaky bits of the floor fairly often. When they do, we catch them. They explain that they were just looking around, and sheepishly go away. They'll try again later. We step on the creaky board, too. Just not nearly as often. It also doesn't hurt that we have quieter shoes.

I think I've made my point. When a submarine goes to its dive point and submerges, it *is* at war. The analogy explains why. If the war starts, we need to be in position to pull the trigger. And, no one can know we were there. That's what makes our submarines such a potent weapon. The bad guys don't know where they are. So when we hear that announcement over the 1MC,

"Rig for Patrol Quiet."

It's "game on", in a very, *very* serious way. The preparations for that condition are very thorough. First priority is to go through the entire boat, checking stowage of all movable items. Pots, pans, dishes, tools, locker doors, and anything else that can move are secured. Then we do what's called "angles and dangles". The boat is put through a series of extreme maneuvers. Extreme down angles, up angles, and turns to port and starboard are repeated several times. Anything that can come loose is noted and taken care of.

One good thing about angles and dangles is a little known sport called "deck plate surfing". Engine Room Lower Level is laid out with a central aisle separating the port and starboard sides of the machinery. These steel plates almost always have some degree of thin oil/grease residue on them. If the proper shoes are worn, and one has a good sense of balance, they can slide down that aisle when the boat takes an extreme up or down angle. Grace or form doesn't matter. It's all about distance.

When angles and dangles are through, the announcement is made to place all watertight hatches "on the latch". A hatch has two positions. It can be closed and dogged, or open and on the latch. A hatch is never allowed to remain free swinging. The reason is very simple. It weighs hundreds of pounds. If the boat were to take a roll, either due to heavy seas or a sharp turn, that hatch would swing. If it slammed shut, it would close with a tremendously loud bang. If a crew member was passing through the hatch at the time, any appendage in the way would instantly be broken. Something like a finger would most certainly be severed completely. The noise is actually the worst option. If the turn was due to evasive action, that sudden bang would be heard for miles and miles and *miles*! The enemy would be able to say,

"There they are. Right *there*!"

By the time Patrol Quiet is announced, all these elements have been addressed. If quiet sneakers aren't already worn, they are quickly donned. Life takes on a silence that is second nature for submariners. No shouting. No slamming drawers. No stomping. No procedures that require pounding. That should have been handled in port. Only a dire emergency would allow any of those actions. We're not perfect. If we could be sneaking into trailing position on a Soviet boat, they could be sneaking up on us. One moment of indiscretion and it would be a Soviet sonar tech saying,

"What was that? Well, looky what we got here."

Well...I seriously doubt the Soviets said things like "looky". But, you get the point.

When on patrol, we act exactly as we would during wartime. The indiscretion rate is kept to the absolute minimum. The indiscretion rate is a ratio of that time spent on patrol, compared to any time when the submarine could be detected visually from the surface. Good examples of situations that could result in this are:

1) When any periscope or mast is above the surface. We come up to PD (periscope depth) for a few reasons. We may need a navigational fix. We may need to "send and receive", in other words, use the radio. We may just need to have a look around.

2) If the boat broaches, which should never, ever happen. But, every once in a while it does happen.

3) When some evolution results in unintended air or fluid being ejected from the submerged submarine. It will invariably float to the surface, marking the boat's position.

While on the surface, all radar contacts are considered potentially hostile until identified. The Electronic Surveillance Measures system is constantly manned, looking for hostile radars and radio signals. When submerged, every sonar contact is given the same treatment. Until we know what it is, we track it and set up a firing solution for a torpedo attack. If the process is going to be lengthy, the Fire Control Tracking Party is stationed.

All torpedo tubes are loaded with live weapons. They are prepped and ready to be fired. A conspicuous sign is hung on each tube breach door that reads "WARNING - WARSHOT LOADED". We don't carry dummies. We have to be ready for the real thing at a moment's notice. If we're tracking a target of interest, and maintaining a firing solution, the weapon waiting to be launched is a real weapon, with real explosives. It *will* make something go *BOOM*.

It all comes down to one thing: a whole new way of living for the neophyte submariner. Come stomping down the ladder to the mess deck, you'll hear about it. Leave a drawer open, you'll hear about it. Forget to bring patrol shoes, you'll hear about it. Especially since the crew is always reminded before a deployment,

"Don't forget to bring your boat shoes."

The concept of silence permeates all elements of everyday life. The submariner walks quietly, talks quietly, opens and closes everything quietly. There are signs everywhere reminding us to never leave a drawer or locker open. Some sub skippers posted signs throughout the boat admonishing the crew that they must always beat the Soviets. They mentioned one type of Soviet boat specifically,

"We have to beat Akula!"

Not only did we need to be silent to avoid detection, but also to allow our own sensors to work to their maximum efficiency. One thought was always in the backs of our very, very quiet minds:

The gun could be at the back of *our* head. There could be a Soviet boat behind *us*, waiting for *their* message telling them war had begun. It was time to shoot.

No submarine wants to be a target. But, sometimes there isn't a choice. That was us. It was called "providing services". That meant our job was to go out to a designated spot in the ocean and play the part of the bad guy. Skipjack was an older boat. She was the oldest boat on the east coast. She was noisier. She used equipment newer boats had long since discarded. There were other characteristics to set her apart that will not be discussed. The end result was that she sounded a lot like a Soviet submarine. We were the perfect rabbit for the hounds to chase. Sometimes we were part of a much larger exercise, involving multiple navies. Sometimes it was just us and another boat. It didn't really matter. We always did our best to stay undetected. Normally we couldn't. We were dealing with boats with modern spherical array sonar, quiet propulsion systems, and skilled seasoned operators. We usually didn't stand a chance. But that wasn't always the case.

I don't know what their problem was. Maybe they had a new sonar tech. Maybe they were just having an off day. Things just shouldn't have gone this way. We had no right to be in the position we were. We were old. We were noisy. We weren't as fast as we used to be. We hadn't been in the yards for a while. We were the ultimate underdog in every sense of the word. They were new. Norfolk was a brand new Los Angeles class nuclear fast attack submarine.

She was the quietest in the world. She had the best of everything. She had a fine crew. She was going to track down Skipjack like the dog she was. It would be over in no time, and we'd be off to bigger and better things.

We went out to the patch of ocean designated as the area for our exercise. We began steaming in the prescribed pattern. It was now just a matter of waiting for the other boat to detect us, track us, set up a firing solution, and simulate the launching of a torpedo. We continued in our circular course, listening and waiting. As soon as Norfolk fired her water slug, we would hear it. The game would be over.

We picked up the newer boat on sonar. She was in the area. She was assigned a contact name, Sierra One. We conducted TMA, Target Motion Analysis, on her as we observed her cruising right past us. She was in the area, alright. But, she was still looking, trying to sniff us out. We continued on our predetermined course, keeping close tabs on Norfolk with our retrofitted towed array.

She began the next leg of her search. Again, we tracked her every move as she sailed past us, obviously clueless to our presence. The Captain began to get impatient as the routine was repeated again. He turned to the OOD,

"Officer of the Deck, increase speed to ahead full. Cavitate."

Our Captain wanted to make a little noise to give Norfolk a hint. Maneuvering did exactly as they were told. We watched for any indications that we had been detected. Norfolk continued her Sunday drive, completely oblivious. The Captain ordered someone to go down to the dry bilge and rap on the hull with a hammer. At his signal, the hammer went to work. After a few raps, we listened intently for any suspicious change in Norfolk's course to show she found us. Nothing! Mr. Mendes reached the end of his patience. Finally, he could take no more,

"Officer of the Deck, I have the con."

"You have the con, aye sir."

We were simultaneously shocked and delighted when we heard his next order,

"Firing point procedures...Sierra One."

"Firing solution set, sir."

"Match bearings and shoot tube three on Sierra One."

On the inside of the boat, a water slug fires just like a torpedo. Instead of pushing the mass of a weapon out the tube, it fires the mass of water taking its place. The torpedo launching system doesn't know the difference. The crew hears the same thump and hiss. The pressure in the hull rises a little for a second. And so it was this time. The only difference was, every man knew why we were out there. Why were *we* shooting? We were supposed to be shot *at*.

Outside the boat, firing a torpedo tube makes a very distinctive sound as well. All sonar techs know the sound. It's essentially the submarine equivalent of one kid telling another,

"Bang! Bang! You're dead!"

The Captain listened with glee as Sonar reported cavitation and hull popping noises on the bearing of Sierra One. Now they were carrying out the drill for "torpedo in the water".

The Captain voiced the rhetorical question in everyone's mind,

"Think you can find us now?"

The exercise was abruptly concluded. Both boats went "back to the barn", and one skipper would have some explaining to do. How could a boat twenty-five years old with an antiquated split spherical sonar array, and rudimentary silencing technology beat an almost brand new Los Angeles class boat? Either they were really off their game, or those Skipjack guys were really, really good. Little did we know we would have a chance to show *just* how good we were.

"We'll be in port for Christmas. New Years, too. No, really. We're serious. We already know it. We'll be in stand down. Go ahead and make your plans, and tell your families to make theirs. Don't worry. It's a done deal! It won't be like before."

We heard that message over and over as we pulled page after page of 1986 off the wall. We had a saying in the attack sub community:

"Cast in jello"

The metaphor is simple. If something is unchangeable, it is said to be "cast in stone". So, if something was "cast in jello", it could change on a moment's notice. Just like an attack sub's operating schedule. We had no recognizable schedule. It was a matter of finding out where we were needed, and when we had to be there, at the whim of COMSUBRON2.

Ballistic missile boat sailors had it easy. Their schedule *was* cast in stone. It had to be, and it absolutely could *not* be deviated from. Our nation's nuclear deterrent force depended on it. They knew whether or not they would be in port literally years in advance. Not so for us. Our fate was to live constantly on the edge of going to sea. That was why we viewed our Christmas status with dubious optimism.

The scratched record played on and on as the year progressed,

"We'll be in port for Christmas(click)We'll be in port for Christmas(click)We'll be in port for Christmas..."

As the pages of the calendar blew away, the holidays crept closer. We noticed something unusual. Well, it was unusual for those unseasoned crew members. We saw unfamiliar people on board. They dealt with certain members of our crew, who seemed to already know them. They spoke in hushed tones, always aware of who was around them. For crewmen like me, it was just peculiar. But the optimism of the experienced members of the crew quickly waned. No words were said, but it was clear something was going to go down. And it would be over Christmas.

"You've got to be kidding!! Please, tell us you're kidding! You've been telling us all year that we'll be in port for Christmas! You told us that *all year*! We had to go out *last year*!"

The Command was duly sympathetic. They were duly empathic. Everyone's holiday was going to be ruined. That didn't do much to take away the sting. Well, not so much a sting...more like a kick in the stomach. They had just announced that we had been tasked with a "mission of higher classification". Everything clicked. The unfamiliar people. The special equipment. The hushed conversations. The grumbling among some of the crew. The lack of conversation about the upcoming holidays. Some people had obviously known about this for a while. Any and all information they were privy to would have been very highly classified. It still was.

They could still get the invisible ball rolling. We were sent to several briefings. One of them was for any crew members still without a will. Oh, boy! *That's* a good sign. One briefing involved what to say to curious civilians, potential rescuers, or potential *captors*. Also…what to say if those captors didn't believe the cover story. Some were for instructions involving circumstances that will never be discussed. A few more days went by. Finally we were allowed to give our loved ones minimal information. It was too late for all of them who had made travel plans. We were given a letter to send to our loved ones, explaining that we had been tasked with an "emergent operation". The Navy was very sorry for any loss or inconvenience, but it simply could not be avoided. We were also allowed to pass on a limited number of "family-gram" forms. The occasional word from home would hopefully soften the blow of being away on such short notice.

That was all virtually erased the next day. The base newspaper, The Dolphin, sent down a photographer to take a publicity shot of a submarine crew with Santa Claus. Guess who got selected…no, really. Guess. Right! It was us! An announcement was made over the 1MC for all available crew members to lay topside. I was in the group for the photo. As we climbed the ladder from the Control Room, there was considerable grumbling about the irony of the situation. Finally, I couldn't hold my tongue. In my typical sarcastic tone I grumbled,

"Ho, ho, *fucking* ho. Merry *fucking* Christmas!"

"Watch the attitude, Smith!"

It was the Executive Officer. He was on the ladder right behind me. We trudged up to the pier. We all put on our "we're so happy" smiles. Finally, Santa and the photographer left us to our holiday-less fate. Our preparations for departure continued unabated.

Finally, the date for our departure arrived. We cast off lines, and made our way down the channel to Long Island Sound. The boat rocked as we got closer and closer to the open sea. It only compounded the somber mood on board. Finally we reached our designated dive point, and grudgingly bade goodbye to the New England coast.

The nature of our mission will not be discussed. I can say it existed, because its existence was made public. The fact that we sailed away on any particular dates is available to the general public. The specific reason, nature, duration, and location of that deployment are not, and never will be, a subject of discussion. I *will* say, it was one of the most fascinating experiences of my already eventful life.

And...we *were* really, really good.

That mission gave me my first good dose of what submarine operations were really about. On assignments like this, the Fire Control Tracking Party was manned twenty four hours a day. Our "subject" was kept under constant surveillance, and their location was confirmed at all times by sonar and fire control. In addition, a manual paper and pencil plot was maintained at all times. This was not for practice. It was an essential, integral part of the operation. Think of it this way: if one is defusing a bomb, and the lights go out, they had better have a friggin' flashlight!

I was assigned to the Fire Control Tracking Party for several days. I found myself immersed in an environment that illustrated the razor's edge on which a submarine operation is balanced. For hours on end, I stood in the crowded, tension filled Control Room. Half the time we were rigged for red, the crimson fluorescent lights bathing everything in a surreal hue. The sense of intense concentration and singular purpose could be cut with a knife.

Each man rid his mind of all thoughts not related to performing his task with absolute perfection. The Helmsman and Planesman had to keep the boat exactly at ordered depth. Too shallow and the boat could broach. Too deep, and we wouldn't be able to use the periscope. The Sonar and Fire Control guys had to ensure their firing solution was accurate up to the second. We on the plot had to keep our target's position constantly updated. The Captain had to use the periscope with the reflexes of a prize fighter, and the intuition of a gypsy fortune-teller.

Trips to periscope depth (PD) were a regular occurrence. We needed to confirm our subject's position, make regular observations, take photographs, and allow the ESM antennae on the periscope to sniff for Soviet radar, ECM, and communications. Each time we went to PD, it was like we were on a trip wire. Nerves ran high and tight. Each observation was an opportunity for some hotshot Soviet lookout to spot our periscope, and bring our mission to an abrupt end. It didn't help any that the seas were very rough, making a broach that much easier.

The Captain would walk up onto the periscope stand. The adventure would always begin with the same statement,

"Prepare to come to periscope depth for observation…Diving Officer, make your depth six zero feet."

As we neared the surface, we could feel the effects of the roiling ocean above. Before we got to PD, the Captain would raise the scope to look for any possible obstacles that might damage our scope. He would angle the lens up toward the surface, and turn in a quick circle.

"No shapes, no shadows. Continue to PD. Okay… scope clear.

Then he would quickly go about the business of locating and ranging his target. My eyes were glued to the small red LED digits on the Periscope Bearing Indicator as I waited to hear the magic word. He would center the crosshairs of the periscope on the target.

"Bearing…mark!"

I looked at the readout on the small display above my head,

"282!"

"Range…mark! Two increments on high power! Down scope!"

The OOD and JOOD had to take the data provided by the Captain and myself, and spit out a calculated range in a second. Fingers flew around Whiz Wheels to take the angle and known height of the target's mast to calculate a range. I would mark the exact point of our own position on the tracing paper on the plot, and write the bearing next to it.

The JOOD would take a ruler, measure out the range, and mark a spot on the plot. A simple dot on the paper said,

You're right...THERE. We know EXACTLY where you are. You have no idea where WE are. You don't even know we're here at all. That's okay, keep playing your games, conducting your experiments, testing your new equipment. Don't mind us. We'll just watch and listen.

Every man in that control room worked under that pressure, felt that same thrill of the chase. Each of us knew we were betting our skins on a pair of twos each time the Captain raised that periscope. Together, we were a precise well-oiled machine...a machine fueled by secrecy and stealth.

I was constantly given information. If I didn't handle it properly, things would go bad. I had to provide information. If I didn't do that properly, things would go bad. We tracked our unwitting target yard by yard, plotting each course change, and predicting the next. The knowledge was always in everyone's mind that the enemy was only a short distance away. They didn't know it, and that condition was crucial to our success. If we were discovered, the mission would be blown. At the very best, we would fail to obtain the highly valuable data our country needed. At the worst, an edgy Soviet submarine captain could decide to put a torpedo in the water. Many of the "entities" we trailed had their own submarines "riding shotgun". And...they didn't like us.

 I'll never forget the time I spent in that Control Room, working with that group of professionals. And they *were* professionals. Maybe they didn't all have college diplomas. Maybe they didn't have big houses or shiny BMWs. Maybe they couldn't afford a first class plane ticket. But one thing is certainly true: those guys did things, saw things, and went through things that would make any Doctor/Lawyer/CEO shit themselves. And, they did them under conditions that would make any other "professional" *puke*.

At the conclusion of our assignment, we were tasked with a virtually impossible task. We were to run the SOSUS line. The SOSUS network is a network of hydro-phones spread across the world's ocean bottoms. Its sophisticated gauntlet monitored all submarine movements with a startling degree of accuracy. Our chances of passing through that cordon undetected were "slim and left town".

Still, a job's a job. We would do our best. At the appointed time, we heard the announcement indicating the beginning of the exercise,

"Rig for ultra-quiet ops."

We shut down all unnecessary equipment. Any unnecessary work was stopped. All personnel not actually on watch were sent to their racks. I was one of those people. It was actually a nice change to be *ordered* to go to bed. Our mission took a heavy toll on all of us. I'm sure I wasn't the only member of the crew to feel that way. I rolled into the rack, curled up with a book, and started to read. The next thing I knew, the Messenger of the Watch was peering in at me.

"Smitty, you can't read."

"Don't be silly! Of course I can read. It's only a rumor that knuckle draggers can't read."

"No, you don't understand. You can't use your reading light. It makes *noise*."

These guys meant business! I looked around. Every other rack was dark. I resigned myself to the fact I would have no choice but to lay back and completely relax. All I could here was the distant hum of the machinery, and the hiss of the ventilators. After a while I couldn't even hear that. I was out like a light.

When I woke, everything seemed to be back to normal. The lights were back on, people were up and about, lots of talking was going on. I wondered if we had made it. Skipjack was old and rickety, but she was still quieter than virtually any Soviet boat. I told myself it wasn't beyond all reason that we could have passed through undetected.

I got up, got dressed, and decided to see what was going on. The normal routine was definitely back in effect. I asked a group of guys in the mess deck if they thought we had made it. The general consensus was probably not. SOSUS was simply too advanced. I would later find out that despite our very best efforts, we had failed. Yes, we were very quiet. Yes, a Soviet boat's sonar would have difficulty detecting us. But, they knew exactly where we were the entire time. I guess it's a good thing they're on our side.

Chapter 14-
The Bonnie Land.

In Scotland, there is no such thing as bad weather - only the wrong clothes.

- Billy Connelly

After running the SOSUS line, it was time for us to go home. Or so we thought. I was standing ERUL watch, when Chief Jardin came over.

"Smith, wanna go to Scotland?"

I looked at him. What had I done now? Was this a joke? Okay. What's the punch line...

"Sure, Chief. What's the deal?"

"Well, it seems Squadron wants to make it up to us a little about having to go out over the holidays. They're offering us the chance to stop at a liberty port. But, they're leaving it up to us. We can go to Scotland, or we can go straight home to our families. So...which one do you want?"

"Do you know where we're stopping?"

"Either Faslane, or Holy Loch."

All right. Faslane is a British sub base in Scotland on the very inside tip of Gare Loch, on the west coast. Gare Loch is a long, narrow, and very deep harbor. Faslane is actually located at a point called Gare Loch Head. The stories about British sub bases are legendary. Especially the stories about the parties, and how nicely guests are treated at these parties. Faslane is also located in a much more rural setting, surrounded by mostly small towns. The nearest one is Helensburgh.

Holy Loch is an American sub base. It's filled with Americans. Over the years, it's been thoroughly Americanized, along with the surrounding area. The nearest city is Dunoon. One characteristic of large American bases overseas is that the locals like to make money from surrounding the boys with the trappings of home. This included women. For some reason, many women in the area were rabid about the prospect of landing an American submarine sailor. We called them "Dunoon Dollies". My decision was really very easy.

"Well, Chief…if we're going to Faslane, I'd like to go to Scotland. But if we're going to Holy Loch, I'd just rather go home."

Chief Jardin nodded his understanding and left. A day or so went by before we learned of the final decision. We were going to Faslane. A ripple of optimism zipped through the boat. Conversations immediately turned to the prospects of entertainment, and the strategies for obtaining it. Even the officers were getting into the spirit. I walked into the Wardroom just in time to hear a conversation between the Engineer and another officer. Lieutenant Commander Riles turned to the other man and said,

"Well, just cycle the bloody valve!"

I had never heard him use the word "bloody" even once the entire time I was assigned to Skipjack. I can't really fault him. I wasn't immune to the magic of our impending adventure either. As difficult as it is to admit, I even found myself "thinking with an accent" from time to time.

Sadly, nothing can go exactly as planned. We set our course for Scotland. We surfaced at the 100 fathom curve. We promptly took an extremely bad wave, and flooded our diesel engine with sea water. I'm not sure how it happened, but somehow it found its way into the induction piping and contaminated the entire engine. Some of us would be partying, and some of us would be dismantling, cleaning, reassembling, and re-oiling our Fairbanks-Morse diesel. After all the contaminated lube oil was removed, fresh oil would need to be pumped in from another tank, *by hand*. With a tiny little hand pump. In an awkward location. Well, no sense crying about it now.

As we made our way up Gare Loch, word started filtering down from the bridge about the scenery. Most of these guys had barely left their home state, never mind gone to a foreign country. One could think these guys were seeing the surface of another planet by the way they were going on and on. Finally, I had a chance to climb the ladder to the bridge and look for myself.

The first thing to strike me was the brilliant sunshine. Okay… that was a complete fabrication . A blatant lie. Oh, come on people! You actually believed me? What's wrong with you? We're talking about *SCOTLAND*! Maybe I should try to push this a little further…there were trolls and fairies everywhere…riding *unicorns*!! Okay, let's start again.

The first thing to strike me was the amazing panoramic view unlike anything I had ever seen before. I couldn't even recall seeing a photo that would compare to this. The sky was a forbidding grey, with low scudding clouds driven by a strong wind. It was cold, damp and raw. I hadn't brought a jacket with me, and I'm not usually affected by the cold, but this was different. I wouldn't want to hang around up there long.

Gare Loch stretched out ahead of us, a narrow strip of frigid steel grey water. Steep hills rose up to either side. Green covered everything. The grey sky cast a muted shadow over the landscape. Strewn across the faces of the hills were dirt roads and old rock walls. Little cottages sparsely dotted the hills, from the very top to the water's edge. These were something right out of a "Why don't you come to Scotland and spend lots of money" commercial. They were absolutely beautiful. They all had white washed walls, rustic doors, and heavy thatched roofs. The finer details were visible courtesy of the Lookout's binoculars, which he snatched back after receiving dirty looks from the OOD.

Finally, I had to go back below. Other people wanted to come up for their own look around, and it gave me a good opportunity to bow out without admitting I was cold. The normal boat routine continued until we stationed the Maneuvering Watch. The normal chaos accompanied our mooring and official arrival at Clyde Royal Navy Submarine Base, Faslane, Scotland.

My first actions upon our arrival was to scope out the two most important jobs waiting to be done, the repair of the Brine Pump, and the restoration of our Diesel Engine. I was to work with another machinist to tear apart and rebuild the brine pump. Gratefully, the Diesel was assigned to somebody else. We worked for a while, and then stopped for dinner.

Dinner was to be a very special treat. It wasn't necessarily because of the food. The Brits knew we were coming, and had some supplies waiting for us on the pier. Among the supplies...milk! It wasn't fresh milk. It was UHT milk. That was my first exposure to UHT milk. It was explained how special treatment of the milk, coupled with a vacuum packaging process, allowed it to be stored for long periods at room temperature. But, it didn't end there. Not only did we have milk for the first time in two months, it was ice cold! It had been sitting on the pier most of the day. Racks of milk cartons were manhandled through the Torpedo Room hatch. Eager hands snapped them up as soon as they made it to the Mess. I'll always remember how good that milk tasted. By the end of the meal, I had guzzled two of them. Each was a pint!

After dinner, we were released for the rest of the night. Many of the guys went to the base's enlisted and officer clubs, to look for a spot in one of those legendary parties. I had other ideas. I changed into civilian clothes, and headed up the quay in search of a British submarine. I had always heard the Brits were very keen on trading uniform articles with foreign navies. The US was one of their favorites. There were multiple occasions when a Brit boat would pull into Groton, or an American boat would pull into Faslane, and each crew would be festooned with each other's submarine pins before the visit was over.

I made my way down the darkened quay. My prospects didn't look good. We had heard we were the last boat on that quay, so any other boats would have to be further up. I walked until I came to a rusty old gate in a chain link fence. I couldn't find a way around it, so it seemed my adventure was over. The next thing I knew, a group of old Scottish yardbirds came up to the gate. It was a very surreal moment. I greeted them through the fence, and we had a conversation. Well...I had a conversation. I could only make out one out of every three or four words they were saying. Standing in the dark, raw night, I played an impromptu game of charades with these old locals until we understood each other. I finally got them to understand that I wanted to visit some British boats to see my comrades. They finally got me to understand that all I had to do was open the gate and walk right through. The boats were "that-a-way". I might be so kind as to close the gate behind me.

So, maybe it wasn't a lost cause after all. I walked further down the quay. I soon came to the low, dark and familiar profile of a Valiant class nuclear fast attack submarine. It looked like a sleeping whale as it wallowed at the ends of its mooring lines. Jackpot!! I walked over to the Topside Watch, and explained my mission. He was very good natured about the whole thing. He walked over to the intercom, and said in true British fashion,

"Below-decks about?"

An unintelligible squawk came over the speaker.

"You're in luck, mate!"

I waited a few minutes, and another sailor came up through the hatch. He came over, shook my hand and introduced himself. He welcomed me aboard HMS Courageous. He was to be my tour guide. He led me to the hatch, and we went below.

It's amazing how different another submarine can smell, and yet at the same time, smell so similar. The basic goblins that haunt the lives of American sub sailors, apparently moonlight for other navies. Present were the same odors -

sweat, oil, steam, food, atmospheric cleansing chemicals. He started the tour in the Torpedo Room, where we entered. It seemed strange to see torpedoes with exposed screws, almost a throwback to World War Two. The space had the same "cluttered functionality" of the Skipjack. As we walked through their boat, we constantly compared notes and experiences. It was like two long lost brothers being reunited for the first time.

The similarities between their boat and ours came to an abrupt end. We had arrived at the Senior Ratings Mess. I looked around. Framed centerfolds were plastered all over the walls! My host noticed my state of shock. I turned to him,

"Where do I sign on!"

It got better. The sailors sat at round pub tables with tall stools. The stools were spare beer kegs with cushions on top. Wait a minute!! Kegs? Yes, kegs. The Senior Ratings have beer on tap! From there we went to the Junior Ratings Mess. No pub tables. No centerfolds. But, they still had beer. We sat down with a few off watch sailors. One came over with several cans of beer. The brand was John Courage. Only fitting for the HMS Courageous, I noted. They quickly corrected me. Their military was just like mine. John Courage was the lowest bidder.

They handed me a can. For cheap Royal Navy beer, it sure hit the spot. Apparently it hit the spot a little *too* well. One of the Brits looked at me for a second, and said,

"You haven't had a beer in a while, have you?"

"No. We've been at sea for a while."

"Well, now. Since there are other submarines here to tour, we'll let you get another one from them. We don't want you walking off the quay into the loch. Bad for public relations and all that."

Everyone got a laugh out of that. I stayed a little longer, and then looked at my watch. Time was getting short. I needed to move along before everyone went to bed. The Below-decks Watch escorted me back up to the brow. After a few parting words with their Topside Watch I was on my way.

A little further down the quay was a shape I recognized instantly. If the Courageous was a whale, then this was a scaly old dinosaur. Sitting there in the dark, looking like an ancient predator, was an Oberon class diesel boat. This was going to be interesting! The Oberons were as much a fixture of the Cold War as anything else. They were reputed to be the quietest conventional submarines in the western world. To those in the proper circles, their exploits were legendary; their silence allowing them to get into all kinds of places no sane man would want to go.

I got to the brow, and discovered just how interesting this was going to be. This wasn't just any Oberon. I was looking at HMS Oracle! Oracle was the boat used as a teaching platform for the Royal Navy's prospective submarine commanding officer school, more widely and infamously known as The Perisher. I knew about The Perisher. Seeing the Oracle was akin to a Greek Mythology fan spotting the Argonaut.

A few words about The Perisher would be appropriate. The Perisher is arguably the most difficult program a submarine officer can endure. Every Royal Navy submarine captain must make it through this guided tour of hell in order to prove themselves worthy of being given a submarine and crew of their very own. Many prospective captains from UK affiliated countries also go through this program. The failure rate is notoriously high. But by far the worst part is the fact that a failed candidate will never set foot on a submarine again. They will be relegated to the surface fleet for the remainder of their naval career. For a dedicated submarine sailor, this is even worse than the burden of enduring the lifelong stigma of being a "Failed Perisher".

The program is known for resulting in nervous breakdowns, divorces, and numerous other problems for failed candidates, and even a few successes.

When I finally recovered from my Oracle induced rapture, I asked for a tour. It almost didn't happen, but the very fact that I knew what Perisher was pushed things in the right direction. The tour began, as usual, in the forward Torpedo Room. As we moved aft, we encountered more off duty members of the crew. Conversations sprouted as I moved from one compartment to the next, and I was introduced to more and more people.

I noticed right away how cramped Oracle was, even compared to my own little old jalopy. It felt more like a World War Two U-boat than a modern submarine. But what struck me most were the sleeping arrangements. Or really, the lack thereof. As I walked from bow to stern, I noticed that racks were stuck in virtually any location big enough to accommodate one. On American boats, even old ones, berthing is located in designated spaces. They may not be luxurious spaces, but they are purpose built none the less. Overflow berthing is accommodated in the torpedo room on folding racks called "trice-up" racks that fold up and out of the way when not in use.

Not so on the "O" boats, as they were called. Sure, there were dedicated berthing spaces, especially for officers and senior ratings. But, a junior crew member or visitor could find themselves sleeping virtually anywhere. As we continued aft from the Operations Compartment to the Engine Room, we passed through a narrow corridor. Set into the bulkhead on the port side, was a solitary rack. Racks like this were spread throughout the boat. It almost seemed as though the designers said,

"Oh, wait! There's a little bit of room right there! Freddie, put one right…there."

Our tour concluded in the aft Torpedo Room. My guide, the small group who tagged along to talk, and I slipped into the cramped, narrow Mess for…you guessed it…a beer. Our questions and storytelling continued for another half hour or so. Then I noticed they were looking at me a bit funny. We all stopped talking for a few seconds. When I started up again, I realized what the issue was. My speech was getting very slurred! As far as these guys knew, this was the effect of one beer. They were taken aback by the lightweights being allowed to serve on American submarines. I quickly clarified the situation,

"Oh, I was over on Courageous before I came here."

That brought quick, awkward responses of "Ah…right." and "That explains it."

Finally I had to bid my new friends goodnight. The walk back to the boat was much easier because I now knew my way around, somewhat. It was substantially more difficult, however, because the ground had gone all wobbly for some strange reason. Finally, I saw the familiar face of Brian Jovanovich, our Topside watch. But, this time he had company. Sitting on the concrete curbing next to the brow, was a soldier. I got closer and realized he was a young Royal Marine. He was wearing the typical British battle uniform, complete with beret. He was holding the universally recognized British L1A1 SLR (Self Loading Rifle) at the non-confrontational ready position, as seen in the gazillion-and-one news stories about Belfast on the nightly news.

I got to the brow, and decided it would be a good idea to talk to him. I didn't get the opportunity to shoot the breeze with foreign military types very often. As I got to the brow, I casually said,

"Hey, how's it going? You pulled sentry duty tonight, huh?"

The Marine silently turned to Brian with a subtle questioning look. Brian said,

"He's okay."

The Marine looked back at me, and gave a slight nod of recognition. I smiled and looked at Brian. He quietly said,

"Smitty...don't talk to him."

It was later that I learned the difference between British policy and ours when it came to security. Our Topside and Pier Sentry watches carried weapons. Topside carried a Colt 1911 .45 pistol. The pistol was in the holster on one side, and the clip of ammo was in a little pouch on the other side. This is, of course, completely useless from a security standpoint. The so-called logic employed here was that the firing of the weapon should be a deliberate act, requiring several steps. This would, in theory, remove any chance of unintended discharge of the weapon. Supposedly, while the sailor was:

1) removing the pistol from its holster
2) removing the loaded clip from its pouch
3) inserting the clip into the pistol
4) cycling the slide to chamber a round

he would have ample time to realize that the terrorist he was about to shoot in the head was, in fact, his XO.

The same applied to the Pier Sentry Watch. He carried a twelve gauge shotgun. The rounds were in a pouch on the watch's belt. Unlike the Topside Watch, he would have to load his five rounds one at a time before pumping the fore grip to chamber a round.

These procedures were intended to make the discharge of a weapon a "conscious and deliberate act". Supposedly, stories circulated about our watches opening fire on approaching violent protestors, and arrogant Admirals refusing to display proper I.D. A sentry actually doing his job was apparently a very disturbing thought in the Pentagon. The British took an entirely different and much more practical approach to this issue. It revolved around this basic philosophy,

"If we can't trust you with a loaded weapon, we're not going to let you *have one*, no matter *when* you load it."

In hind sight, I have to come to two conclusions. First, considering the nature of some of my activities toward the end of my naval career, it's probably a good thing our watches didn't have loaded weapons. Secondly, violent protesters threatening vessels carrying nuclear weapons and arrogant Admirals refusing to follow regulations actually fall into the same group, and should both be shot anyway. To this end, the Royal Marine sitting at the end of our brow was carrying a fully loaded weapon, with a round in the chamber. His finger was resting on the frame of the weapon, just above the trigger. What was keeping him from errantly shooting his best friend who probably owed him drink money? It's simple. The gun's safety was on. And, he had a functioning brain.

The next day was spent on the boat. I had the duty, and it was someone else's turn to explore our surroundings. I spent the day standing Shutdown Roving Watch, and buttoning up the diesel with another machinist, Keith Albans. The time came to refill the lube oil sump with fresh, clean oil. The next few hours were spent sitting in an awkward position on the deck, next to the diesel, turning a pathetic little hand crank until our arms fell off. Finally, the job was done. They really should find an easier way to do that. Maybe an adapter for a hand drill or something.

The rest of the day was spent hanging around the boat, talking and drinking coffee. The conversation revolved around the escapades of the previous night. Listening to these stories had a very predictable effect. I really, really needed to take some leave before we left Scotland. Later that evening, I ran into Chief Jardin. I asked him if I could have two days leave, starting tomorrow. He stopped and thought, going through a mental checklist of equipment status, maintenance, and watch bills.

"Sure…I can't see why not. It won't be tomorrow, it'll have to be the day after."

My leave couldn't start the next day, but I found myself on a chartered Royal Navy bus anyway. A group of us signed on for the daytrip to Edinburgh. As the bus tooled along through the Scottish Landscape, I flipped back and forth between taking in the beautiful scenery, and being shocked out of it by noticing we were on the wrong side of the road. Finally, we arrived in Edinburgh.

I got off the bus, and as it drove away I turned around. The first thing a saw was Edinburgh Castle. It was a life changing moment. It wasn't a Disney castle. It wasn't a little wooden playground castle. It was a real castle, centuries upon centuries old. Here was a truly historic place where real royalty lived, experienced the cutting edge of primitive life, wielded their power, held lavish banquets, and chopped other peoples' heads off. I stood there in awe, just taking this sight in.

Finally I realized I would need to look at something else. I slowly looked around myself. This was the first time I'd ever stood in the middle of a truly foreign city. It was really pretty daunting. The only similarity to any previous experience was that everything was still in English. I was startled out of my surreal bubble by a little old lady. When I say little old lady, I mean *very* little and *very* old. She was wrapped up in a shawl one would expect to see in Scotland. She had a pleasant but pointed little face, a curly poof of snow white hair, and small thick glasses.

In her thick Scottish brogue, she began talking quickly, pointing out and giving directions to anything of interest. If I went down this road, I'd find that museum. Around that corner was this or the other pub. She went on for a few minutes. When she was finished, I very politely said,

"Well, thank you very much. That's all very useful information. But, what I really need right now is a bank."

She looked at me as if I asked for shoes when I was already wearing them.

"Oh! Well, the bank is right there!"

Sure enough, directly in front of me was The Royal Bank of Scotland. Not only was it right in front of me, it was labeled with a huge sign with huge lit up blue letters. I thanked her, and went in to get a Visa advance in British pounds.

On the way, I realized I was by myself. This was something we were specifically told not to do. The briefing we received before being turned loose on Scotland was very clear on one thing: Everyone knows where you're from. Everyone knows who you are. Everyone knows what you do. If you're found in the wrong place at the wrong time, you're going to disappear. The Soviets would just love to get their hands on an American submariner.

Luckily for me, on the way out of the bank I saw one of the guys from Seaman Gang in the same position as me. We decided to pair up for the evening. He quickly realized he would be better off with the Soviets. It became my mission to find some authentic fish and chips. As we tromped around Edinburgh, I dragged him into restaurant after restaurant to see their fish and chips. At one point we went into a department store to have a look around. One of the men working there was dressed very professionally, in a very professional looking kilt. I started a long and involved conversation with him about kilts. It was then that my shipmate quietly slipped away. I can only assume he decided to try and find some Soviets. I never did find my fish and chips. That's just my luck. Here I am in the middle of Scotland, and I can't find a decent plate of fish and chips. I had to settle for a milkshake. And…a lesson in Scottish.

As I walked down the street, I saw a fast food restaurant. Maybe some Scottish fast food would fit the bill. My prospects plummeted as I scanned the menu. Nothing I recognized seemed overly palatable. I settled for a milkshake. For 87p I could have a milkshake. I was getting pretty hungry by then, and it seemed as though it would be a milkshake or an unfortunate rat in some alley. The milkshake won out.

The young girl behind the counter handed me the milkshake. Then she said something that struck me as odd,

"87p, please. Take it away or set in?"

I stood and stared. I thought I'd heard her correctly, but there was no way I could have. Maybe it was the accent. Maybe I was tired. She stood and stared back. She found herself in a bizarre Mexican standoff, with nothing but a counter between her and a crazed Yank. Finally, I broke the awkward silence,

"What?"

"I said, take it away or set in."

"Okay, I know you're trying to tell me something, but I have no idea what it is."

With exaggerated patience, she explained the phrase she had said hundreds of times that day with absolutely no problems. Until now.

"Do you want me to put it in a *bag,* so you can *take* it *away* and have it somewhere *else*…or do you want to sit *down* and have it *here?*"

It suddenly clicked. I knew exactly what she was saying. My face brightened as I said,

"Oh! You mean for here or to go!"

She stared at me blankly. The line was building up behind me.

"What?"

"Never mind. Take it away. Take it away."

She smiled as she handed the shake over, either because smiling was her job or because she was genuinely relieved the ordeal was all over. I looked at my watch and realized the bus would be back soon. I sucked down the shake as I made my way to the spot where we had originally arrived. My day in Edinburgh was anticlimactic, but it was a day in Edinburgh none the less.

My leave started the next day, after several hours of delay. It left me feeling as if I was abandoned barking at the end of my chain. It all turned out for the best though. I ended up leaving at the same time as a few other guys, and I was able to share their cab. As we made our way down the winding back roads to Helensburgh, one solitary goal filled my mind.

I was hearing one term more and more often over the last few months: Bed & Breakfast. The concept was very appealing, for a number of reasons. A homey atmosphere. No noise. A home cooked breakfast, my favorite meal of the day. Spending time with locals. This could only be a win. Even better, B &Bs were getting more and more popular. These things were popping up all over the place. This was going to be easy!

The first omen was the weather. The singular element that kept Scottish meteorologists securely employed was coming down in a soft drizzle as we got into the cab. In the time it took to careen down the narrow Scottish roads to Helensburgh, it had turned into a hard steady rain. By the time I got out of the cab, it was a torrent.

The second omen was the timing. As we piled out of the cab, I noticed almost all of the shops were already closed. The streets were empty. Only one was open, a liquor store. I fumbled through my pound notes to get my share of the fare, thanked the driver as I closed the door, and headed for the dim fluorescent lighting. By the time I slogged through the downpour and rushed into the store, I was soaked to the skin. My jacket, a cheap "Members Only" knock-off, was plastered to my skin like a wet t-shirt. My hair was pounded flat, and my drenched glasses were beginning to fog over. What a sight I must have made for the two early middle aged women behind the counter. My first words couldn't have helped much,

"I need a place to stay!"

The two ladies looked at each other with expressions that clearly asked which one of them was closest to the phone. I must have looked for all the world like a desperate fugitive.

Quickly, I spewed out my story of how my submarine had pulled into Faslane, I managed to get a couple of days leave, and I wanted to stay at a B & B. Their next words caught me completely off guard,

"I don't think you'll find one here."

I asked if they were joking. That started a dialogue between the two of them.

"We had a few of them close."

"They might be out of rooms."

"Wait! Isn't there a new one?"

"Ooooh, yes! But it's very nice"

"They might be booked up."

"It's bound to be expensive. It's brand new."

I ensured them it didn't matter, if they could only tell me where it was. That started an entirely new conversation.

"What's it called?"

"Oh, I don't know. The Sicilian?"

"Why on Earth would they call it that? This isn't London!"

"I don't know!! I'm guessing! Maybe it's the Cincinnati."

"Oh! Now, you're just saying that because he's a yank! Wait…it starts with an S."

"Sin…sin…"

"Sinclair House!! The Sinclair House! That's what it is."

I asked them if they could tell me how to find it. That started a whole new argument between the two. They garbled out directions, constantly contradicting each other and trying to talk over each other. I gratefully held up a hand and thanked them for their help and understanding. I was able to gather that the Yellow Brick Road was a left turn up a hill. I went back out into the pounding rain.

I took my first left. It was up a hill. It was getting late, and I wondered if alleys in Helensburgh were nice and homey. It was even odds I'd be sleeping in one. Up the hill I went. I got to a patch of the road that was unlit. The pavement was a little broken. Things were looking bad. I kept going, mostly because I really didn't have much else to do, or any better leads to follow. A few more steps wouldn't make the difference between where I'd sleep if things went totally bad.

I couldn't believe my eyes. A large house sat on the left hand side of the road. There was a light over the door, with a small sign. I didn't even bother to read it. I rang the doorbell. What did I have to lose? If it *was* the Sinclair House I'd find out soon enough if I had a place to sleep. If not…well, maybe they could give me directions or take pity on me and let me crash on their couch.

A man came to the door. He was middle aged, balding, a little heavy, wearing trousers and a sweater. I really hoped that was what a Scottish inn keeper looked like. He looked at me as if I was the drowned rat I actually was.

"Can I help you?"

"Is this the Sinclair House?"

'Yes."

Yes!! Payday! Now if only my luck would hold...

"Do you have any rooms?"

PLEASE, PLEASE, OH PLEASE...

"Yes, we do."

"How much are they?"

He looked at me with an expression that asked if I was in any position to haggle.

"Twelve pounds a night."

"Really?"

"Yes."

"*With* breakfast?"

"Yes."

"I'll take it!"

I couldn't believe my luck! I actually found the Sinclair House, against all odds. They actually had a room for me. For twelve pounds. Twelve pounds!! That was eighteen US dollars. He led me inside. He showed me my room. I asked where I could take a shower. He showed me the bathroom I would share with another room. I asked when I should pay, and he told me it was tomorrow.

I threw my little bag with my toiletries and fresh clothes on a chair. I stripped out of my soaking wet clothes. I grabbed a towel, wrapped it around my waist, and peaked cautiously out of my room down the hall. The coast was clear. I went into the bathroom, and proceeded to take a nice, long

Hollywood shower. I scrubbed the submarine smell and Scottish rain off my body, head to toe.

I went back to my room, and changed into my fresh clothes. I happily noticed they only smelled a little like a submarine. I went back down to the TV room. Several other couples were already there. As soon as I stepped into the room, all the "Yank alarms" went off. I gave everyone a very humble and pleasant greeting, and spent the next few minutes answering questions about where I was from, what I did, how I got there, and what my plans were.

We finished up just in time to watch the end of a game show. It was very homey. Then it was time for one of their evening dramas. It was reputed to be quite scandalous. It was very homey. I figured out that was what I was probably in for over the next couple of days. I wasn't very put out.

After watching a couple of hours of TV, we all decided it was time to turn in. We all wished each other pleasant dreams. I returned to my room and collapsed into my bed. It was soft, warm, quiet and solitary. After all the rubbish I went through that evening, I was absolutely exhausted. I wasn't awake for long. I don't even think I dreamed.

I let the sun wake me up the next morning. I woke up and looked at my watch. 8am. I decided I could lay in for a while. I let myself relax. I savored the soft, warm cocoon in which I was wrapped. It was so nice, so peaceful, so soothing, sooooo peaceful.

It was my stomach that finally urged me out of bed. I hadn't eaten since lunch the previous day. My belly was barking for food. I got up, got dressed, and went downstairs. I was looking forward to a nice big heavy breakfast. The innkeeper greeted me with a smile, since he now also knew I wasn't a fugitive. I peeked around the corner into the dining room. It was a little difficult to see what was going on. I could only tell people were eating and talking. A TV chattered on in the background.

The inn keeper said,

"There's cereal and milk over there. Help yourself."

Cereal? Really? I was really hoping for more. I was hoping for eggs, toast, sausage, maybe some tea. I sighed. Well, I might as well get my money's worth. Maybe I was being too optimistic for twelve pounds a night. I found a seat at an empty table. I poured myself the largest bowl of Cornies I possibly could. I added the milk, and started to eat.

I had gotten about halfway through the Cornies when he came back with a pot of tea, along with a little pitcher of milk and bowl of sugar. Maybe things weren't so bad. I was getting my tea after all. I made myself a cup. It was really good tea. I'd finished the cereal and started my second cup of tea when he came back again.

"Does eggs, sausage, and toast sound good?"

I froze. What was he trying to say? Was he giving me grief because of the size of my bowl of cereal? Had I done something wrong? Had he changed his mind about me being a fugitive? It took a few seconds, but I finally realized he was telling me what they had for breakfast. Apparently, the cereal was only intended as a starter.

"Oh, that would be great! Thank you very much."

I couldn't believe my luck. I was going to get a real breakfast. I now had no place to put it, but I was going to get it anyway. He brought a rack of roast, along with butter and marmalade. The toast was toast, but the marmalade was incredible. Next came a plate of sausage and eggs. I was starting to think Bed & Brunch might be a better name for this place.

The conversation had died down, and the room began to pay more attention to the TV. A morning show named Breakfast Time was on, very similar to Good Morning America. The hosts said something about the next guest coming up. After the break, they would be speaking to an American feminist. I should have taken that as a warning, complete with flashing lights and blaring siren. Oh, no. The day just wouldn't be complete without me being the solitary awkward American in the room.

The commercials were over, along with any chance of me avoiding the devastation soon to come. Out stomps the American feminist. At first it wasn't so bad. Then she got down to business, describing exactly how lousy the British were at being American feminists. Then she went right for the jugular,

"Here's a prime example. You people finally get a female Prime Minister. And, what do you call her? Maggie!"

"But, what's wrong with that?"

"It's demeaning!"

The hosts tried to smooth things over. An angry mob with flaming torches could form very, very quickly in that part of the world. They probably still run drills for that sort of thing, complete with stopwatches. Sadly, angry mobs with flaming torches hadn't been covered by insurance for years now. Even those who didn't like her referred to Margret Thatcher as if she were a deranged yet lovable aunt. Perhaps an explanation of their old tried and true traditions,

"But you don't understand. That's the way we are. We give our leaders affectionate nicknames. We've always done that."

"*I don't care!! It's DEMEANING!!*"

Ever so slowly, every eye in that room turned to look at me. Uh…oh. The angry mob with flaming torches was sending a committee headed this way! I had a mouth full of food, but desperate times called for desperate measures. I swallowed some large bits of something without chewing, and blurted out,

"We're not all like that! She's an idiot. Please divert your angry mob with flaming torches!"

I didn't actually say that last bit. But, I sure was thinking it. I tried to be as endearing as I was the previous night, and replace a bad memory with good. I finished up the last of my breakfast. I happily handed over my twelve pounds, and started my day long exploration of Helensburgh. It was going to be much better than last night. The ground was still wet from the soaking it got overnight. But, gleaming off the wet pavement and countless puddles, was the *sun*.

I decided to make it my mission to see as many sights, browse through as many shops, and converse with as many people as I could. The hardest part would be the walking. For a small village, there sure was a lot to see. There weren't a lot of people to talk to, but those there were turned out to be very friendly. If they have the time, British people love to talk. I wandered from place to place, my deliberately unhurried pace allowing me to take it all in. Every now and again I would stand for a while, facing into the crisp wind coming from off the loch. I thought of the stifling Engine Room. If only I could take some of this with me.

Helensburgh had a small department store, and a decent sized supermarket. I spent a lot of time in those two shops. Browsing through everyday items was more of a guide to the nature of the locals than a travel brochure. I bought a model kit in the department store, and talked to the locals about the produce at the supermarket. I bought souvenirs for my Mom and Dad, and searched for hours for a little special something for Yvette.

The last thing I expected to see thousands of miles from home…was home. But there it was. A little after lunch time, I stumbled across this little bakery. Figuring the Scots had to be good at baking *something*, I figured I'd have a look. I walked in. The lady behind the counter pegged me right away as American. We started talking, and I started looking around for something to eat. She mentioned haggis cakes. I was tempted. But I'd heard the only way to try haggis, and have one's taste buds survive, was to have it fresh. I declined. We were still talking when I saw something I never thought I'd see outside of my Mom's kitchen…

A stack of SODA FARLS!

Many people have heard of Irish soda bread. By this day and age, it's even served in some restaurants. But, it's always in the form of a loaf, traditionally called a "Bannek". Slices are cut off the loaf to make sandwiches or toast. But, in Northern Ireland soda bread is often baked in the form of an enlarged version of an English muffin, called a "Farl". Farls are split like an English muffin to be toasted or used for a sandwich.

Before I could stop myself, I pointed and shouted,

"Oh, my God! You've got soda farls!!"

With shock every bit the equal of mine, she exclaimed,

"Oh, my God! You know what those are!"

After I had recovered my composure, I told her about how my Mom grew up in Belfast. I told her how I was raised on soda farls baked by my Mom, as she was raised on her mother's homemade farls. She listened to my story with a bright grin on her face. Soon I was walking out the door with a split and buttered farl.

Soon the daylight was fading. As I stood looking out on the loch, I heard a voice calling my name. One of the guys was standing at the open door to a pub across the street. He waved me over as he stepped inside. I followed him in, and found myself in a very typical Scottish pub. Cigarette and pipe smoke hung in the air. People were perched precariously on bar stools crowded much too close together. The bartender was busy pulling pints, pouring small glasses of scotch, and mixing the occasional martini for the local eccentrics. Guys from the boat were dispersed through the crowd, buying drinks and chatting with the locals. The din of conversation all but drowned out the music coming from some indistinguishable location.

I found a rare empty stool and claimed it. I looked up and down the bar. Glasses filled with the usual list of suspects sat there in various states that could keep an optimist and pessimist arguing for days. One thing quickly drew my attention. Some of the people had large angular pilsner type glasses in front of them. The color of the liquid in them was like the reddish brown hue of maple syrup. A faint hint of a head lingered on top. I waved the bartender over.

"Wha' would y' like, laddie?"

I asked him what was in the glasses. He told me it was cider. That was the first time I'd ever heard of fermented cider. It looked too good to pass up. I ordered one. It was unlike anything I'd ever tasted before. The flavor was just incredible. No cider in this country has ever come anywhere close to it. It had this wonderfully smooth taste of what can only be described as what would result if a barrel of rum, a cask of brandy, and an apple tree had an orgy, and a child. One could only speculate on who the father was.

That first glass went down very quickly. I called to the bartender and asked for another one. He brought it, along with a brief lecture about caution and bad surprises. I sat with my glass and looked around. I finally figured out where the music was coming from. Against the wall next to the door, was what looked like a video game. It had buttons all over it, and a large screen. I watched someone walk over to it, slide some coins into a slot, and push some buttons. The screen came to life, and began playing what I instantly recognized as a video for a recent popular song by Dire Straits.

I asked the bartender what it was. He told me it was the latest fad for pubs lately. It was a video jukebox. For 50p, it would play the video for any song in its library. The selection wasn't huge, but the novelty could keep it in business for a while. My eyes became glued to this technological wonder. I asked for some change...and another cider.

"Are y' sure, laddie?"

I waved away his concern. I wasn't even feeling the first two yet. He walked away with a wry smile and some comment about that being exactly the problem. I have no real idea how long I watched and put money in this thing. The songs all blurred together, with the expert help of another cider. Finally, the moment had to come. The guys were ready to leave. The cab was waiting. I downed the last of my last cider, waved goodbye to all my new friends, and jumped down off my stool.

No one had the courtesy to inform me that the floor had been removed from beneath my stool. One would think that was the neighborly thing to do for someone who had been drinking deceptively mild beverages the entire evening. I mean, wouldn't international relations come into play at some point? I contemplated the funny feeling that came with acceleration due to gravity. The feeling of floating in space was lasting a curiously long time. I was shocked out of my existential reverie by the sudden *deceleration* due to the floor. I was aware of a sudden silence, then the sound of laughing Scotsmen. The round curious face of the bartender peeked over the side of the bar, which was strangely where I thought the floor should be. I absent-mindedly wondered if that might be the problem. I could hear his voice coming from a distance,

"Are y' a' reet, laddie?"

My friends came over and carefully lifted me back into a vertical position. I felt hands bracing me up like a rocket at NASA. Voices asked me if I was okay. I told them all I was. They all held me very still, and then all pulled their hands away, to see if I would stay upright. I stayed upright. See? I told you guys the cider couldn't beat me. Having found the floor that someone cleverly tried to steal from me, I followed the rest out the door to the cab.

It has often been said that there are no atheists in foxholes. Foxholes are, as I was about to learn, where atheists go when they feel they're not quite up to a Scottish cab ride. Our cabbie used an Audi for his vehicle of choice. Apparently, it had a very powerful engine. Apparently, our cabbie was quite fond of using it. The scenery changed quickly from a curbside in Scotland to something one might expect to see when making the jump to hyperspace. Roads, streetlights, fences, cars, and terrorized sheep became a dim multicolored blur.

I was sitting in the middle of the back seat, so I had the perfect view of the scene of our almost certain demise, *and* the speedometer. Out of morbid curiosity, I looked over the driver's shoulder to read the speedometer. It was steady at seventy five. *Seventy five!!* On this little twisty turny road? With rocks, and poles, and water all around? That can't be right! No one would be that crazy. I must be reading it wrong. I must have been looking at seventy five *kilometers* per hour. Yes, that must be it. That makes much more sense. That would make it forty five *miles* per hour. I should look once more just to make sure. I should, in fact, have *not* looked again. It was, in fact, seventy five *miles* per hour.

Many people say that a feeling of peace and acceptance washes over you when you realize you're probably about to die. That's a load of tripe! The only thing that washed over me was an ominous sweat. The only feeling I had was that of my head bouncing into the ceiling of the Audi that would soon be my expensive, German made funeral pyre. Apart from the whining of the engine, and the occasional screech of the tires, that was the quietest cab ride of my life. Little did I know, the roads and cabbies of Scotland would be tame in comparison to its seas, as I would later learn.

Early the next morning, we bade good bye to the bonnie land of Scotland. The howling wind was a harbinger of things to come. We slowly made our way down the loch, swaying softly in the heavy wind. The transit to the Atlantic Ocean took about ninety minutes. When we reached the open sea, things quickly changed. The North Atlantic has always had a reputation for being extremely rough, especially in winter. Vessels of any size have a rough time, but it's especially hard on submarines. The trials of Germany's U-boats in the First and Second World Wars were legendary. The North Atlantic was an area in which they loitered. Fifty meter seas were common. That means the waves were fifty meters high from trough to crest. Fifty meters is between 150 and 160 feet. Do the math. The waves were often well over the height of a ten story building.

Being a student of military history, concentrating on submarine warfare, I was familiar with the conditions we might be facing. Not even that could prepare me for the difficulties we faced. The boat began taking heavy rolls almost right away. People began getting seasick, only this time it was as if they really meant it. One of our electricians was pushed to the point of passing out. I was relieved of my station for Maneuvering Watch. The only place any sane man would be in weather like this was their rack. I wedged myself in, and tried to get some sleep. Just as I fell asleep, the boat took a forty five degree roll. Out I went, sliding across the deck into the opposite bulkhead. I climbed back in and tried to make myself more secure. It happened again. I finally found a way to wedge my feet under the mattress, and tuck my arms between the mattress and frame. I finally fell asleep. I was awakened by the boat rolling over, and feeling as if it had run into a huge granite wall. I was about to curse the weather gods and go back to sleep, when I heard two very alarming things. One was the Chief of the Watch yelling over the 1MC,

"Check shut the Battery Well hatch!"

The other was the sound of rushing water. I leaned out of my rack and looked up the ladder to Ops Middle Level. A torrent of water poured down the ladder from the Control Room to Middle Level, and headed straight down the ladder to the Battery Well. If the seawater got into the battery, it would react with the battery acid and produce chlorine gas. Chlorine gas is poisonous. Breathing it is fatal. Many crewmen wouldn't get to emergency air in time. Those people would be dead. There was only seconds left. As the water neared the bottom of the ladder, another crewman ripped his mattress out of his rack, and dove on the hatch.

 Soon other people were piling mattresses around the hatch. More people began dragging foam mattresses up to the Control Room. The frantic call came down for more mattresses. Deciding to make our mattresses out of cheap foam rubber had finally paid off. They made excellent sponges. The flow of seawater from above finally stopped. Crewmen bolted from one compartment to another, tracing the flow of the water, trying to keep it away from anything critical or anything that could short out and catch fire.

Now the laborious process of hauling these waterlogged mattresses back aft became our top priority. Man handling these huge sopping wet blocks of foam rubber through the tight confines of the "knee buster" watertight hatches was quite a problem, but we eventually figured out a system. Once they were back aft where the wet bilges were, they could be rung out.

Now we had an engine room filled with damp mattresses. What to do? Someone decided the best way to dry them out was to hang them over the turbines and steam piping. Soon the engine room was transformed into a mattress lover's Hanging Garden of Babylon. The humidity immediately soared. It was obvious the Engineering Spaces were going to have their own weather for the transit back across the Atlantic.

The Captain immediately determined the "100 fathom curve" rule wasn't so crucial. He asked for a sounding, and quickly determined we were close enough. We dived. Now we were where we were supposed to be during weather like this. The Brits had a clever little saying for this,

"Happiness is 400 feet in a force ten gale."

This time, even submerging wasn't a relief. At 400 feet, we were still taking twenty degree rolls. It wasn't until we had room to increase our depth to 700 feet that we had any relief. I was to later find out the seas were worse that day in the North Atlantic than they were when we surfaced in the middle of Hurricane Gloria. The difference? That day off the coast of Scotland, there was no hurricane. That was just their typical winter weather.

But, here's the most unusual aspect of all this. We used a lot of mattresses to sop up all that water. Those mattresses were all now hanging back in Engine Room Upper Level. That meant a lot of sailors were sleeping in empty mattress pans. Stainless steel isn't very comfortable. I was still a very junior crew member at that point. Yet, I had a complete, intact rack the entire way back. How the fuck did *that* happen? Did everyone just forget that I had a rack with a mattress? It would be easier to explain Jimmy Swaggart, the Grand Unified Theory, or Sweden's tax codes…than how I ended up with a cozy rack while senior members slept on metal.

I'm just saying…

Chapter 15-

No, really...what am I doing here?

If fate decrees that I should fail, then fate will not have watched my tail.

-inscription on the side of a Hawker Typhoon fighter on D-Day, June 6, 1944

When I arrived on U.S.S. Skipjack, the sting of S1C was still good and fresh. The feeling that no matter what I did, it would turn out bad, was always in the back of my mind. The end result was that I postponed any involvement with the boat as long as possible. What had started out as a proud dream had become a waking night mare.

The boat pulled in shortly before the weekend. Tom and I reported aboard, and met our superiors. We were told the boat was going into "Cold Wet Layup", a long term idle condition used with PWRs (Pressurized Water Reactors). I instantly turned to Tom,

"You can do it. I need to go home to attend to some business."

The Engineer looked at me with puzzlement.

"You know, this is something guys usually fight over. This doesn't happen very often."

I quickly stuttered,

"I'm sorry, sir. I'm not usually like this. But, these matters are very important. If at all possible, I need to clear them up this weekend."

The important *business* was getting the hell off Skipjack and back home. The Engineer said he understood. I got the weekend off. I was able to postpone hell for a few more days. I went back home that Friday night. The weekend was good, but knowing I would have to eventually return to Groton loomed over me like a dark cloud of piss.

Sunday night finally arrived. I drove back to the base. Monday morning dawned, and I steeled myself for the failure that would surely come. I reported aboard for quarters. The routine began. Quarters in the morning. Then work assignments. If the work was finished, we could study for quals. Lunch and dinner were spliced in where there was room. At quitting time, if we met the curve on quals, we could leave. If not, we stayed on board until we got some signatures on our qual card. The next day, we would start it all over again.

The next twist in the road was duty days. We ran a three section duty schedule. Every third day I would be required to remain on board from 0700 to 0700 the next day, at which point we'd be relieved by the next section taking over the duty for their own twenty four hours. Many of these days were spent awake the entire time. There was always something to repair, maintain, or calibrate. There was always cleaning to do. There were always watches to stand. And, the ever present pressure to qualify.

As bad as they could be, the duty days were sometimes a blessing in disguise. Sleep was replaced with time when the only thing to do was study. I quickly learned how I would fit quals *and* work into the same period of time S1C gave for quals *alone*.

I would simply forfeit sleep.

I found myself slipping into the routine. I was able to stick to the same program, and achieve the same results for the same requirements.

But just barely.

Learning and retaining the vast amount of knowledge required to qualify in submarines was an almost insurmountable task. If I learned something, I quickly forgot it. It took enormous amounts of concentration to learn even simple procedures. Operating parameters were a little easier, if I spent copious amounts of time memorizing them over and over. Even when I *did* learn something, I would question it repeatedly, sure in the knowledge that I had done it wrong. All these elements ensured that my performance would lag behind the others.

Which only served to remind me that I had already failed.

It was then I also discovered I was dyslexic. Reading wasn't a problem, but numbers were a major obstacle. And, as if that wasn't bad enough, I couldn't tell my left from my right! I remain like that to this day. I'm so bad with this, people who ride with me often have learned that instead of saying,

"Turn left up here." or "Take your next right."

They point conspicuously and say,

"Go down *that* street." or "Go *that* way at the intersection."

When seeing road signs advising that a lane is closing, I need to imagine myself holding up my hands to see which one makes the "L" for left. Sadly, that is also the reason I felt the need to quit flying lessons. A screw up on the road is one thing. A screw up at 10,000 feet is another matter entirely.

These disabilities caused a number of incidents that were laughed about later, but not at the time. They only reinforced the belief that I needed to analyze and re-analyze every action multiple times. The end result was my looking as if I had frozen, forgotten what to do, or neglected to memorize some critical operating figure. In reality, history was repeating itself. Mentally, I was right back at Knowles. I had come to the correct conclusion, several times over in fact. But I just didn't trust myself to have the right answer.

Others around me joked about my needing better glasses, or how I needed to watch Sesame Street to learn my numbers again, or how we needed to paint the engine room red on the port side, and green on the starboard. That way they could say,

"Petty Officer Smith, shut down the *green* Main Seawater Pump."

I took a fair amount of ribbing for these incidents. That was nothing new. Humor is used quite often for entertainment and reducing the stress or tension of those conditions inherent to submarine duty. Submariners have, and have always had, a very keen, albeit indiscriminate sense of humor. People who screw up are usually the first target of opportunity.

The difference was how I received it. In anyone else's mind, it was just well deserved ribbing. That was how I appeared on the surface. Inside, it was an entirely different matter. Outside, they were laughing *with* me, or making me the butt of a well-earned joke. On the inside, they were laughing *at* me. They were realizing what a loser I was. If I poked fun or abuse at someone else, and the others laughed, it wasn't because I was part of the group. It wasn't because it was simply someone else's turn to attract the dubious attention. It was that I was being *tolerated*. Inside, they were all wondering how a creep like me could feel justified in teasing someone else who was obviously superior to me.

The other weight hanging over my head was the issue of trust. Trust is extremely important on a submarine. A crewman who can't be trusted quickly becomes a liability on a vessel where one bad crewman can kill *everyone*. I quickly became convinced the other crewmen were constantly watching me. It seemed perfectly logical to me that people would watch me discreetly, or follow along behind me to catch and fix any mistakes before they became serious.

The fact of the matter is, even in a critical environment like a submarine, no one is perfect. Mistakes are made. It just happens. There was one major difference between the others and myself. If someone else made a mistake, it was okay. If I made a mistake, no matter how trivial, it was just one more example showing the others that I couldn't be trusted. It was one more example of how much a liability I really was. And, with each error, *everybody* knew it.

It got to the point where I assumed my incompetence was common knowledge. M Div was the legion of the damned, simply because they were the ones saddled with *Smith*. I became convinced I was the subject of every conversation in those compartments where I wasn't present. If I walked into an area, I assumed people were discussing my latest failure. When someone expects to see something, it's much easier for them to interpret what they see to be exactly what they expect. I was seeing exactly what I was expecting.

If the mistakes weren't bad enough, I also had those times when I was actually *right*. In those incidents, it seemed that people didn't notice, or take me seriously. I truly felt as if every mistake was magnified, and every redeeming moment ignored. It only closed another door, another escape route, from the slowly shrinking room of expanding depression. Here are some good examples:

1) Is it my fault that my Dad was a spook? No! Is it my fault that I was a freak, an outlier as a child? No. Is it my fault that I spent hours upon hours with my nose buried in books about Soviet military hardware, when the other boys were reading Sports Illustrated? Not that I know of. So, why was it such a crime when I poked my head into the Wardroom to ask my Division Officer a question? They were in the middle of a "flash card" session on Soviet ship recognition. One of the senior officers was using an overhead projector with slides of various types of warships. He would slap a slide on the projector for a quick instant and pull it away, simulating the quick glimpse one might get through a periscope. Whoever recognized it first would shout out the name. Slap…Kashin! Slap…Kiev! Slap…Moskva! Slap…Kotlin-SAM! Slap…Kanin!

The room fell into a stony silence. The last two had been me. I'd stuck around, and with everyone intent on the screen, no one noticed in the darkened room. The eyes all turned in my direction. The look on my face said "Was I wrong?" The looks on their faces said "Why the fuck are you still here?"

They could have given me a kudos. I would have been happy with a pat on the head and a shoo out the door. Maybe a quick thumbs-up? Nothing doing. No such luck. I felt my face flushing hotly.

"Sorry. I was just leaving."

I allowed myself a brief celebration of my hollow victory. I knew my shit…just as good as they did. I was a typical middle class kid who never joined the Boy Scouts, never played football, and never had a prayer of getting into Annapolis. And I knew their job before they did. What they were learning now, I had learned as a *child*.

2) I spent as much time as possible on the Bridge when we were surfaced. I loved seeing the sky, feeling the wind, enjoying the fresh air. We were transiting out to our dive point on the start of another patrol. We had cast off lines in the morning. We had long since passed Race Rock and Block Island. The 100 fathom curve was approaching. I went to the Bridge for one last time before we submerged. I basked in the brisk fresh air, riding with the subtle rolling of the boat. The squawk of the speaker snapped me out of it,

"Bridge, Plot…radar contact bearing 350, range 20,000 yards. Designating this contact Romeo five. Can you get a visual?"

The Officer of the Deck was Lt. McGuire. He and the Lookout both raised their binoculars. They stared intently for a few seconds. They looked at each other for a moment. Their expressions both said they were coming up blank. I squinted into the distance. All I could see was a white dot on the horizon. I turned to the Lookout and asked if I could use his binoculars. I focused the glasses on the target. It appeared to be playing peek-a-boo with me as our vessel and theirs took turns cresting the waves and sliding down into the troughs.

I finally managed to get a decent look. It seemed pretty obvious to me what our target was. Through the glasses, the dot became a white rectangle. Portals appeared scattered across its front. It was the superstructure of a ship. Why did it look like that? We were viewing it from head on. But, it looked like a building floating across the sea. Why? I caught a glimpse of a black painted bow for just a split second. That's why…she's hull down.

I turned to Mr. McGuire,

"Sir, this may not mean much coming from me, but I think it's a freighter. She's hull down, and her target angle is 000."

McGuire looked at me for a long moment,

"You're right, Smith. It doesn't mean much coming from you."

I gave the Lookout back his binoculars. I shouldn't have even opened my mouth. All I did was make myself look like a pretentious idiot. I decided to remain on the Bridge for a couple more minutes before dropping back down into the stuffy steel tube. The speaker squawked back into life,

"Bridge, Plot…we got a visual on Romeo five. It's a freighter, bearing 345, target angle 005. CPA is 10,000 yards at time three two. She'll cross ahead of us, left to right"

Mr. McGuire didn't even look at me.

3) We were out on a routine mission. I had taken over the Engine Room Upper Level watch. A little while later, we were surprised with a High Chloride Drill. We would need to locate the source of the corrosive compound, and flush out the affected side of the Engine Room.

We quickly narrowed down the source of the leak, and the word was passed,

"Shut down the starboard side of the Engine Room!"

Before I could make a move, another crew member reached out and hit the Emergency Shutdown for the *port* Ship Service Turbine Generator. Chief Jardin immediately noticed the silence coming from the wrong side up the Engine Room. He spun around.

"Smith!! What the fuck did you do!"

I started to point to the port SSTG, my mouth agape. It didn't matter. I didn't even get a word out. It was the first time I saw a Chief Petty Officer split down the middle, and climb out the top of his own head. There was no opportunity to defend myself. Wrong-way Smith had struck again.

4) We were in port, shut down, during a brief upkeep period. It was a typical duty day. The normal routine was cruising along in its typical apathetic manner. I had just finished lunch, and was heading back aft to do some work. I heard a strange sound as I walked through the reactor tunnel. When I got to the hatch leading to Machinery Space Upper Level, I realized it was the muffled sound of a scuffle.

I quickly discovered the source of the noise. One of the off duty Reactor Operators, wearing a conspicuous red hat, was trying to "smash" one of the nuclear instrument panels with a very large wrench. An Electrician was desperately trying to fend him off and subdue him. The RO was playing the part well, looking just like a crazed lunatic, eyes wide and foaming at the mouth.

I sprinted to Engine Room Upper Level. I poked my head into Maneuvering and yelled,

"Security breach!! Security breach, Machinery Space Upper Level!!"

The SRO and an Electrician sat there staring at me, looking as if I just asked for a rat shit pizza. I gave up, and bolted back to subdue the "intruder". The two of us were able to wrestle the man to the ground and disarm him. Right about that time, the Electrician from Maneuvering showed up with a Machinist.

The drill was declared over. I sat there on the deck, leaning against an instrument cabinet, panting like a drunken Saint Bernard.

"You guys didn't even listen! You just sat there and looked at me like a bunch of chickens with the gapes!! Why the fuck do I even bother?"

After a few seconds, one of them said,

"Oh, Rich…we listen."

But this, by far, was the one for the books:

5) When I was completing my quals for Engine Room Supervisor, one of the evolutions I needed to complete was operating the Propulsion Clutch in manual mode. Yes, a submarine has a clutch, just like the old truck sitting in your drive way. Granted, it's a lot bigger than the clutch in a truck. It's about four feet long, and about three feet in diameter. It has friction plates like the clutch in a truck, but it has quite a few more…like, say, by

multiples of ten. It opens and closes like any other clutch. But, the clutch in a truck is operated by a driver's foot. The clutch in a submarine is operated by its own dedicated hydraulic system. As everyone knows, hydraulic systems can fail. So, if one needs to open or shut the clutch, and that nifty system is broken, it must be done manually.

The process is deceptively simple. Instead of an electric pump, a small hand pump is used. Instead of an automated manipulation of valves, secondary valves must be opened or shut by hand according to a specific procedure. Obviously, a non-qual isn't going to do this by himself. A qualified ERS is there with him, watching every move the student makes.

We got the procedure, set up communication with Maneuvering with sound powered phones, positively located all valves involved, and declared ourselves ready to perform the task. The preparations were made, and finally we heard the order,

"Engine Room Supervisor, Maneuvering…open the Main Propulsion Clutch in manual."

"Open the Main Propulsion Clutch in manual, Engine Room Supervisor aye."

We located the valves, realigned the valves, and I pumped the little handle. The little brass needle slowly moved across the scale on the bulkhead. Finally, it reached the end.

"Maneuvering, Engine Room Supervisor…the Clutch is open in manual."

"Very well, shut the Main Propulsion Clutch in manual."

And that, my friends, is where the so-called poop hit the proverbial propeller. We reversed the process we had so carefully carried out. The procedure was consulted. The valves were re-aligned. I started to pump the handle. After several seconds, we should have seen movement in the indicating needle. We didn't. I quickly expressed the obvious,

"It's not moving."

We double checked the procedure, double checked the valve line up, and tried again. The needle didn't move.

A voice crackled in my ears,

"Engine Room Supervisor, Maneuvering…report status of the Main Propulsion Clutch."

"The clutch is unresponsive. Troubleshooting."

We reviewed the procedure. All valves were rechecked. I pumped the little brass handle frantically. I could hear the dim sound of obscenities being shouted. The needle refused to budge. I saw a shadow over my shoulder. It was the EWS. He was leaning over, looking down into the little cubbyhole the ERS and I were squeezed into. He was sweating. He began telling us about how everyone was getting nervous in the Control Room.

"Engine Room Supervisor, report status of the Main Propulsion Clutch."

"Maneuvering, the Clutch is still unresponsive. Continuing to trouble shoot."

"Engine Room Supervisor...*expedite* the shutting of the Clutch!"

"*Expediting*, aye!"

The EWS poked his head down into the small Clutch Bay. He reminded me that with our Clutch in its present condition, open and unresponsive, we had lost *all* of our propulsion. He reminded me of how Thresher died. They lost *all* of their propulsion. Very softly and deliberately, he said,

"If you don't get that fucking clutch to shut, we're all going to die."

The ERS picked up the wall mounted phone and called Maneuvering,

"We're doing everything we can! We're doing everything right! We're following the procedure *exactly*! I don't know why it's not working!"

He listened for a second, and then hung up.

"Control Room's getting' scared."

We decided to cycle each valve. We checked, double checked, and triple checked the lineup. I pumped the handle for all I was worth. I concentrated on that little brass handle. He watched the needle for any sign of movement. It was unresponsive. I kept pumping. I heard jumbled voices muttering from the deck above. We had an audience now. I pumped that little handle to save my life. That's when we heard it. It wasn't the cracking of the hull. We'd heard that plenty of times before. It wasn't the nervous voices. We'd heard that before as well. It was a low dull roar. The Control Room had enough.

We were doing an Emergency Blow.

"It's moving!"

I looked up, and sure enough the needle was starting to move. I pumped faster. Ever so slowly, the needle crept across the scale. My arm felt as if it would burn off and plop on the floor, but there was no way I would stop now. Finally, after what seemed like an eternity stacked on top of two more, the indicator showed the Clutch as being fully shut. I keyed my headset,

"Maneuvering, Engine Room Supervisor…The Main Propulsion Clutch is shut. Control is returned to Automatic Mode."

> The rest of the watch went well. I finished the evolutions that were scheduled for my quals. That was child's play compared to what I was about to face. I was relieved, and went forward to grab something to eat. The Inquisition was awaiting my arrival. I found myself facing a nasty, jittery mob. I disappeared beneath an onslaught of angry, accusatory questions. These people were clearly very unhappy! The only thing that saved me from being drawn and quartered was the qualified ERS with me.

He quickly quieted them all down, telling them there was nothing he or I could do, or had done wrong. Now that my grizzly death had been called off for lack of interest, I heard the full story.

Even in peacetime, an Emergency Blow is an absolute last resort. It's an extremely noisy evolution. The wartime posturing required by our mission, our line of work, the constant uncertainty regarding what the enemy could or might do, made actions like that an act of utmost desperation. Even in peacetime, the sound of an Emergency Blow is the sound of a submarine saying,

"Please, God…don't let me die."

That was the point those men in the Control Room had reached. They felt the need to use their last resort. They had been pushed into that nasty corner, and as far as they were concerned *I* was the one who put them there.

Eventually, the stress died down, and the event took its proper place in the storyland that houses all the other stories told over drinks, or to wide eyed grandchildren. I finished my quals for ERS. Time plodded on, one more reason for me to lose a little more hope reared its ugly head, and one more nail was driven into the coffin.

Finally, my depression had reached its peak. I wasn't sleeping. I couldn't concentrate. My memory was almost nonexistent. I was constantly making mistakes, reinforcing the ideas behind the depression. I had managed to skillfully construct a perfect storm of vicious circles. What made the situation even more difficult was the requirement to appear perfectly normal on the surface. On that incredibly slim chance they really were laughing *with* me, it would do no good to erupt at someone, and alienate myself for nothing. That was a very painful lesson from my schoolboy days. The other possibility was being disqualified for submarine duty, which would be the very worst of all. So, while all these desperate screaming voices were ringing in my ears, on the outside I was just…peachy.

I did allow a crack to form in my flawless façade on one occasion, and it was in front of the worst possible person. I had gotten off watch one night, during a routine patrol. Things were quiet. Not much was going on, and many of the guys were asleep. I walked into the Mess Deck to see what the cooks had laid out for mid-rats. Three other guys were already there, grazing on cold cuts and distracting themselves with idle conversation. I quickly joined in.

"Hey, guys. Whatcha doing?"

"Oh…hi, Smitty. We're having a SART meeting."

"SART? What's SART?"

"SART stands for Skipjack Anti Retention Team. We basically just sit around and bitch about how bad everything is."

"Sounds like fun! Where do I sign up?"

"You? Oh, *you* can't join SART."

"Why not??"

"Your attitude isn't bad enough. You need to have a really bad attitude to join SART."

"I have a bad attitude."

"You don't have a bad attitude. Trust me, your attitude isn't *nearly* bad enough for SART."

"Oh, yeah? Well you listen to me…"

I then proceeded to explain, in fine detail, just how bad, lousy, rotten, and generally malcontent my attitude was. As I went on, their faces showed more and more shock and alarm. I was having fun. It was true, I was venting. But, I was playing it up as well. Yeah, that's right guys! I'm bad. I figured they were finally seeing someone with a truly *bad* attitude. Who knows, maybe they would make me the new President of SART. One of the members of my audience was actually blushing by the time I was finished. I awaited their rebuttal. What could they possibly say in contempt or criticism to what I had just said?

"Uh…Smitty."

"Yeah?"

"The Skipper was standing right behind you the entire time you were talking."

Thus began another period of waiting for the axe to fall. It didn't take long. A couple of days later I was in the Control Room, heading to the ladder to go down and get a bite to eat. Coming up the other way was the Skipper. I gave him a smile and jovially said,

"Good morning, sir. How are you?"

"I'm doing fine, Petty Officer Smith. Thank you. How are *you* doing? How are things going for *you*?"

I looked at his face. There was a look of genuine concern on that sea worn face. I felt a little guilty for giving him cause for concern over something that was really not much more than a good natured rant. It was time for a little damage control.

"Oh, I'm fine. I mean, it's true there are some rough spots from time to time. But, it's nothing I can't handle."

He gave a slow, concerned, half believing nod. I gave him a smile and went on my way. The theatrical aspect of my display was, for the most part, well...theatrics. But, the meat of the issue was every bit as real as it always was. I told the guys I had a bad attitude. I didn't mention how I was the boat's official loser, the one everyone had to watch, the one that put the pain in everyone's ass. I left unmentioned the whitewater of undercurrent that lay just below the surface. It was still there, pulling me closer and closer toward that ultimate dark place.

And, I finally reached my breaking point.

Under the pretenses of studying, I locked myself in the Ship's Office. I contemplated my circumstances and options. My position looked grim. Every possible route led to either misery through failure, misery through being ostracized, or misery through doing nothing at all. The last strand broke. For the next hour, as quietly as possible, I cried like a baby.

A couple of weeks later, a light appeared at the end of the tunnel. The senior Corpsman from Squadron Two rode us for a two week operation in the NBOA. I finally worked up the courage, and tapped on the Goat Locker door. I asked the Senior Chief if we could talk. Around the corner from the Goat Locker was a little work shop for A Gang. We stepped inside.

It all came out. The constant feelings of failure, condemnation, paranoia, and shame. He listened quietly as the flow of misery slowed to a drip. Then he voiced his concerns regarding my abilities to be useful during emergency conditions. He felt my concerns should be addressed immediately. I needed to be confident and competent should the worst happen. He then gave me the worst piece of advice he could possibly ever give.

"I think you should start by running these concerns past the XO."

Let me explain this assessment by running through two scenarios. One is how things would have gone if Commander Ulriche was there. The second is how things actually transpired with Lieutenant Commander Forbes.

Scenario One: I would have gone into the XO's stateroom. I would have voiced my concerns. He would have asked several pointed questions.

Do I have any concrete proof that what I suspect exists?

Has anyone else made any direct statements to support my suspicions?

Have your Chief or Division Officer registered any specific complaints?

Should I ask them myself if they have any complaints?

That conversation could have quite possibly quelled my concerns, directing me onto a much more rational path, and radically altering the remainder of my time on Skipjack.

Sadly, that is *not* what happened. Mr. Ulriche wasn't the XO. He was most certainly the Captain of his own boat by this point. Mr. Forbes was the XO. So, *this* is what happened.

Scenario Two: I went into the XO's stateroom. I voiced my concerns. He made several pointed statements.

If I am that concerned about how I am viewed, I need to requalify.

If I need to requalify, I will be removed from the watch bill.

If I'm not standing watch, my shipmates will have to do my work on top of their own, thus burdening them because of my weakness and failure.

"So, Petty Officer Smith, do you want to proceed with this concern?"

I stiffened, standing next to his little fold out desk. Finally I answered,

"No, sir. I do not."

At that moment, any support or prospect of support from the command vaporized. I was completely on my own.

Upon our return to port, my next stop was the Psychiatrist's Office. The Corpsman had made an appointment on my behalf. At the appointed time, I showed up at his office. It was a basic, non-descript room. It was minimally decorated and furnished. A chair was provided so the patient could sit near his desk, which was very military issue. He, however, was not. He was a civilian. That raised my hopes a little. I felt it was unlikely that I would be told it was all in my mind, although I recognized the irony of his potentially saying so. For the first time, they'd be correct.

He collected some preliminary data, and then settled down to the task of figuring out what was wrong with me. I began by giving him a detailed description of what I was feeling, and why I felt it was valid. He nodded and took notes as I spoke. He had some questions.

Was I considering harming myself?

Yes, I was seriously considering it.

If I did, how would I do it?

Pills. Nothing painful or messy.

Where would I get them?

Over the counter. It couldn't be that difficult.

He then had me take the Minnesota Multiphasic Personality Inventory, or MMPI. This was a standard test given to anyone suspected of having any kind of personality disorders or pathology. I carefully went through the test, taking extra care to answer as accurately as possible. He sat down and perused the test after I finished. His diagnosis?

I was definitely depressed. Determining exactly how depressed would take further poking and prodding. His solution?

He took out a scrap of paper. He scribbled something on it. He handed it to me. It was the title of a book.

The New Guide to Rational Living.

By Albert Ellis and Robert A Harper

"Buy this book, and read it."

I looked at the paper. I looked back at him. I was thinking of killing myself, I had a method picked out, and knew where to get what I needed. *This* was his treatment?

"Just go down to the mall. They'll have it there."

The awful truth dawned on me. I truly was on my own. Whatever I did to make it through this, it would be entirely of my own doing. Don't get me wrong. I bought the book. I read it. It *was* a really good book. It provided some insights I still use to this day. It actually helped take the edge off the pain. But in the end, the military medical system had won out. They had "addressed" the issue, "solved" it, and managed to keep someone from leaving a hard to fill seagoing billet.

I started working on a strategy. Conditions on the boat wouldn't change. It would be naïve to expect otherwise. That was the one constant I would work around. There had to be a way to counteract the boat's impact on me. I knew I had to endure the daily routine. I had to endure the patrols.

My time spent away from the boat would have to be used to its maximum effect. If I could make my time away from the boat as pleasant and relaxing as possible, I might actually break even.

PLAN A:

I decided I would go back home any time it was even remotely feasible. My time with Yvette was always the best cure for the toxic steeping the boat provided. If I couldn't make it home, I'd go to Mystic.

I figured out how I could maximize my time at home. On Friday night, I would leave for home, regardless of the time I could get away. If I could get to Feeding Hills before 10pm, I was on the road. I should have left to return to the boat on Sunday night. I didn't. I wanted to sleep at home as much as possible. So, Yvette would get up with me at 4am. We would quietly sit in the kitchen while I wolfed down a bowl of cereal. I would steel myself, and get in my car. Time to go back. On the road at 5am. I would get back to the boat at 6:30am. I'd have just enough time to stop at my room, change into my uniform, and make it aboard for quarters.

PLAN B:

If I couldn't make it home, I'd spend my evenings in Mystic. Mystic reminded me of Maine in many ways, so it was always a comfort. I had some favorite restaurants picked out. The area was perfect for a long after dinner walk. Mystic has a sizable historic section. Restored homes that once belonged to ship builders, Captains, tobacconists, coopers, and sail producers lined the streets. I picked out a long meandering route that was perfect for walking off a meal, burning off some steam, and grounding myself.

So, Operation Hey Don't Slit Your Wrists went into full forward motion. I tolerated the time on the boat as best as I could. I did my best to chalk up the bad parts to experience, reminding myself that my enlistment had an end date. I enjoyed any and all positive aspects of submarine life. I kept my attitude as upbeat as possible. I did my best to get along with my shipmates, angering as few as possible, being as nice as possible, and appearing as normal as possible.

Every opportunity to go home was pounced upon. It didn't matter what condition I was in. There were times I'd been awake for well over thirty six hours when I started the engine and aimed my car for Feeding Hills. Each time Monday morning came, I would roll out of bed with a feeling that is difficult to describe. The combined effects of alcohol, a destroyed circadian rhythm, stress, and the early wake up times left me with a feeling that truly made me yearn for death on countless occasions. It was all still worth it. Those few days spent away from Groton, distracted by Yvette, made the ledge on which I stood just a little wider.

Almost every free evening during the week, and during short weekends, I went to Mystic. Over time it became a familiar comfortable routine. With few exceptions, I would go to Nana's Margarita, a long established Mexican restaurant that became a pillar of Mystic's ambiance. It was almost something out of a movie. I had the same waiter almost every time. I ordered the same dish almost every time. Jose' got to the point that upon seeing me, he would automatically put *two* baskets of nachos with *two* bowls of salsa on my table. He had long since learned one was never enough. The looks of puzzlement from the other tables only conjured a knowing smile. I'd order a beer, and then he'd say that classic line,

"The usual?"

Those times were a priceless tonic for my ragged soul. After a good meal, I'd set off on my walk. It didn't matter what season it was. Every time of year had its own advantages. Whether it was a cool breeze off the water, classic New England foliage, or the abundant Christmas trees and decorations, there was always something to distract me from the torment waiting just a few miles up the coast.

I knew it all could only help so much. I knew it would only help for so long. It was really just a delaying tactic, postponing a moment I knew would eventually come. The operational pace was becoming increasingly hectic and unpredictable. More medical issues were starting to crop up. Trying to balance tactical commitments with the Navy's version of treatment was getting more and more difficult. Their attempts at diagnosing my problems led to unpleasant events at home, when I was supposed to be forgetting the Navy.

Sadly, that moment finally arrived. The boat had won. My time away, no matter how skillfully used, could not counteract the time spent on base or at sea. Mystic wasn't working anymore. My trips home to see Yvette weren't working anymore. The last door closed. No more doors, no more windows, no more escape routes. My situation quickly degraded, and plummeted toward rock bottom.

But, one small spark of sanity remained, like a solitary star on a cloudless winter night. It was a good thing, too. That little spark kept me mesmerized just long enough for salvation to arrive. And, it arrived in a most curious form, a most unexpected form, quite out of context, but not one unknown to me...

Pain.

Chapter 16-
Yer outta here!

"Destiny has two ways of crushing us.... by refusing our wishes and by fulfilling them."

-Anonymous

Submarines are known for their comfort. They have copious space, and leisurely, almost idyllic routines. The crew is provided with entertainment by a marching band that accompanies them on their journeys. At least the ones painted yellow fit this description. Just ask The Beatles, who apparently frequented one of these vessels on a regular basis.

Sadly, the ones painted black are nothing at all like the yellow ones. The black ones are cramped, noisy (at least on the inside), hot, and have a complete total lack of marching bands. Trust me, not a one! Unfortunately for me, I was assigned to one of the black ones. Space is at an extreme premium. Many components are located, not where they can be conveniently reached, but where they will *fit*. Often, half the battle of conducting maintenance is physically getting to the object being maintained.

A prime example would be the Feed System Relief Valves. Early in my time on Skipjack, I was tasked with reinstalling those valves when they returned from the valve shop. Their location was very awkward and inconvenient. To reach them one had to lay on the deck, reach over and then below the deck plates, and stretch as far as they could into the maze of piping. Working with both hands was almost impossible. One slip, and a valve would drop into the bilge. An extremely difficult job would become a nasty, painful, drawn out ordeal.

As carefully as I could, I reached out with a valve in one hand. Snaking and turning my hand, with a twenty pound valve in my sweaty death grip, I found the threaded seating surface for the valve. I was able to get a second hand on the valve, but in that position I couldn't see what I was doing. My arms quickly fell asleep as I scrambled to steady the valve and engage the threads on the fitting. If I let go before they were secure, the valve would end up in the bilge. I couldn't feel my hands anymore. I couldn't see what I was doing, working strictly by touch. Finally, I thought I had things where I needed them. I let go. I waited to hear a clang and a splash. Silence! I did it!

Only three more to go. I took a deep breath. Time for number two. Then the next…and the next. By the time I was finished I was simultaneously sore, numb, and breathless. Now it was time to tighten them all up. I took a quick breather, and then lay back down on my side, reaching into the piping with a heavy adjustable wrench. I could see about half of what I was doing. My muscles ached as I groped to find the fitting at the base of each valve. It seemed an eternity for each fitting to be tightened to the point it hopefully wouldn't leak. The close confines and awkward positions made it impossible to exert full strength.

Finally, I was finished. I sat up, panted, and then got to my feet. I cleaned up and reported my success to Chief Jardin.

He seemed content, and everything seemed to come up roses.

Not for long!

The Feed System was started up for testing. The longer the system ran, the less coolant filled the system. A leak was the obvious cause. Men traced out the system, peering intently with flashlights. Then they found the culprit...

MY RELIEF VALVES.

They were spraying like lawn sprinklers! What I thought was "tight enough" was no match for the discharge pressure of the Feed Pumps. We now had a bilge full of the cleanest, purest bilge water money could buy. I wasn't there when the testing took place, so I was spared the immediate rage of the Chief. The merciless abuse I took upon my return made up for it. Everyone else was laughing, but for me it was just one more incident proving my failure.

Over the next few months, I became adept at the acrobatic gyrations necessary to reach the parts of the boat for which I was responsible. I could shimmy through piping to the outboard sides of the Main Condensors, squeeze into the back corners of Shaft Lube Oil Bay, and weasel my hands into the deepest, darkest recesses of the engineering space bilges. I actually had a reputation for putting my hands where others were afraid to.

Slowly, almost imperceptibly, that began to change. The flexibility in my left arm became reduced. The strength in my left hand went next. It became a struggle to reach certain valves and apply full torque. Pushing on wrenches and lifting myself up on pipes became increasingly difficult and painful. Finally, I had to talk to the Corpsman. We decided it would be a good idea to have it looked at.

Off to the New London Naval Hospital I went. After an exam, it was decided to try immobilizing the wrist for couple of weeks. They sat me down and constructed a plaster half cast. They placed it against my fore arm and wrapped it all up in an ace bandage. I was sent back to work with an order for light duty.

Chief Jardin listened to my status with one ear while he listened to a steady stream of bad news with the other. We were in the midst of an abbreviated refit, and nothing was going as planned. Finally he turned to me,

"Light duty? Okay, no problem…go ahead and start taking apart the Brine Pump."

Dutifully, I went to work. Things were progressing nicely, until the cast got wet. The cast weakened the first day, and the next day it got wet again. The cast broke. I went back up to the hospital for a new cast. The Corpsman showed open irritation as he constructed the new cast. I was sent back to the boat with a reminder that I was on light duty.

We continued to struggle to pick up the pace of our refit, swimming against a tide of broken and obsolete equipment. Duty days were a non-stop blur. We all provided maximum effort. The Chief waited, tapping his foot like a frustrated mother when I got back. I got my work assignment and went down the ladder. A couple of hours later, my cast was soaking wet...

"What the frig are you doing back here!"

The Corpsman at the hospital looked at me in complete disbelief. What part of light duty was I getting stuck on? He grumbled as he constructed a *third* half cast, molding the hot plaster to my arm and wrist. I tried to defend myself, explaining the urgent situation of our refit.

"Light duty is light duty. If you keep doing this, you won't heal. I don't give a shit what your commands issues are. You're not coming up here again. I'm going to make sure of that!"

When I returned to the boat, I found a furious Chief Jardin waiting. I soon found out what the Corpsman had done. He complained to his boss, who then complained to *his* boss, who then climbed the ladder until a rank above my Captain was reached. That person then called my Captain, and the process reversed itself, gaining momentum on the way down. By the time it reached my Chief, it was a free-fall torrent of poo.

"Can't work, eh? Light duty, eh? Can you do *anything*, you useless fuck??"

I stared blankly.

"Can you stand watch, you fucking no-load??"

I thought for a moment, and then nodded dimly. I really didn't know if I could or not, but the intense guilt I felt meant I had to do *something*.

"Okay! You're going to be our official watch stander. Take over the SRW watch. Technically you can only stand twelve hours of watch a day, so each four hours someone else will sign the log. You'll stand all the watches."

It actually felt like a huge relief. At least I would provide some kind of useful support. I fell into a very predictable routine. I felt like a burden. The other guys understood. They knew I couldn't help it. It didn't make it much easier. The Chief cringed every time someone relieved me so I could eat or go to the head. Work was going undone.

My third cast survived, but that only proved it wouldn't solve the problem. It was time for the next step. I reported to the hospital for a cortisone injection. I was put in a chair, with my wrist bent over a rolled up towel. A low level X-ray emitter was set up, and my wrist bones were projected onto a monitor. The doctor used the image as a guide as he maneuvered the long needle deep into my wrist. I looked at the monitor once. It was a big mistake. A wave of nausea rolled over me and left me feeling faint. That was something I could go without ever seeing again.

I returned to the boat with instructions to pay close attention to how my wrist felt as the next week or so passed. Luckily for me, that didn't include any sea time. The Chief would have had an aneurysm at the thought of taking someone to sea that couldn't stand watch. As I predicted, my condition didn't improve. It continued to worsen. The doctors would have to think of something else. Everyone involved knew it was time for surgery.

The next day, I sat in a small, claustrophobic office. The orthopedic surgeon, Lieutenant Brian Alecher, moved my wrist around, feeling the bones move. It seemed as if he knew what he was doing. I found that a source of optimism. After a thorough exam, and a few X-rays, he declared his diagnosis.

Rotary Subluxation of the Scafoid.

Whaaat??

Apparently, one of the bones in my wrist called the Scafoid had moved out of position. This was causing all of my problems. The cause? Unknown. The solution? Fuse it to two adjacent bones. The end result would be one big bone instead of three small ones. I would lose some range of motion, but otherwise I'd be fine. The decision was made, the date was set, and something unexpectedly came to an abrupt end…my time on Skipjack.

I was assigned to COMSUBRON 2 for the duration of the medical process. They didn't have much for me to do, since they weren't really expecting me. A couple of slow directionless days passed by. Finally, I reported to the hospital.

The mechanics of the operation were explained to me.

1) They would make the incision.

2) They would go into my wrist, and locate the three bones targeted for the procedure.

3) They would scrape all the cartilage off the bones.

4) The bones would then be pinned together into the intended configuration.

5) Bone marrow would be taken from a donor site, and packed between the bones like brick mortar.

6) The end result would be a solid mass of fused bone.

They doped me up, brought me in, and did the deed. I woke up in the recovery room to a cast running from my knuckles to my bicep, a tube down my throat, and lots and lots of pain. So much pain, in fact, that "pain" was the first word I said to the nurse when she came over to check on me and remove my breathing tube. Someone returned with some morphine and shot it into my IV.

That began my three day stay at Hotel Morphine. The days were a blur of pain, drugs, and bad food. Eventually they let me go. I was driven back to the barracks, and given a week of convalescent leave. I called Yvette, and she came down and picked me up. I was going home.

I quickly adapted to a routine where my left arm could never get wet. Showers were the worst, providing the ultimate paradox of getting clean without a quarter of me getting wet. Yvette took advantage of the blank canvas that was my plaster cast. Soon it was covered with drawings of cats, ostriches, sheep, and anything else I hoped would not get me sent to the brig. A couple of guys at the barracks also made their contributions to my quickly swelling art collection.

I was assigned to the staff of the barracks in which I lived. That was convenient, providing the shortest commute possible. My room and the office were only four doors apart. I was put on the watch bill for security watch at the front desk. I stood the 0800 to 1600 security watch, from Monday to Friday. Every once in a while I'd pull weekend duty. On those weekends not requiring my presence, Yvette would drive down Friday night to pick me up. Sunday night she would drive me back. This was certainly a routine I could get used to.

Entertainment during the week was hit or miss. I was dependent on others for any kind of transportation. I found myself treating for dinner or drinks quite often. It didn't bother me, and it obviously didn't bother any of my friends. I was still able to associate with some of my shipmates from the Skipjack. One person was always adept at making things interesting, Mike Jeeves.

One of my regular haunts in those days was a strip club called The Horse and Nail. I discovered the wonderful world of strip clubs during my assignment in Orlando. I always knew where the closest one was located, since it was a critical part of my "cheering up" process. There is a right way, and a wrong way to frequent strip clubs. I learned early how to do things the right way and usually found myself a welcome and popular visitor.

This one night, we found ourselves back at The Horse and Nail. We quickly found prime seats directly in front of the air conditioning vent, and set ourselves up for a good night of "cheering up". One of the dancers quickly spotted us and sashed over. She was about to start her dance routine when she noticed my very conspicuous cast. The conversation went something like this:

Dancer: Oh, you poor thing! What happened to you?

Me: Well, I…

Mike: He got shot!

Me: What?

Dancer: He got *shot*?

Me: No! I…

Mike: Yup. He got shot. Lucky to be alive.

Dancer: Oh, my God! What happened?

Me: I didn't really…

Mike: He can't talk about it. It's classified. TOP SECRET.

Dancer: Oh, you poor thing! I'm gonna make you feel all better.

Me: Okay, Mike. You win. I got shot.

It was an interesting night. Not all nights were like that, but I usually managed to keep myself entertained. Another good friend, an ELT named Fritz Gurthe, managed to keep me in trouble much of the time. We were constantly driving off somewhere in his old beat up Volkswagen Bus. He had elaborate plans to decorate it up nicely for his girlfriend. But for the time being, it was the burger and booze bus. Between the bunch of us, the time went by quickly enough. It was time to have my cast removed.

I'll never forget my shock upon seeing my arm and hand fresh from the cast. Without the effects of the sun, all the hair that had been shaved off for the surgery had grown back thick and jet black! A quarter of me had turned into the missing link! The dead skin cells that would normally come off in the shower had nowhere to go. They formed an unsavory layer along with the hair. But, it felt so good to be able to move my arm again. Life could return to normal.

I started physical therapy. That was when I formed my first opinions about physical therapists. Apparently they were all very pretty. Apparently they all enjoyed causing intense pain. It seemed so paradoxical for this beautiful young woman to sweetly tell me what she was going to do…and then *do it*! Surely a pure angel like her wouldn't be causing pain like that. All the while I was biting my lip, sweating, and stomping my foot on the floor, she would be softly cooing about how it was all critically necessary to fold me up like origami.

Therapy progressed. The bone fusion finally solidified to the point that the pins could be removed. "Pulled out" would be a more accurate description. That's exactly what he did. He located the ends of the pins. He made very small incisions at the ends. He fished around with a pair of needle nose pliers until he found something to grab onto. Then he just yanked then out. The sickly and unnatural felling it produced turned my stomach into one of those balloon dogs clowns make at birthday parties. Over time my strength began to return. My range of motion was beginning to return. But, there was a problem. My strength wasn't returning fast enough, and my range of motion was less than they were expecting. Something was clearly wrong.

The surgeon and physical therapist decided to run some tests and take some X-rays. It was discovered that the bone fusion had broken up during physical therapy. The surgeon knew right away what had happened. He sat me down, and explained it to me. This was where he was very lucky. He was a medical practitioner for the U.S. Government. He was practicing on military personnel, who were government property. If he made a mistake, his patient had no legal recourse. That was why he sat down at his desk across from me, and with no signs of regret said,

"Usually the bone marrow for a bone fusion is taken from the crest of the pelvis. It's the highest quality, and has the best characteristics for this application. But, I didn't want to go to the trouble of dealing with two incisions. So, I used bone marrow from the forearm, right next to the fusion. It isn't as good, and I knew there was a chance it wouldn't work. I knew it was a shortcut, but I decided to take the chance and do it anyway. We'll have to do the procedure again, and this time I'll go into the pelvis for the bone marrow."

If he had said that to a civilian patient, as a civilian doctor, he would be charged with malpractice. Odds are he might also be stripped of his license. But, he wasn't a civilian doctor, and I wasn't a civilian patient. So, he was able to sit there with complete impunity as he told me of how he screwed up the operation by taking a deliberate shortcut he knew might not work. The words of a senior naval officer echoed in my mind,

"Because your medical care is free, you *will* accept substandard medical care."

What I *wanted* to do was tell the doctor that he was nothing more than a butcher, and that he would never lay a finger on me again. What I *wanted* to do was tell him he'd better learn to operate with his nose, since I would break off all his fingers like chicken wings if I ever found out he had a civilian practice. But I *couldn't* do that. All I could do was smile and nod.

The operation was rescheduled, and I reported to the hospital again. The same routine was followed. I woke up in the same recovery room. But, the pain I awoke to was much worse. It was then that I learned one of the obscure facts about bone fusions. The pain at the site of the fusion is *nothing* compared to the donor site. The pain in my wrist was very bad. The pain in my pelvis was *excruciating*. It was time for my good friend, morphine, to pay a visit. This time morphine brought luggage and bed slippers. This was going to be a longer visit. This was the first time I'd felt real post-op pain. This was going to be rough.

That day and the next were spent in a drug induced haze. Friends came and went, usually leaving when they realized I couldn't stay awake or recognize them. I had no appetite. I was on fluids only, but this only served to highlight one of the nasty elements of being on morphine. It works very well as a pain killer, but it has side effects. One of the most inconvenient is that it virtually paralyzes some voluntary muscles in the body. Among these are the muscles that squeeze the Urinary Bladder when the time comes to pee.

A Corpsman walked into my room, looked at my chart, and put an unhappy expression on his face.

"Mr. Smith...according to your chart, it would appear you haven't urinated in eighteen hours."

I responded with a fuzzy nod of recognition. He stared intently at me, as if he was try to bore his way through the haze.

"This isn't a good situation. I'm coming back in a half an hour. If you haven't urinated by then...I'm going to catheterize you."

He turned and walked out. I had never been catheterized before. From the stories I'd heard, I wasn't about to start now. Stories of garden hoses, laughing nurses, and thumb sucking filled my mind. I began to focus on the situation at hand. I was now required to do two things. I had to get out of bed. Wait...I was now required to do *three* things. I had to get out of bed. I had to actually walk into the bathroom. Then I had to pee. Specifically, I had to pee *in the toilet*.

This wasn't going to be easy. Just getting into or out of bed was a project all its own. The bed was in a position that helped alleviate the pain in my pelvis. But, that same position made it almost impossible to get up. To walk, I'd need to use my cane on my right side, and hold onto the IV stand with my left hand. Those times I spent on my feet usually ended with me starting to pass out. So, I might be able to get up. I might be able to shuffle into the bathroom. I could use the cane and IV stand for support. What the hell am I going to use to aim at the toilet?

This logistical nightmare ran through my groggy mind over and over. It wasn't looking good. I probably wouldn't be able to get any help. Everyone was busy. I would have to "sprint" to the bathroom and back to finish the mission before I passed out. Hopefully my ego would take over, and I'd end up pointing at the toilet just on default. I was still undecided regarding the entire venture, when the Corpsman poked his head in.

"Did you go yet?"

I slowly shook my head. He looked at his watch, looked at me, and went about his business. It was now or never. I gathered my strength. I took a deep breath, and did the granddaddy of all sit-ups. Amazingly, I found myself sitting upright. So far, so good. Okay, let's try swinging our legs over to the floor. Not so easy. That took a few tries, which also meant it was time for a break. Time to stand up. I searched for my cane. Now I had a cane on one side, and the IV stand on the other. Ally-oop!! Now I was on my feet. No time to celebrate now! I quickly began the shuffle to the bathroom. My wobbly legs ran a death race against the catheter, past the chair…around the meal tray…around the corner. There it is! The bathroom!! I got to the toilet, took careful aim, and squeezed.

Plink. Plink-plink. Plink…plink.

I'd forgotten the damned morphine! My bladder muscles were almost useless! I strained. I thought about the garden hose that would soon be making its way up my…I strained more. If someone had seen me, they would have thought I was trying to roll a car off my Mom.

Plink, plink, plink.

Close enough! My vision was beginning to narrow. I felt that numb swimmy feeling. I heard the blood roaring in my ears. I was going to pass out. I turned and half shuffled, half limped back to my bed. Except for one spot in the center, my vision had gone completely yellow. I quickly positioned my IV stand so I wouldn't pull out my needles, and let myself fall back on the bed. The pain in my right hip cut through the morphine like a fog horn. I lay on the bed, panting like a sled dog. The Corpsman walked back into the room.

"Well? Did you?"

"Just did"

"Really?"

"I'm too stoned on morphine to lie to you."

Technically, I didn't lie to him. If eight drops of pee landed in my pants while I was sitting at the bar, everyone would be talking about how I pissed myself. So there.

Over the next two days I weaned myself off the morphine. I peed for real, started eating solid food again, and recognized the people who came to check on me. I was released and given more convalescent leave. It was decided I would go to Florida this time. I experienced something quite unusual during this flight. When I left the ticket counter, someone summoned a cart to take me to my gate. When I got to the gate, a staff member helped me aboard. Someone carried and stowed my bag. In Melbourne, someone helped me off the plane. They brought out my bag and gave it to my parents. They had a wheel chair waiting for me. They wheeled me out to the car. For the first time in my life, I asked myself if I was important.

My parents doted on me each and every moment. I relaxed, and finally recovered to the point I would only ask for the basic essentials, like helping with the plastic bag on my arm. By this time I'd gotten fairly accustomed to having my left arm completely incapacitated. My Dad and I swapped military stories, and my Mom asked how things were up in Massachusetts. That was life until the time finally came to return to Groton.

When I got back, it was time to get back into the physical therapy regimen again. The cast was removed at the proper time. I began my treatment with that beautiful, angelic demon again. Things began to progress. It was different this time. I made headway ever so slowly. It was decided that the unusually long period of immobilization was a setback that would greatly delay my recovery. They would need to consult with the Pentagon to determine the future of my military career.

I was summoned back to the surgeon's office. The situation was explained to me. When I went in for my first operation,

I was placed on six months of limited duty. That was acceptable. I had since exceeded that period due to the complications. That too was acceptable. But, to allow enough time to properly heal and recover my strength, they would need to start another period of limited duty. That would result in a period of limited duty greater than one year. That was *not* acceptable. Chances were, the request for more time would be declined. What would that mean? I would be discharged.

That caused me instant alarm. Any successful future plans based on my naval service required an honorable discharge. I was quickly assured I would get an honorable discharge. The injury was service connected. It didn't involve a disciplinary action. The circumstances would be entirely honorable. The surgeon asked me how I felt about the prospect of a discharge. There were two answers:

The external answer: If the Navy decides to keep me, I will carry out all my duties willingly and cheerfully. My medical condition would determine my path at the end of this enlistment.

The internal answer: I want out of here so friggin' bad I can't see straight.

The request for additional time on limited duty was…declined. I would be discharged. My status at COMSUBRON 2 was changed to reflect the decision. But, I fell into an interesting category. Many people assigned to squadron were there because they were waiting to get a *dishonorable* discharge. Many people working for squadron were there because they were caught using drugs, had civilian legal issues, were claiming conscientious objector status, or sexual orientation issues. The reliability rating of these people was considered low. Granted, it was good to have them around when the workload was high, but they were generally considered less than desirable.

Those people assigned for reasons like mine were viewed differently. The assignments we were given reflected that. Easy, if not outright desirable assignments came our way.

I was maintained on the barracks staff, continuing to stand security watches on day shift. My physical therapy continued until it got to the point another therapist could take over without difficulty. I settled into a comfortable, foreseeable routine. It was now a matter of just waiting for the paperwork. The timeframe used to measure how fast something happens at the Pentagon is officially: GLACIAL.

This was going to take a while. I knew it, and I was ready for it. I had an easy daily routine, minimal off watch or weekend duty, plenty of spare time, and best of all…a steady paycheck. The people I worked with were good quality people. There was rarely strife on the job. Visits home were a regular occurrence. During the week, I spent many evenings in Mystic. Life was good.

Working the security desk was interesting most of the time. The people coming through the door were almost always good for a joke, a funny story, or just some idle chit-chat. I treated the tenants well, and the overwhelming majority of the time they knew a good thing when they had it. But, it was a "white bread" job. What it made up for in easy going nature, it lacked in excitement. But, that was about to change.

"Hey, Smitty. Squadron wants to see you."

I looked up, and it was my boss MS1 Will Baylor. He brought down a sailor to take over my watch. I asked him if he knew what the issue was. He just shrugged. I grabbed my hat and I walked down to Lower Base. I entered the Yeoman's office, and Ski was sitting at his desk. Yeoman First Class Ski was actually called something else according to his name tag. But, in time honored naval tradition, long Polish names were automatically shortened to "Ski" or "Alphabet". Ski was the enlisted "Nerve Center" for everything that went on at squadron. He was their organizational backbone.

"Hey, Ski. What's up?"

Ski looked up and smiled. It was as if he held some juicy little secret that only I would appreciate. He twiddled his fingers and raised his eyebrows as he spoke.

"They were asking for someone this morning. It's something people don't usually like to do, but something they don't like to order people to do either. It's strictly voluntary. You were the first person I thought of. Want to hear about it?"

"Sure." I mused.

"Do you know what a Zulu Five Oscar is?"

I did know what it was. One of our guys was disqualified from Topside Watch because of one. A Zulu Five Oscar was the infiltrator. They were named after the original Zulu Five Oscar exercises carried out by the SEALs, to test the security of high value and sensitive facilities. One of those facilities was the Weapons Depot at Groton. By weapons, I don't mean pistols and shotguns. By weapons, I mean torpedoes and missiles. Many important and high ranking people were very embarrassed by those exercises. They vowed it would never happen again. One step toward that goal was to run their own Zulu Five Oscars on a much more frequent, although less elaborate basis.

COMSUBRON 2 was responsible for running Zulu Five Oscars on the waterfront. They wanted someone with a "spooky" background to do them. Some of the people at squadron knew about my family. I had told some of them about my Dad's adventures doing infiltration exercises between two friendly rival Air Force Bases in Japan. I was equally intrigued and flattered by Ski's announcement. I told him I'd be happy to give it a crack.

Ski began by giving me a quick rundown on what the exercises actually entailed. There were rules. There were certain things I would not be allowed to do, for instance, impersonate a commissioned officer or Chief. If someone was on to me, the drill was over. But, for the most part, I could beg, borrow, steal, cheat, bluff, or lie my way onto any submarine on the wharf.

"Hell, you could even swim over to one if you have the grapes to try."

(That would end up being very interesting advice. And that's all I'm going to say.) NR-1 was obviously off limits. She was an extremely sensitive high value asset. They would probably kill me on the spot, exercise or no exercise.

I officially accepted my assignment. I sat down to strategize and cook up plausible cover stories. I used my mechanical experience the most. Making up tools used on obscure valves and equipment would be very valuable when trying to snow my way past a young non-qual. I looked out uniform articles I hadn't worn in a while. One would be surprised just how memorable a paint stain on a shirt collar can be. Finally, I went to work.

Over the years, I've often told stories about doing Zulu Five Oscars. They always made for great drinking stories. After all, how many people are tasked with sneaking aboard a guarded nuclear submarine? I was always extremely careful to avoid saying anything damaging, anything that could compromise a boat's security. Or, so I thought. I will always remember the night that changed. I was at a restaurant called Dr. Deegan's. It's in Chicopee, Massachusetts, right next to Westover Air Force Base. I had gone with some friends for after work drinks. The drinking and talking was in full swing. The topic of my old Navy days came up. One question and story led to another, and soon the Zulu Five Oscar stories started.

During a lull in the evening, things got quiet. Some people left, and some late people showed up. I was standing at the bar, chatting with the bartender as he mixed a drink for a woman at the other side of the bar. I noticed a man walking over out of the corner of my eye. I realized he had come over to speak with me. There was nothing overly remarkable about him, but he was obviously military. He stood leaning against the bar, facing away from the bartender, with the bar at his back. He took his wallet out, and produced an active military ID card. He was an Air Force Captain. He leaned over, and spoke softly into my ear,

"I wanted to show you my ID card so you wouldn't think I was just being a prick. I've been listening to your stories. I think you should stop talking about those exercises."

I looked at him closely. He seemed completely genuine. I thought for a second.

"You know, I put a lot of thought into what I say. I grew up with these kinds of issues. I don't think there's any harm. After all, I'm only telling stories about the times I got caught. There can't be any harm in that."

He held up a finger.

"Think of it this way. You're telling stories about what *didn't* work. Now imagine someone is here listening to you, someone looking for information. By telling them what didn't work, you're helping them narrow things down to what *might* work. Put yourself in their place. It sure would help if you didn't have to start from square one."

I felt as if I'd been punched in the gut. He was right. Why didn't I think of that? I felt as if I was a dim witted recruit who just got caught cleaning a loaded weapon. I decided at that point, it wasn't important enough to be entertaining. It wasn't important to be "cool" to the other guys. It didn't matter what I'd seen that other people will never see. I was going to keep my mouth shut. I already had enough stories to tell that were harmless. I'd stick to them.

But, there is one thing I *can* say. At one point, I had an absolutely furious Navigator screaming at his crew members, demanding that I be "proned out" on the deck with a loaded shotgun held to the back of my head. Furious Navigators get what they want…especially when they scream.

My time doing Zulu Five Oscars finally came to an end. I complained about the treatment I was receiving from the boats I selected, not that I could blame them. I was starting to burn out a little, as well. I received my promotion to Petty Officer Second Class, and began training so I could be rotated into the watch bill for COMSUBRON 2 Duty Petty Officer. I was also reassigned to the barracks, but this time with a change. I was going to be management. I was elated at the news of my new assignment. I would be working with MS1 Baylor. It didn't last long. Will Baylor was retiring. I would be working with his replacement.

MS2 Steve Traut was on limited duty for medical issues. He had a problem with his kidneys that caused him to piss blood all the time. I also learned he was going through a very rough separation period with his wife. His kids were angry and alienated. All this together resulted in his being a real bear to work for at times. His frustrations often ended up being directed at his subordinates, whether they deserved it or not. We ended up knocking heads a few times when he wanted someone's head on a plate, and I tried to convince him to take an calmer route.

I got a very clear picture of Steve, one late night during the holiday season. I was coming back from an evening in Mystic. I had to walk past the office to get to my room. I noticed the door was open and the light was on. That was unusual, unless there was a problem bringing Steve in from off base. I poked my head in. Steve was very drunk. He was fumbling with a large box, some wrapping paper, and some tape. Watching him try to wrap this box was, as my Dad would say,

"Like watching a monkey trying to fuck a football."

I felt bad for him, so I asked if he wanted some help. He looked at me as if his fairy godmother just popped in for a drink. I smoothed out the paper and went about the business of salvaging his Christmas gift. I listened to him talk as I wrapped. In his sad, slurred southern drawl, he spilled his guts. All the frustration and sorrow poured out. I really felt bad for him. I couldn't even imagine trying to be married under these circumstances. He had an unhappy wife, confused bitter kids, and a serious medical condition that wasn't responding well to treatment. I decided from that point forward I'd give him as much slack and help as I could.

The boat came back to haunt me several months after I left. One of the guys I worked for was in the same situation I was. He had been pulled from his boat because of an auto accident. He remarked every once in a while that a boat would take revenge on someone who left before their time, especially if they were left shorthanded. I found this difficult to believe. The military evaluation system was put in place for a reason. I attributed his remarks to bitterness over the circumstances surrounding his accident. He was absolutely right, as I would soon discover.

Ski called me at the barracks, and told me he had a paper for me to sign. I got to his office and waited as he finished up some business with a Chief. Then he turned to me and handed me a paper. It was my separation eval from the Skipjack. I was looking forward to seeing the eval, because I'd been told the command was very happy with my performance in the last ORSE. I had to look twice. I felt my heart stop. The eval was terrible! I couldn't believe what I was seeing. I had essentially been given a "kiss of death" eval. According to this form, I was an unreliable, angst ridden loser. I was livid!

"I'm not signing this!! I'm not signing this! I don't have to sign this!"

Ski calmed me down. He explained that I *did* have to sign it. But, I could include an official rebuttal statement, which they *had* to include when the eval was routed to Washington. I gathered my wits, and called my Dad. I explained to him what had happened and the probable reasons for it. Together, we drafted a rebuttal statement that successfully shed doubt on the command's decisions. I brought the statement down to squadron and showed it to Ski. He read it and gave a subtle approving nod.

"That's good. That's very good. I'll include this with the eval when it goes back to Skipjack."

I stomped back up to the barracks. One of the first people I encountered was my friend recovering from his auto accident. I spewed out my story and confused anger. He only gave me a sympathetic, understanding look.

"I told you they would screw you."

"But…but…right before I left, they told me what a good job I had done!"

"It doesn't matter. You left them early. And, as I recall, they were shorthanded already. It doesn't matter how good you were. They were going to screw you. It's what they do."

A few days later, I was summoned back to squadron. Ski was waiting for me. He looked agitated.

"Skipjack refused to route your rebuttal statement."

"*What?* They can't do that!! They *have* to route it! That's the procedure!"

Ski held up his hands. I realized why he looked so edgy. He knew what my reaction would be.

"You don't need to worry. *I'm* going to route it. Trust me. Don't worry. It'll be in your service record. Skipjack is going to look very bad for this."

I started to calm down a little. It took a long time to realize it, but I actually had people who liked me. I had people going to bat for me. It was a very good, albeit unfamiliar feeling.

Daily life continued. Being an assistant manager for a barracks with 390 rooms and over 1500 tenants was more of a challenge than I expected. That was okay. It was still gravy compared to the boat. Only one issue made working in the barracks difficult: the suicides. The submarine service is known for its relatively high suicide rate. The idea of suicide certainly wasn't new to me. We lost three guys in Orlando, and one more at KAPL. I suppose I expected those guys to be fully weeded out by the time they got to a boat. I was wrong.

Between the time I arrived in Groton to the time I left, we had three more guys driven to suicide. One was found hanging in his shower. One locked himself in his bathroom and slit his wrists. I still remember how we discovered him.

The bathrooms in the barracks had doors that would automatically unlock when the door was closed. The idea was that it would be impossible for someone to lock themselves out of their own bathroom. The only way to lock the door was to go into the bathroom, close the door, and then lock it from the *inside*. It wasn't uncommon to enter a room for room inspection, and find the bathroom door closed and locked. We would rap on the door and yell,

"Barracks Manager. Room inspection."

A muffled voice would reply,

"Okay."

It was a bad sign when the door was closed and locked, and we got no reply when we knocked. Maybe he fell asleep on the pooper. Maybe he was still passed out from the previous night. Maybe it was something else. We were doing the weekly room inspection when it happened. Knock, knock. No answer. Time for the master key. We went into the room. Everything looked normal. The bathroom door was closed. Knock, knock. No answer. Will tried the knob. It was locked. He knocked again. No answer. This time he pounded. Still no answer. He yelled into the bathroom. No response.

Will got this expression on his face that I'll never forget. It was a classic "not again" look. But it was mixed with a profound sorrow. He quietly said,

"Oh, no. No, no, no. I've got a bad feeling…"

It was a feeling he'd obviously gotten too many times before. We went back to the office. Will called security. They knew the routine, too. They would bring a locksmith…and an ambulance. He waited for security to arrive. I left and finished the room inspections. Will was right. They disassembled the bathroom door knob. When they opened the door, they found a young man lying in a pool of blood. Will was right…again. Frantic action quickly erupted. He was bundled up and whisked off to the naval hospital. As the cars pulled over for the speeding ambulance, they had no idea the blaring siren was actually saying,

"There goes another one! We lost another one!"

The hardest one to take was a friend of mine. His name was Pete. He started on the boat in the Nav ET area a little while before I left. He was a young guy, but he had a lot of baggage. He was married with a child, but he was separated. His wife had maxed out his credit cards. Bill collectors were contacting the boat. The command could have helped him, but they didn't. Instead of running interference for him, they essentially delivered him on a silver platter. Finally, the stress was too much.

He went out riding with Roni, a fellow crew member, on one of the routes popular with the motorcycle enthusiasts on base. It was at night, but the weather was clear and dry. The two of them tooled down 391North for a while. Then Pete suddenly took off. He wound up his bike to over ninety miles per hour. Then, to his friend behind him, it looked as if he simply stepped off his bike. There were no obstacles in the road, and he was an experienced rider. It just didn't make sense. He died in his friend's arms, on the side of the road. Roni said the whole thing just didn't seem right. I asked him if he thought Pete had dropped his bike deliberately. All I got was a slow, sad nod. Then he walked away.

One day in early April 1988, I got called down to squadron. Ski smiled at me as I walked in. Obviously, he had good news. I sat down next to his desk.

"Ever heard of Home Awaiting Orders?"

I shook my head.

"Well, it goes like this…instead of you staying here, breathing government air, eating government food, drinking government water, and filling government poop tanks…they send you home. You live at home, grow your hair long, start looking for a job, and they mail you your paychecks."

"What about my discharge papers?"

"You pre-sign them before you leave. When the paperwork is done, they mail them to you. You cut up your ID card, put it in an envelope, mail it back, and you're officially a civilian."

I looked at him with a questioning look. This all had to be too good to be true. Ski leaned over his desk toward me,

"Smitty…they only do this for people they *like*."

It looked as if the end game had begun.

It wouldn't take a rocket scientist to figure out my response to this proposition. They got the ball rolling. The papers were filed, and that enormous red-white-blue glacier that is the Pentagon slowly began to move. A tiny little speck named MM2(SS) Richard A Smith was at one end, pushing for all he was worth.

The days continued to march by. My routine of working, drinking, eating, walking, and strip clubbing transformed itself into a comfortable blur. Home had an irresistible draw. Each time I went home I knew I was closer to coming home for good. Yvette and I were filled with nervous anticipation. Soon it would be time to start a crucial new chapter of our life.

I began shedding unnecessary articles. I donated my stereo to the front desk. Extra uniform articles were dispensed to willing recipients. Unfinished models I was working on were abandoned. Valuable objects were brought up to Yvette's house. My room was taking on a sparse, temporary look. It no longer looked like home.

A funny thing was happening around me. The people who worked with me were being transferred, discharged, or returning to sea. A new crop of guys was coming in. Those who worked in the barracks long term were accustomed to seeing this. But, it felt very strange to me. It felt as if I was being left behind. At the same time, Skipjack was deployed in the Med, taking away the friends I still had from the boat.

I was at the point when a sailor usually found himself surrounded by friends, and well-wishers. He was going to parties celebrating his moving on and "having a nice life". But, the course of events took that all away. I found myself looking at this key point in my naval career from an entirely different perspective. I found myself strangely alone. I tried to find comfort in the places I usually frequented. It didn't help. I felt like a stranger, even in those places I was once considered a fixture. I felt cheated. I was cheated out of a contentment, happiness, and excitement others felt when they were leaving. The only consolation was apartment hunting with Yvette when I was home for the weekends.

The day arrived for my debriefing. I walked down to one of the administrative builds for my appointment. Soon I was sitting in a stuffy office with a Lieutenant. He spread out the myriad of forms I was going to sign, put a pen on the desk, and began going down the list of restrictions accompanying my separation.

1) I was not to discuss or disclose any classified information regarding equipment, hardware, or

operations with which I was involved. No, speeds, depths, ranges, procedures, locations, or anything else that might reveal classified information. If I did, I would go to prison.
2) I was not to write or speak in detail about any classified or sensitive activities in which I was involved. If I did, I would go to prison.
3) I was not allowed to travel to any communist country. Ever.
4) I was not allowed to travel to any socialist country without first obtaining specific permission from the U.S. State Department.

I signed all the documents outlining what I had just been told. They were filed away. I signed my separation eval. I couldn't believe my eyes when I read it. After my experiences with the boat, I expected another kick in the lugs. It was the exact opposite. These guys made it look as if the sun rose and set on my ass. I felt a warm glow of appreciation. Was this how it was supposed to feel? I signed a blank DD214, my discharge papers. It would be mailed to me when it was fully filled out. He then began the portion of the debriefing that dealt with the VA. He warned me that many young people being separated ignore this portion of the process. Their eyes glaze over, and they quickly discard the stack of pamphlets given to them. They want the information later, but they've thrown it all away. I wasn't really hearing what he was saying. My eyes were almost fully glazed over by that point. I got tired of hauling around all those heavy pamphlets, so as soon as I returned to the barracks, I threw them away.

Finally, my last night in Groton arrived. I went down to Mystic for dinner and drinks. Mystic had lost its magic. I left and went for a drive down through Groton Long Point.

It too had lost its appeal. I stopped at one of the cheesier strip clubs on Route 12, just outside the base. I sat down, had a beer, and then left. The effect was like staring through the window of a wonderful store or restaurant, knowing you could go in, but knowing you'll never be welcome there.

The next day, I packed my belongings in my car, shook the hands of those few people who still knew me, and drove north. The military chapter of my life had come to a certain irrevocable end. It was the ultimate hollow victory. But, I reminded myself, there were plenty of battles ahead to lose.

Chapter 17-
The long road back.

All paths are the same: they lead nowhere.

-Carlos Castaneda

It was summer of 1982. My brother and I were sitting, talking about how things were going for him in the wonderful, magical world of submarines. He was assigned to U.S.S. Tullibee, SSN 597. It truly did seem wonderful and magical for me. At this point I was chomping at the bit to get things started. My own naval career wouldn't start for another six months. The conversation turned to the stories he'd heard about post-Navy employment opportunities.

The stories he had heard involved nuclear power plants sprouting up like big, nuclear powered dandelions. Corporations were scrambling to staff them. Navy Nucs were considered the gold standard for operators. Headhunters were waiting outside the gates of Navy bases, doing battle for the coveted operators that would be walking out the gates at any minute. All a newly discharged nuc had to do was pick the best offer, and begin their easy, lucrative new life. This would be the reward for all the stress, long hours, and hard work.

When I was on Skipjack, a couple of the Machinists were getting ready to leave the Navy. They took leave to get their affairs in order, find a place to live, and find a job. Both came back with reports of quick success. Soon they were on their way to the nuclear promised land, reaping their just rewards.

Then why the hell wasn't it happening for me?

I arrived at home. Yvette and I had just moved into a small apartment in West Springfield. I had nothing to do, since I was still on the Navy payroll. I quickly went about the business of preparing a resume. I sifted through all the information I could think of, that might look good on a resume. It was looking good. I had a list of schools, jobs, and experiences that few could claim. It was all due to my naval career. I went to a resume service in Springfield to have it all polished up.

The writer at the resume group looked at my material, and gave an appreciative whistle. Out of the different branches of the nuclear field open to me, I picked what I thought would be the most versatile. Obviously, I wasn't going to have any problems. He went about the business of formatting, cleaning up, and rewording some of the content. When it was finished, even I was impressed. With a door opener like this, how could I have a problem? True, I didn't have a college degree. But, from a technical standpoint the Naval Nuclear Propulsion Program was considered a very close second. Anyone looking for my type of person would already know that.

The next step was determining who I would send my resume to. That question had to be answered according to one very important condition: I did *not* want to relocate. I knew that would put a limiting factor on my options. But, I had a very important reason for that restriction. Yvette had established a career at a well-known life insurance company. She had gone to a great degree of trouble to work her way through college, search for a job, and actually find a good one. I wasn't about to put all that in second place in favor of me finding my own employment. Also, I figured my options would be open enough to find work within living distance of Western Massachusetts. There were several nuclear power plants within a radius that would allow us to move to a location halfway between Yvette's work and any place that would hire me.

Obviously, I would start with the nuclear industry. I had a beefy list of sites from which to choose.

Vermont Yankee

Rowe Yankee

Pilgrim

Seabrook

Millstone 1

Millstone 2

Combustion Engineering

This was going to be easy!

WRONG!! Things had changed in the few years between my brother's time and my own. Nuclear power was not as popular as it was in the old days. Political administrations changed. Environmental issues had changed. A powerful anti-nuclear movement was in full swing. The construction of new power plants had ground to a halt. Some were being shut down. Options were knocked off my list like cans in a shooting gallery.

Vermont Yankee: no openings.

Rowe Yankee: shutting down.

Pilgrim: hiring freeze.

Sea brook: hiring freeze.

Millstone 1: hiring freeze.

Millstone 2: hiring freeze.

Wait! That's okay. I don't have to run a nuclear power plant. The field I picked in the nuclear program would allow me to run *any* type of power plant. As long as it ran on steam, it didn't matter how they heated the water. There were countless oil fired and coal fired power plants in the area. I'll just work in one of those.

WRONG!! Almost all of them were run by Northeast Utilities, who also ran some of the nuclear sites. They were under a hiring freeze. It was time to expand my search. I had other talents. I had a quality control background. I had a maintenance organizational background. There had to be someone out there who needed me. I started sending resumes to Bay State Gas, Smith & Wesson, Tennaco, City of Springfield, and Monsanto.

I was sitting at home one morning, trying to figure out what I'd do that day, when the phone rang. It was Monsanto! They wanted to talk to me! I tried to contain my overwhelming glee as I scheduled an appointment. I called Yvette at work. I would need to get my suit cleaned. I would need to sit down and review all the tips my Dad had given me regarding interviewing. I called my parents to give them the good news, and ask them to keep their fingers crossed. This was something I could *not* drop the ball on.

The day for my interview arrived. Things got off to a rocky start. I got lost on the way to the site. I misunderstood the signs at the gate, and sat there at the security gate tooting my horn for the gate to open, when I was supposed to park and walk in through a separate entrance. I hoped this wasn't going to be an omen. It wasn't. Not exactly.

It turned out I would be interviewed by four separate people, each in their own office. I would be shuttled from one office to the next in assembly line fashion, until all interested parties had their shot at me. The interviews went very well. I established a repoir with each interviewer quickly. The questions and conversations went smoothly. Everyone seemed to be happy and impressed with my answers and stories. Then it all came to a screeching halt.

I was sitting with the last inquisitor, and the interviewer was almost finished. He got quiet for a moment, then continued,

"It isn't unusual for someone to start out here as a janitor, while they wait for a more advanced position to open up. Is that something you would be willing to do?"

I thought *very* carefully about this. What was really being asked here? In my experience, a janitor was a janitor. That's where one started, and that's where one stayed. This was my only bite on my resume. I had to step lightly here.

"Yes. I think I would. I'd be willing to *start* as a janitor, providing it was understood that I'd be moving into a higher position."

"Okay…I can understand that. What if you were required to remain in that position for up to a year?"

I now knew the route my responses would take. I would be patient, as long as a reward was certain.

"Yes. I think I could do that for a year. But, again it would be with the understanding that a position would be opening up for me in a reasonable period of time."

He leaned forward, and looked me in the eyes.

"What if it were two years?"

I spoke without stopping to think. I slipped directly into "honesty mode", without running what I was saying through any kind of filter.

"No."

He stared at me. The expression on his face showed he was genuinely surprised. There was no going back now. It was time to put all my cards on the table, win or lose.

"Absolutely not. I ran nuclear reactors for a living. I've put a great degree of time and effort into what I can offer today. Working as a janitor for that length of time would be something I just couldn't do."

There was a long silence. I had plenty of time to kiss my prospects at Monsanto goodbye. I had blown it, without a doubt. I got cocky, and shut every door open to me with a bang. He looked at me, and said,

"Okay…let's talk about salary. What did you have in mind?"

I already had an answer waiting to go. I knew Steve was at Vermont Yankee, bringing in $36,000 dollars a year.

"Well, I have an idea what other candidates with my experience are being paid. So, I'd say…$35,000 a year."

He laughed out loud! Okay, if my arrogant answer to his janitor question hadn't blown the deal for me, *that* answer did it. I would need to remember these mistakes for next time, if there *was* a next time. Then he said something I did not expect to hear.

"Trust me. You'll have absolutely no problem making at least $35,000 dollars a year. But…you'd be working shifts. Can you do that?"

I put on my most reassuring smile,

"After five and a half years in the Navy, after serving on a submarine, I could work shifts standing on my head."

That's where the interview ended. We stood; he shook my hand, and told me they would be in touch. I immediately wrote a follow up letter, and mailed it to each of the four people who interviewed me. It was my last chance to smooth things over after such a huge blunder. I didn't see much chance of me making it in.

About a week later, I was sitting alone one afternoon in our apartment. The phone rang. I reached over to the end table and picked it up.

"Hello?"

"Hello, is Mr. Richard Smith available?"

"Yes, this is Richard."

"This is Jeannie Cabot from Monsanto Company. You interviewed at our Indian Orchard site a few days ago. I'm calling to offer you employment. Are you still interested?"

I couldn't believe what I was hearing! After what I viewed as an unforgivable error during my interview, they still wanted me. I assured her I was still quite interested. She told me when and where to report to receive a security badge, and continue the indoctrination process from there. After she was finished, I called Yvette to give her the good news. I felt as if I had just pulled off the impossible!

Now I just had one more impossible task left to complete. I needed to prove that I was worthy of any kind of admiration, whatsoever. My mind was is utter turmoil over what happened during my naval service. On one hand, I thought of what my brother said,

"Don't get disqualified, don't get disciplined, and don't break the plant. If you can make it through your career without doing those three things, you're doing fine."

It was a solid fact that I fulfilled those requirements. But on the other hand, I had all those years of doubt, fear, discouragement, guilt, and self-condemnation. Any time someone said anything positive or favorable about my naval service, I felt like I was lying to their face. It was obvious what I would have to do. The only way to make up for my past failings was to be absolutely perfect from then on.

My integration into Monsanto went smoothly, for the most part. My experiences dealing with people on the submarine came in very handy. It didn't matter who I spoke to, everyone was an angel, and they were all at least my equal. It didn't matter if they were a fellow operator, a salary employee, or a janitor. Everyone got the same treatment. I was pleasant. I never asked for much. I kept a low profile. I assumed everyone knew more than I did. I got along with everyone.

The culture shock caused by the extreme differences between a submarine, and a union shop, made for some unusual circumstances. My intense desires to fit in and make everyone happy only made the situations more pronounced. What other employees viewed as minor exchanges and decisions, were life changing milestones for me. It was very difficult to let go of the old ways of thinking, and remind myself that I was in an entirely new world. I wasn't on a submarine anymore, but I had severe problems letting go of that constant sense of urgency.

The members of a submarine crew are very dependent upon each other. When people say we put our lives in each other's hands, it's not an exaggeration. It's vital that each member be a competent, contributing, supportive part of the machine. Those people who cannot fulfill that requirement are the recipients of derision and contempt. They're considered slackers, or in the case of married crew members, called "my-wife-she's". This implies they're using their wife, or other family business, as a reason to get out of work. The terminology is handles thus:

"My wife, she needs to go to the doctor." or "My wife, she went to see her Mom. No one can watch the kids."

Used in a sentence:

"Of course Ron can't pull duty this weekend. He's a my-wife-she."

This ghost from the past was brought into sharp focus the first time I was asked to stay for overtime. I was still in training. I had been there maybe a few weeks. I knew just enough that I could provide some support, albeit minimal. The trainer came to me and had this exchange:

"Hey, Rich. You want to stay tonight?"

I, in fact, did *not* want to stay. I never wanted to stay late somewhere ever again. I was in sheer heaven just realizing I could go home after eight hours, without begging for permission. But, before I could think anything else, my mouth opened:

"Uh...ah...I really can't. I've got so much to do. I'm really sorry! I'm so sorry! I really want to, honest. But, I just can't!!"

Ernest, the trainer, looked at me like I was having an epileptic fit with a live grenade in my hand. He just stood quietly, watching me. Finally, when I stopped, he said,

"Rich...are...you...okay?"

"Yes, I'm fine. But I've only been here a few weeks. I don't want to get the reputation for being a no-load this early!"

"What on Earth are you talking about?"

"They need me to stay. If I don't stay, someone else will have to do my work. The guys will hate me!!"

"Are you out of your mind? What are you talking about?"

"I'll be gone, and someone else will have to work harder because I slacked off."

"Rich, I have no idea what you're thinking. If you go home, they don't *have* to do your work. They *get* to do your work.

And, they get paid extra to do it. It's called *overtime*. If you go home, they get to earn that money instead of you. You're not making them angry. You're making them happy."

My first assignments at Monsanto weren't difficult. There was a lot of work to do, and a lot of things to remember. But, it certainly wasn't like the boat. I tried my very best to keep my errors to a minimum. When I did make a mistake, the reaction was much less than I expected. Any ribbing that resulted was usually good natured, and not excessive. This helped me try to view my mistakes in a rational light. I fell into the shift routine easily. It was much easier than any schedule I worked on the boat.

About two years into my Monsanto career, I won a job in the Quality Control Laboratory. A friend of mine worked there, and seemed a good mesh with my SUBSAFE QAI background. SUBSAFE was the program instituted after the loss of U.S.S. Thresher. It was an extremely stringent program, second only to NASA. It was used to ensure the quality of all components used on American submarines, and to ensure all work conducted on sensitive and critical equipment was done according to approved procedures. These procedures were called "Controlled Work Packages". QAIs wrote those packages. Each boat had to have a certain number of QAI qualified people on board. I was one of those people. My association with SUBSAFE was the cause of my first real conflict on the job.

I was approaching the end of my training in the lab. I was "on my own", but being observed from a distance. My trainer was there just in case I had a question or screwed something up. We had an issue with the thickness profile of the product. In English, that means it had a bump in it that was too big. I was standing there looking at the trace, which resembled an EKG trace. The foreman walked in with one of the control room operators. The foreman took one look at the trace, and turned to the operator,

"Don't scrap, and don't overrun."

In other words, pack the material out as A-grade, and don't make any extra to use as a backup. I went ballistic! This was a flagrant disregarding of specifications and procedures! Those specs were important, and there for a reason! Who the hell did this guy think he was? Before I could stop myself, I shouted,

"YOU CAN'T DO THAT!"

The foreman turned and looked at me, eyes wide. Nora, the operator, quickly put a hand on my arm to calm me down. She looked intently at me.

"Yes…he can."

It was my introduction to the world of internal specs, customer specs, and waivers. These were all a routine fact of life in the business world. It was one more instance where I had to remind myself that I wasn't on a submarine anymore. But, if truth be told, it took me many years to get accustomed to the idea of an out of spec product being acceptable for release.

The lab and I got along very well. The work was well suited to me. I caught on quickly. I got along well with the other analysts. I quickly gained confidence. I was trusted by those above me. It got to the point that special assignments were deliberately reserved for me. Other analysts actually asked me for my opinion. This was a feeling unlike anything I'd encountered before. I was truly happy.

I spent a total of eleven years in the QC Lab. I felt good. I was established. I went to work each day confident that I could handle anything I might face. It was the perfect combination of challenge, respect, and predictability. I worked with people I fit in with well. They were people who would have done well on a submarine. I was truly comfortable. But, there was one other position constantly catching my attention. The entire time I was in the lab, something else was there, waving…whispering…yoo-hoo, over here…

The Control Room.

I found myself spending more and more time in the Control Room. I was getting a feel for how the mechanics of the process affected the quality of the product. It was becoming very useful. I found myself having an insight most others in the lab didn't have. But there was something else. The Control Room resembled the boat. I saw a unique opportunity awaiting me if I could get a job as a Control Room Operator.

I could redeem myself.

It was a chance to "go back in time", a chance to "qualify" again. It was a chance to find myself in a similar environment as before, but this time I would do everything *right*. It was a chance to convince myself that I was okay. I was good enough. If I could put myself into this situation, and succeed, truly *succeed*…I could put all the toxic quicksand of the past behind me. I would feel worthy when someone complimented me for my military service. If I was good enough *now*, maybe I really was good enough *then*. If I could be as good in the Control Room as I was in the lab, it would be a whole new start.

I finally got my chance. As steep as the odds were, finally a chance came along. An opening came up; I had enough seniority, and had the right department privileges. I made it into the Control Room. On the Monday morning after September 11, 2001, I officially became an SEO1, the company designation for a Control Room Operator.

I found that training would be similar to KAPL and the boat. The process was broken down into specific systems, each with their own operating parameters, schematics, and procedures. These were covered one at a time. Classroom time was followed by field time, tracing out lines and locating components. Instead of the "hull" that KAPL had, we had a simulator to use for panel time. This was a very complex system that could replicate any condition we might face. The control panels were identical to the actual equipment in the control room. All actions would be the same. All alarms would be the same. All reaction times would be the same. All *mistakes* would be the same.

Training progressed. I found myself to be an average student. Some aspects were difficult for me to grasp. Others came to me quicker than the other students. We were all very well matched. Again, my submarine experience came in handy, especially when dealing with certain mechanical and engineering principles the others were seeing for the first time. I was matching the curve, and soon it would be time to go on my own.

That time finally came. No SEO1 is ever truly ready to go on their own. They need to just grit their teeth and jump in. The other operators know how the rookie feels. They were all rookies themselves. They understand the jitters, the hesitation, and the self-doubt. The atmosphere in the control room was always one of support and patience.

Such a pity I didn't realize it.

I wanted to do that job because it was so much like the boat. In the end it was a poison pill for my psyche, because it *was* so much like the boat. Gone was the confidence of the lab. My old demons from the boat resurfaced. They were never gone. They had only gone deep, sat silently on the bottom, waiting for a chance to come up again and take their shot. I made mistakes. Everyone made mistakes. It was understood, and recriminations seldom happened. But, my mistakes were different. My mistakes were proof that I would *never* be good enough. My mistakes were a huge red flare floating down next to a sinking ship.

Instead of the Control Room at Monsanto, I was standing in Engine Room Upper Level. The others weren't laughing *with* me, poking well deserved but good natured fun. They were laughing *at* me because I'd humiliated myself again. They were talking about me when I was gone. They were following me, fixing my mistakes before they became catastrophic. My team mates were pitied for their unfortunate fate of working with me. Every error, no matter how slight, was a reminder of how much *nothing* had changed. Every time a fellow operator questioned anything I did, it was a glaring indictment of how much the others couldn't trust me. What on Earth was I thinking? Why would I ever assume I had even a snowball's chance in hell of improving my situation? My true nature? My fate?

The compounded stress of years of shiftwork, family issues, and health problems opened the door to depression again.

In it flooded, filling a void that I'd hoped would be filled with newfound confidence and self-esteem. The vicious circle of poor sleep, failing short term memory, and increased errors quickly got back up to speed. It reached the level of my Skipjack days, and kept going. On top of that was the irrevocable requirement that I appear completely normal on the outside at all times. I couldn't afford to be snippy or hostile, no matter how bad I felt, no matter how much the pressure and depression affected me. On that ever so slight chance that I had read the situation incorrectly, I couldn't afford to alienate anyone or draw adverse attention to myself. Nor could I bring myself to leave the control room. My Nuc School era stubbornness was at full strength as well. My past had caught up with me, and had its slimy, stinking hand around my throat. The clock was ticking again…

In the same way an old car seems to have an autopilot that can magically drive a drunk home from his favorite bar, my psyche instinctively turned to what it knew best. All the sorrow, shame, and self-hatred from the past were just itching for a ride. But, my psyche now had a nitrous system under the hood…validation. Just like an outcast scientist feels, after finding out he was right all along, my demons came back with more power than ever.

It was too good to be true.

You should have known better.

How could you expect things to change?

How dare you not accept your fate?

Who are you to change your destiny?

One night things finally came apart. I was on the panel that night. My partner was working the field. She had a busy night, one of those ones that never seemed to let up. We had process issues that made A-grade production seem like walking a tight rope. I decided to make a stand. I wasn't going to call her back in to help. I wasn't going to make her do my job on top of hers. I wasn't going to be a pain in the ass, the burden I always was.

I was going to do this myself. I reasoned out the process as best as I could. I factored in the issues with the other operators I depended on. I thought I'd found a balance between keeping the line running and making good product. I made the modifications, and let the process run. Wouldn't she be happy that I saved her the trouble. She didn't have to babysit me. I could be trusted. The other operators wouldn't have to put a bell around my neck.

Unfortunately, the adjustments I made to keep the process running, threw one of the quality parameters out of spec. After running her ass off in the process field, my partner finally came back to the Control Room to rest. When I told her what I'd done, she went ballistic! Why hadn't I consulted her? We're supposed to work as a team. We were making rubbish now! Why did I take matters into my own hands?

All those good intentions and optimistic ideals went right down the tubes. I was hopeless. My fate was sealed absolutely airtight. I had things in my life going good, and I had ruined everything. The rest of my hopeless life was going to be an endless shitty hell.

My drive home was very interesting. I had a one sided conversation with my solitary passenger. He was a little irritating. His robe and hood were cutting down my visibility, and I had to open his window so his sickle wouldn't poke holes in my roof. Without saying a word, Mr. Grim Reaper made a very convincing argument.

Don't think of it as killing yourself.

Just think of it as not being alive anymore.

Imagine the benefits.

Things will go so much smoother.

No more stress.

You'll find it so much easier to cope.

There's no one at home to talk you out of it.

Now's the perfect time.

I found myself in a dark place that made run-of-the-mill dark places look like a sunny day at the beach. I was ready. This time, I was really ready. Everything I strived for to prove my worth, was a miserable burning sinking failure. I had nothing holding me back, no reason to live. Except one. Yvette. Yvette wasn't there. She was in Maine, visiting her sister. But one thing kept going through my mind. She told me about a horrible dream she'd had once. In this dream, she was downstairs in the bedroom, and I was upstairs in the office. She heard a shot ring out. She realized I'd killed myself. She described to me the horrible feelings she felt right before she woke up in a cold sweat. My wife, Yvette, was the only reason I decided not to kill myself that night.

She was the one thing that inspired me to hold off, to let reason have a say, to let new alternatives finally have a shot.

One thing on my side was the fact that I wasn't alone, as I was the other two times. I was getting competent treatment. I was now in therapy. After years of senseless and self-destructive resistance, I also finally agreed to go on anti-depressants. I had finally found a gifted therapist who really seemed to understand my problems. The down side to that was my diagnosis of probably being at least borderline PTSD. But, at least I'd gotten things moving in the right direction. That, along with the rock solid patience and support of my wife, was keeping my floundering head above water. I also vented some frustration through my writing. Because the Control Room reminded me so much of the boat, that is the subject my writing gravitated toward. Two pieces in particular will always stand out in my mind. One was happy, and one was sad.

PIG BOATS

You can't see where you're going,

And you can't see where you've been.

You just sit and strain to listen,

To the sounds that might come in.

And the time goes on forever,

Outside it's always night.

The sun has turned fluorescent,

From black to red and white.

You sit there in your armchair,

And you watch it on TV,

But don't tell me about it.

I've already been,

On the Pigboats.

Your life becomes a number,

A point upon a chart.

Your soul turns to machinery,

No mind, no voice, no heart.

The tension and frustration,

Grow stronger day by day.

You always end up twisted,

But you're better off that way.

I can't say when I'm leaving,

Or if I'll ever come back.

Don't bother trying to find us.

We're off the beaten track,

On the Pigboats.

I can name about a million,

Places I'd rather be,

Than on this goddam pig boat,

Punching holes in the sea.

I try to maintain sanity,

But it's hard to keep up hope,

When the only view of reality,

Comes through the periscope.

I say I've served my time in hell,

You say I'm the one who chose.

But when the others turn their backs,

I'm the one who goes,

On the Pigboats.

Or maybe this one…

THE FLOUNDER SONG

The Navy sent me to the Flounder,

We spent all our time around her.

Chip and paint her up and down,

We hardly ever went to town.

Get along boys.

Better turn to.

Get hot boys,

Be handy-oh.

Rig the planes out.

Clear the bridge too.

Get hot, boys!

Be handy!

The skipper was a little hazy,

On account that he was crazy.

If his choo-choo jumped the track,

The XO tied him to his rack.

Get along boys.

Better turn to.

Get hot boys,

Be handy-oh.

The Ensign is stuck,

In the TDU!

Get hot, boys!

Be handy!

The navigator was so grand,

As long as he had sight of land.

He claimed Atlantis had been found,

When he ran the boat aground.

Get along boys.

Better turn to.

Get hot boys,

Be handy-oh.

Rig the planes out.

Clear the bridge too.

Get hot, boys!

Be handy!

The cook served up filet of cow,

He smuggled her aboard somehow.

He boiled her up in diesel fuel,

So it tasted just like mule.

Get along boys.

Better turn to.

Get hot boys,

Be handy-oh.

The Ensign is stuck,

In the TDU!

Get hot, boys!

Be handy!

Nothing left to eat but taters,

When we saw a string of freighters.

Ice cream would have hit the spot,

When they said no we sank the lot!

Get along boys.

Better turn to.

Get hot boys,

Be handy-oh.

Rig the planes out.

Clear the bridge too.

Get hot, boys!

Be handy!

They say we've sailed the seven seas,

From Java to the Hebrides.

Just don't mention Morotai,

The Master Chief will start to cry.

Get along boys.

Better turn to.

Get hot boys,

Be handy-oh.

The Ensign is stuck,

In the TDU!

Get hot, boys!

Be handy!

The first piece made it into my second book, "A House Of Words". The second is printed here for the first time. As usual, the creative process of writing had a therapeutic effect.

I was just starting to level off, when the opportunity came to move my career along to its next step. It was time to get a day job.

The natural order of things at Monsanto was that a person would start working there when they were young. They would get a production job, and work rotating shifts. They would make their money, and save their money as they worked the years away. As time went by they would gain seniority. After they had frugally prepared themselves for their later years, they would then use that seniority to snag a day job. They would spend their remaining years in the relative ease of a day job as they waited for their time to retire. I had spent seventeen years working shifts. Not as much as some, but more than many others. It was time to start looking for that day job.

It is still up for debate whether I found the job, or the job found me. Whatever the circumstances, I soon found myself looking at the prospect of bidding on a driver's position in the warehouse that supported our operation. I bid on the job, along with a couple of other SEO1s with the same ideas. As the expression goes, a watched pot never boils. It seemed to take forever to receive word on whether or not I won a job. I finally learned that I had, in fact, won a job. But how many jobs were there? Which job did I win? What hours would I actually work? Over the next few weeks, I learned that I had actually gotten a permanent day shift driver position. Finally, shortly before Christmas 2005, I was released from the Control Room.

As I transitioned into my new job, my stress level dropped…a little. My depression lessened…a little. My outlook on life in general improved…a little. I was making progress, but something was still holding me back. It was like being a beautiful Rolls Royce V-12 engine, smooth and silky, strong and sinewy, firing on three cylinders. My concerns, my trip-ups, my pitfalls all came back to the same issue time after time:

The Boat.

I just couldn't shake the self-loathing, the assumptions, the shame, the regret, the uncertainty. *The not knowing.* How was I? Did I do okay? Were they laughing *at* me or *with* me? Did they *like* me, or were they *tolerating* me? Was I the one everybody had to watch? Or was Steve right? I never got disciplined. I never got disqualified. I never broke the plant. Was it really good enough? I didn't know.

I had nothing to refer to for a reality check except my own mind. How reliable was *that*? I desperately needed an independent standard of some kind. But that was twenty five years ago. How would I ever be able to objectively look back on those years, and retrieve any kind of reliable observations? It seemed hopeless. I would be permanently stuck in this frame of mind forever.

Or so it would seem.

It was late evening. I was sitting in front of the computer. I had just finished answering some messages on Facebook. Yvette came in to talk to me, on her way to the shower. It was therapy day for me. We usually chatted about how the appointment went that morning. I told her about the things we discussed. I mentioned how the subject of the boat came up again. I complained about how the uncertainty of those years was holding me back. She hesitantly observed that I may need to find a way to get around it, put it in my past, and forget about it. It was then that I made a key statement.

"You know something, Yvette? I wish there was a way I could talk to those guys, just sit down with them and ask them what I was like. How was I as a shipmate? Did I do my job? Did I help? Did people like me? Was I trusted? I wish I could just ask those questions."

Yvette looked at me for a second.

"Why don't you? You just finished looking at Facebook. Why don't you try looking up some of the guys? They've got to be out there, I mean, *you're* on there. Right?"

It felt like I'd just been given the last piece of the puzzle, hiding under the Lay-Z-Boy for the last twenty five years. *That* was why I was married to her! She thought of things like that while I was busy being stupid. Figuring out why she was married to me would have to wait 'til later. I logged into Facebook again. In the search window, I typed in,

"U.S.S. Skipjack SSN 585"

A few entries popped up. I clicked on the first. It was a page set up by some old Skipjack crew members. I began scrolling down the page, looking at names, reading posts and stories. The names, pictures, and memories put a lump in my throat. I called Yvette back into the computer room. She beamed as I pointed out people, named them, and showed her photos of the boat they had shot over the years. I went down the list of members, picking out the ones I remembered, and the ones I hoped might remember me. Soon I had a long list of messages and friend requests awaiting responses.

The days went by. I became more and more nervous as responses failed to appear. Yvette watched me with concern as I became increasingly convinced no one wanted to contact me. Was this the sign I was going to get? Yvette kept reminding me that people often go a week or more without checking Facebook. People go on vacation. People may not remember me. Finally, responses began to come in. I decided the best way to go about this was to come clean from the beginning. I decided to post a message on the page.

I explained who I was. I listed the years I served on board. I explained that I was at a crossroads, and needed accurate, reliable feedback about my time there. I explained the issues I faced while aboard Skipjack. I needed honest opinions and observations, *good or bad*. Both would be equally useful. Their input about the past would help me navigate the future. Could they please help?

Over the next couple of weeks, e-mails, Facebook messages, and IMs poured in. The responses covered a wide variety of possible replies.

1) It's good to know I wasn't the only screwed up person on Skipjack.
2) I don't really remember you, but if you were an asshole, I'm sure I would have!
3) We spent a lot of shut down watches together, you probably reset the heater breakers for me a lot!
4) Now, I remember you. You were ERLL, and I was AEA. We spent a lot of time talking. You were a good guy.
5) I remember you. You were moody a lot. I guess now I know why.
6) We all had problems. Don't think you were alone.
7) Don't worry. You were just fine.
8) Now I know who you are. We stood a lot of watches together. You were a good guy, and always willing to help.

The tears rolled down my cheeks as I read these replies. It was too good to be true! I was okay! I wasn't able to get ahold of all the guys I wanted to hear from, but it was enough. I may never be able to find the words to describe how it felt to have twenty five years of guilt, doubt, sorrow, and shame lifted from my shoulders. Steve was right. I didn't get disciplined, I didn't get disqualified, I didn't break the plant. And...I did okay. I fell right in the middle. Some guys didn't even remember me. I blended in with everyone else. That alone was better than I could ever hope for.

Now I look back on those years with true, unbridled fondness. I think back to those incidents when I was teased, and know it was only teasing. I think of the times we laughed, and I know it really was *we*, not *they*. I remember how people always said,

"If people screw with you, it means they like you. If they don't, they just leave you alone."

They really meant it. It's so much easier now to regard myself as a true member of the crew. I can feel truly proud of those years, now that I realize I actually contributed, instead of being the dim-witted leech I always assumed I was. It's very difficult to quantify how significant that really is. I was accepted all along. I was one of them all along. The extreme depth of my depression made seeing things rationally next to impossible. Would it be better if I knew that twenty five years ago? Of course it would. But, better late than never. That knowledge has proved absolutely invaluable over the last several months. It has been crucial to my continued progress and recovery. Being able to compare my *perception* of the past to the *actual* past is a tool I use every single time I find myself slipping back into old ways of thinking, old ways of viewing myself. It doesn't mean I see myself as a hero. It means I can allow myself to see myself as…okay. Adequate, instead of a failure. Participant in something critically important, in a desperate period in history…instead of a burdensome bystander. It's been a miracle drug for my soul. Never doubt the value of being able to believe in your own past. It's the only way you can believe in your future. In hindsight, I now realize I was lucky I lived long enough to have one.

Chapter 18-

The Silent Bastards and the Rolex Watch.

"The unexpected always happens"

-*proverb*

Robert Frost spoke of the "road less travelled". There are many such roads. But they all have something in common. My brother Steve and I both travelled such a road. We can both describe one inevitable feature of the road less travelled. It is very, very lonely. From beginning to end, very few companions will be seen. Of those, fewer still can be spoken to. Our road less travelled was a special road. It was paved with secrets. Every paving stone was a number, a principle, a material, a procedure, or a place...that we could never discuss. Just by the nature of military service, those who choose this road are young. Old people don't join the military. The military wants young people, people filled with fire, wind, and piss. They want people who still believe they are immortal, indestructible.

But Steve and I were different. We were *destined* to walk a road less travelled. I have mentioned in the past that our military service was not ordered, preordained, or coerced. It was simply the natural way of things. It was natural the way a plant grows toward the sun, instead of into the Earth. It was also natural that we would seek out something valuable while in the military. We would look ahead, not behind. We would move forward, not loiter. We weren't going to get an education in *a* field of work; we would get into *the* field of work. Whatever we became involved with, it would be on the forefront. It would be cutting edge. And, my Dad realized one common aspect to all the different fields of work that might attract us:

THEY ALL START OUT BLACK.

All advanced technology, in one way or another, begins its life in the dark, murky, deceptive, ambiguous world of "CLASSIFIED". Very few people get to see it in its early stages. Very few people can qualify for the security clearances necessary to be involved in those early stages of a technology. Here's a perfect example: GPS.

I have a GPS in my car that can plot my position anywhere on Earth down to a few meters. It can follow my progress as I drive. It can tell me exactly how fast I'm driving. This is actually a little irritating because my GPS and my speedometer *never* say the same number. But, the point is, this technology is available to anyone with $150 dollars. I even have a GPS in my cell phone! WOW! Where did it all start?

GPS was originally developed for the military. Specifically, it was developed for the Special Operations community. Someone decided it would be a good idea for the SEALS and Green Berets hiding out in the middle of nowhere to have a good way of knowing exactly where in nowhere they were. It would have to be a passive system, so signals couldn't be traced. It would need to be portable. It would need to be reliable, giving repeatable results every time. An infrastructure would need to be put in place to support it. The foundation of the system would be satellites.

When those satellites were launched, they were TOP SECRET. When they were tested, it was TOP SECRET. When the receivers were developed and tested, it was TOP SECRET. All the people involved in this program had to qualify for the clearances required to be there, to do the work, to be a part of it all. Those few lucky people able to be in that position all got to that point in the same fashion. They all took the same path, the same road.

They took the road less travelled.

My Dad foresaw all of this. He learned most of this the hard way. He was bound and determined that we would not have to. He knew we would be taking the road less travelled. So, he set us on that road early. Priorities were established early.

1) Education: We learned quickly that getting the highest possible quality education was paramount. Nothing would be allowed to interfere with that goal. School sports were discouraged. Having a job was discouraged. After school activities were closely watched. If my grades dropped, a cause was found, and it was eliminated. My Dad actually told me at one point that my only purpose for living was to get the best education I possibly could. All else was secondary.
2) Clean Record: This was actually not the case. We were required to maintain an absolutely *spotless* record. A police record was the kiss of death for a security clearance. Even a small infraction, early in life, could keep someone from passing a background check. That would have a direct impact on what I would be allowed

to do once I was in the military. No misbehavior of any kind was tolerated. There would be no partying, no drugs, no drinking. We were not allowed to associate with anyone with a questionable background of any kind.

3) Responsibility: Both my parents had to assume adult responsibilities at an early age. They learned painful lessons early in life. They didn't want us to face the same situation. Those lessons they learned the hard way, we would learn the easy way: through *their* experience. The result was that we acquired an adult perspective much earlier than our peers. This put yet another boundary between us and them.

The end result was that we got a taste of the road less travelled much earlier than anyone else. If the others went into the woods to party, I was nowhere to be seen. When the others were winning the big game, and dating the cute cheerleaders, I was nowhere to be seen. When the joint was being passed around, I was nowhere to be seen. While others were interested in sports, movie stars, or pop culture, I acquired an interest in the military. My father's background steered me toward an intense interest in hardware, tactics, strategy, and above all...the intelligence community. The good news was that by the time I was ready to join the military, I was a prime candidate for any classified program in existence. The bad news was that by the time I graduated from high school, I was almost completely isolated and alienated from my school mates.

Nothing changed when I enlisted in the Navy. I was involved in a classified program, and upon completion, I would be part of a highly classified community. Again, keeping one's nose clean was paramount. "Demonstrated

Unreliability" was a sure ticket out of any classified program. No trouble with the authorities was tolerated. Drug use was highly illegal. Drinking problems were nipped in the bud, usually with potent pharmaceuticals. No disciplinary issues were tolerated. I had no problems. I was right at home. Others found the strict rules to be an irritation, but this was how I'd lived my entire life.

Civilian life was little different. I had to pass a drug test to be hired by Monsanto. That was certainly no issue for me. I had to deliver my best performance. It's difficult to get "fired" from the military. Getting fired from a civilian job is easy. I had to focus, keep my nose clean, and keep my head in the game. I was expecting things to lighten up a little when I became a civilian. It didn't feel like it was going that way. I had put in the hard work and the long hours. I endured the restrictions and isolation. I passed up the glory, the parties, the friends, and the sense of belonging. I was hoping it was time for the big payoff. It was time for a change of scenery. But, the scenery didn't change. I was still on the road less travelled.

Don't get me wrong. I had gotten to the destination I had chosen. I was very grateful for that. The disappointment was *how* I'd gotten to my destination. Plenty of other people got to the same destination I did. But, their experiences were far more liberal than mine. Imagine watching the Boston Pops…while wearing ear plugs. Or, driving through Yosemite National Park…in a vehicle with blacked out windows. Sure, you get to the end point you wanted, but what did you experience on the way?

I found myself wondering…would it have been so wrong if I played football? What if I went to a few parties, assuming I would have been invited? What if I had smoked a little weed? Many people who really know me consider my childhood to be something right out of a science fiction movie. The level of obedience I demonstrated is mind blowing. In hindsight, I started to feel cheated. What did I really have to show for myself, besides a good job, and some really cool stories?

The occasional point of light would pop out when I met a fellow submariner. The common bond between those who endure extreme conditions is something one has to experience to understand. It was uplifting to hear people in other lines of military work say,

"I don't know how you do it!" or "I could never do that!"

But two specific events helped to "take away the sting", so to speak. One in particular proved to be the payoff for forty seven years of very, highly unusual life.

Back in the mid 1990's, I found myself "playing bachelor" while Yvette went to visit her sister. I had a weekend all to myself. I weighed my options. I wasn't really in the mood for a trip to a strip club. I was ready for a change of surroundings. I decided to spend the weekend in Mystic, Connecticut. Spending time down there always made me feel good. I called the Whaler Hotel, and reserved a room.

I made the rounds of all the old favorite places. One of my coworkers in the QC Lab was from the area, and reminded me of a place I hadn't stepped into in far too many years. Right down the street from the drawbridge was a little Irish pub called John's. Small, dark, cramped and smoky, it was the perfect poster child for little bars near the coast. Several nautical facilities were right down the road in various directions, which only made the clientele that much more interesting.

I stepped inside, and immediately took in all the familiar sights, sounds, and smells. The jumbled conversation sounded just like before. A worn out pool table stood before the only unblocked window in the place. Across the old wavy wooden floor were a table and four chairs in the far opposite corner. Seven old swivel stools lined the bar, which was sorely in need of a new coat of urethane. The original had long since cracked and blistered. In other words, nothing had changed a bit.

I took the last stool at the far end of the bar. The friendly old bartender came over, and asked me what I'd like. I ordered a Guinness. As I waited for my pint to settle up, I spun my chair around and surveyed the room. Fishermen and mechanics occupied the bar. A young man with two pretty girls played eight ball on the thin faded felt of the old pool table. At the corner table were three men. They were all roughly middle aged. Their faces were tan, but not very weathered. I had them pegged as leisure boaters. I briefly listened in on their conversation, and then turned back to my Guinness. A round of sudden laughter erupted from the table, and I heard a voice cry out,

"I always said you bubbleheads were sneaky!"

I spun around in my chair and stared. As the laughing died down, one of the men grinned and pointed at me.

"He heard that."

I smiled and nodded. Then man looked at me for a moment.

"You a bubblehead?"

I nodded. He motioned for me to join them. I grabbed my now half full pint glass and sat down. We made introductions. The other two men started in on their own conversation, while he started asking about my boat, my service, where I was from, and other small talk. More drinks were ordered. Our conversation continued, and after a while the other two joined in. I heard a voice call from the door, and one of the men at the table turned, looked, and waved. Another man walked over to the table. Soon he too had a beer.

The picture came together slowly. The man who just walked in was a former Marine. One was former Army. One was a skimmer off of a carrier, and the last was a submariner like myself. The conversation turned to sea stories, and everyone had stories to tell except the Army guy. For the next hour and a half, we drank and swapped stories. The other submariner had us in stiches over a story of one of his patrols getting extended due to the unexpected arrival of a Soviet boat. No one at home knew what was going on, except one guy working at Squadron who had access to radio traffic. He found an old postcard from some exotic place somewhere. He wound it into a typewriter, and typed a brief message on it about how he had gone AWOL with two women, and would never be home again. Then he mailed it to the storyteller's wife. Meanwhile, our friend is nowhere to be seen, and no one knows where the boat is.

"My wife almost fucking divorced me over that one!"

I turned and looked at him.

"And I thought *I* had a good story. I think you just trumped mine."

"Well, let's hear it."

So, I told them about the winter patrol we went on, after telling all our family members we'd be in port for Christmas. I told them about how rotten it was having to tell my parents to buy plane tickets and come on up, knowing full well I wouldn't even be there. The sailing date was highly classified, and not even the slightest hint of our departure was allowed.

"My Dad understood. He was very unhappy, but he understood. But, my Mom was *sore as hell*. All that plane fare for nothing. And on top of that was the disappointment"

There was a sudden lull in the conversation. Then one of them spoke.

"I think we've got ourselves a Silent Bastard."

I was befuddled at the prospect of being called a silent *anything*. I looked around at all of them, waiting for the punch line. Finally one of them explained.

"Ever heard of the Order of the Silent Bastards?"

I shook my head. He continued.

"It's similar to the Shellbacks and Blue Noses. It's a bit smaller. A lot of folks don't know about it. You cross the equator to become a Shellback. You cross the Arctic Circle to become a Blue Nose. The Silent Bastards are different. It doesn't matter *where* you go. The Silent Bastards are all about secrecy. A Silent Bastard is someone who has kept military secrets to the point that it affected their personal life…their family life…or their marriage. You heard my story. I never did tell my wife where I was. I couldn't. The patrol ended up being a mission of higher classification.

That bugged her for a while. For a time, she really didn't trust me. It sounds like you've had a similar experience. I bet there are things your wife would love to know, that you can never tell her."

I nodded my head. I strangely didn't feel like talking.

"Your parents sure got burned by our wonderful compartmentalization system."

Again I nodded.

"Well, it looks like you're in."

I looked around at all of them. Were they putting me on? Was I the joke of the night? Was I the pigeon they were going to use for their entertainment? It certainly seemed probable. Until...

"Now you've got to get a ring."

He held up his right hand. He was wearing a military signet ring with a black stone. The others all held up their hands. They were all wearing some form of signet ring with a black stone.

"A military ring with a black stone is the symbol of the Silent Bastards."

It took me many years to finally decide to get a ring. The story seemed far-fetched. Questions loomed. Was it real? Why would they actually go to the expense of buying identical rings, solely for the purpose of screwing with *one random guy*? Was it all rubbish? What were the odds of *me* having the chance of getting into a cool, exclusive group like this? Finally, I stopped caring. If someone didn't believe it, screw them! Who do I have to justify myself to? *ME!*

I got the ring.

But, one event did come very close to providing that one big payoff. In late 2010, I bought a model of a Soviet submarine. Model companies have always come up a little short when tooling up a kit of a Soviet boat. Years of secrecy took their toll on kit designers who had to resort to guess work or grainy photographs in place of accurate plans and drawings. But, this time it was different. It was a smaller kit manufacturer, part of what hobbyists call the "Cottage Industry". That didn't stop them from producing an absolutely wonderful kit of a Romeo class submarine.

I ordered one from them, and a couple of weeks later it arrived in the mail. I opened it up, not really sure what I'd find. I was very pleasantly surprised! The castings were beautiful. Not one pit or bubble marred that smooth resin hull. The conning tower was perfectly reproduced. The subtle contours of the stern were dead on. I wrote an e-mail to the kit producers.

I told them what a wonderful job they had done. I told them they had gotten everything right and just how rare that is. They had obviously taken their research very seriously. I told them to take my word for it. I had studied Soviet military hardware virtually my entire life. I had access to classified references during my military days, and had excellent references in my library now. I knew what looked right, and *they* had gotten it right.

I didn't expect a reply. I was just one person in a huge sea of customers. But I hoped I had made them happy. But, I was wrong. I did get a reply, and it wasn't the reply I was expecting. A couple of days after sending my e-mail, I received a reply. If that was my background, and I had such good references, would I be willing to help out a friend of theirs? Could they pass along my e-mail address to them? I noticed the people producing the kits had eastern European names. I was intrigued. Sure, I said. Why not?

A couple of weeks later, I received an e-mail. In this e-mail were three files of photographs. The writer explained that one file was photos of Project 885. The second file was photos of Project 955. The last was a couple of photos of a class of Soviet boat he couldn't identify. Would I be so kind as to look at the files, and verify them? I was glad he asked. There were problems with the first two files:

Project 885: This is Russia's latest nuclear fast attack boat, originally known as the Severodvinsk class, now also known as the Yasen class. For the Russians, this is cutting edge stuff. It features design aspects they were far too long in implementing. It has a spherical sonar array in the bow, which we've used for decades. It has vertical launch tubes for cruise missiles. It uses their latest version of a quiet screw with a "skewed back" design. It could be a major thorn in the side of western submarine commanders and strategists. There was just one problem. None of the photos were of Project 885. What he had was photos of a Beluga class research boat. It was a high speed test bed. It looked very sleek and fast, because it *was* very sleek and fast. If one wanted to design a new boat, it could very well look like Beluga. But, being a test bed, the only weapons it carried were the AK-47s for the security watches.

Project 955: This is Russia's latest nuclear ballistic missile boat, also known as the Borei class. It too is very advanced. It's also the first Russian boat to be driven by a propulsor, instead of a traditional screw. This was a big step for them. This boat would be very quiet, and very difficult to detect. Again, this was very advanced stuff. Reader, you see it coming, don't you. His photos were not of Project 955. It was the India class. The India is another research boat. It's designed to use DSRVs, or other types of small submersibles in deep water work. But, when the wells for the submersibles are empty and covered over, the India looks just like a ballistic missile boat.

The last file contained photos of a Charlie 2 class cruise missile submarine. Some photos of these boats are difficult to identify for the uninitiated. Here's why: the Soviets started out with the Charlie 1 class. It was a very efficient, practical weapons platform. But, then newer equipment came along. This newer computer equipment was more accurate, and faster operating. This resulted in quicker and tighter fixes on their targets. To accommodate this new equipment, the Charlie was lengthened by one compartment forward of the conning tower. This was the Charlie 2. If the viewer didn't know about the Charlie 2, and the photos only showed a little of the boat above the surface of the water, this would result in lumps, bumps, and contours in places they weren't expected. That was why he didn't know what he was looking at.

I was a little suspicious. Yes, there were rational reasons for the misidentifications. Few people know about Beluga and India. They *do* look like fast attack boats and missile boats, respectively. With them being relatively unknown, someone could stumble across photos of them, and not recognize them. That would make them appear as brand new. And it's true, some people know about Charlie 1, but may not know about Charlie 2. I reminded myself that I was accustomed to dealing with people with a little higher knowledge level. I decided to answer the e-mail.

I crafted the e-mail with care, softening the blow as much as I could. I told him of his mistakes, but explained why his conclusions were so easy to come to. I told him about Charlie 2, and directed him to some suggested web sites where he might find better photos, if he was interested. I ended on an apologetic note, saying I was sorry to be the one to bear bad news. I hoped I was able to help.

A couple of days later, I received an e-mail in return. He told me he was sad that his information was incorrect. He appreciated my time and expertise. He ended by asking for my mailing address, telling me he wanted to send me something for my trouble. I thought for a moment. His friend already mailed me a model kit. I was in the phone book. If he wanted to send me a bomb or a rattlesnake, I would be giving him information he most probably *already had*, or could easily find. I thanked him and included my mailing address. I would just wait and see.

A couple of weeks later, a notice appeared in my mailbox. The Post Office had a package waiting for me. That wasn't a surprise. I was always ordering something. I would probably remember what it was when I saw the box. I went down to the Post Office the next morning. The box looked odd. Small and rectangular, it was taped up like a national treasure. The mailing label was covered with a mix of English and some variation of eastern European language. I brought it home. There was no way I was going to tear my way into this box. I went straight for the scissors. The box contained a wrapped paper package. This I could tear. The wrapped paper package contained a smaller bundle of bubble wrap encased in packing tape. I cautiously felt and squeezed the package, trying to decide where I could cut it without damaging the contents. Back to the scissors. I carefully cut open the end. I turned the bundle over on my bed. Out tumbled...

A watch. Aaaaw...that was nice. He sent me a watch for looking at his pictures. I picked it up and looked at it. So nice. Silver and black. He sent me a...

FUCKING ROLEX WATCH?

I looked very closely at the watch. It was a Rolex Submariner. It couldn't be real. There's just no way it's real. Over the next couple of days, I combed the internet looking for information regarding counterfeit Rolex watches. It turns out there are quite a lot of them floating around out there. I learned some interesting things. I sat down with my watch, a magnifying glass, and my information.

Sweep second hand. CHECK. (Rolex made very few quartz watches.)

Small Rolex crown etched just below the six o' clock position. CHECK.

The crown must be smoothly engraved. CHECK.

Small Rolex crown on end of stem. CHECK.

Small black O-ring on stem. CHECK.

The date at the three o' clock position must be magnified to the prescribed size. CHECK.

Finally I took it to a local watchmaker to get the band sized. It turns out I could have done it myself. Instead of pins, Rolex bands are held together with tiny fine thread screws. All I would have needed was glasses. While he worked, I told him I suspected it may not be real. When he was finished, he gave it a thorough examination. He told me he often works on Rolexes. He saw nothing indicating it was counterfeit. But, it was stainless steel. It was a cheap Rolex, only worth about $6,000 dollars.

I began to get a warm fuzzy feeling. I may have just found it. My payoff. My place in the sun. My game winning pass. My party in the woods. The prettiest cheerleader in the world just stepped onto the road less travelled, and planted a big, warm, wet sloppy kiss on me! With *tongue*!! This wasn't just a watch. This was a trophy. I now owned a watch the vast majority of people couldn't even fathom purchasing. It was all because I had information few others had. It was because of all those times I'd stayed on the road less travelled. Every decision in my life had somehow led me down the twisting, turning, winding path of probabilities to this event. Forty something years of alienation, solitude, exhaustion, and unending stress finally paid off.

I stopped for a moment, stepped off the road less travelled, and showed a friend of mine my new watch.

Author Biography

Richard A Smith was born in 1964 to an unlikely couple, his father - a U.S. Air Force intelligence analyst from Southern California, and his mother - a book keeper from Belfast, Northern Ireland. The melding of two completely diverse worlds made for a very interesting childhood for Richard.

Upon completion of public school, he followed the family's strong military tradition. He enlisted in the United States Naval Nuclear Propulsion Program, and volunteered for submarine duty. Classified work in general, and submarine duty in particular, provided all the adventure and intrigue advertised.

After a naval career cut short by an injury, he was hired by Monsanto Company where he's worked ever since, spreading his experience over the areas of Quality Control, Production, Plant Operations, and Logistics.

After his naval career, he also married his high school sweetheart, Yvette. Their blessed union survives to this day, and has produced not one, not two, not three, but *four* beautiful cats.

Today, Richard resides in Western Massachusetts, near UMASS. He lives with his wife, and two cats, Rosie and Fleetwood. He continues to pursue his interests in photography, acting, military studies, world theology, scale modeling, mixology, sunsets, and long walks on the beach.

www.ingramcontent.com/pod-product-compliance
Lightning Source LLC
Chambersburg PA
CBHW051812090426
42736CB00011B/1436